Ricoeur, Rawls, and Capability Justice

Continuum Studies in Political Philosophy

Continuum Studies in Political Philosophy presents cutting-edge scholarship in the field of political philosophy. Making available the latest high-quality research from an international range of scholars working on key topics and controversies in political philosophy and political science, this series is an important and stimulating resource for students and academics working in the area.

Titles include:

The Concept of Justice, Thomas Patrick Burke
Morality, Leadership, and Public Policy, Eric Thomas Weber
Nozick's Libertarian Project, Mark D. Friedman
Perfecting Justice in Rawls, Habermas and Honneth, Miriam Bankovsky
Rawls, Dewey, and Constructivism, Eric Thomas Weber
Rousseau and Revolution, edited by Holger Ross Lauritsen and Mikkel Thorup

Ricoeur, Rawls, and Capability Justice

Civic Phronēsis and Equality

Molly Harkirat Mann

Continuum Studies in Political Philosophy

continuum

This book is dedicated to my teachers:

John, Frank, and Gautam

Continuum International Publishing Group
The Tower Building
11 York Road
London SE1 7NX

80 Maiden Lane
Suite 704
New York NY 10038

www.continuumbooks.com

British Library Cataloguing-in-Publication Data
A catalogue record for this book is available from the British Library.

ISBN: HB: 978-1-4411-9850-1

Library of Congress Cataloging-in-Publication Data
Mann, Molly Harkirat.
Ricoeur, Rawls, and capability justice : civic *phronēsis* and equality / Molly Harkirat Mann.
p. cm. – (Continuum studies in political philosophy)
Includes bibliographical references (p.) and index.
ISBN: 978-1-4411-9850-1 (hardcover) – ISBN 978-1-4411-5524-5 (pdf) – ISBN: 978-1-4411-7757-5 (epub) 1. Equality. 2. Justice. 3. Distributive justice. 4. Ricoeur, Paul–Political and social views. 5. Rawls, John, 1921-2002–Political and social views. I. Title.
JC575.M35 2012
320.01'1–dc23

2011035029

Typeset by Newgen Imaging Systems Pvt. Ltd, Chennai, India
Printed and bound in Great Britain

Contents

Acknowledgments

This book has been taught to me by my teachers. I have simply tried to write it so as to honor what I have learned from them.

I would like to thank my endlessly generous colleagues from the Society for Ricoeur Studies, especially George Taylor and Dan Stiver, for their encouragement and support. I would also like to thank David Pellauer and Peg Birmingham for giving me the opportunity to teach this book at DePaul University and for believing in me. I am so grateful to Howard Adelman and to David MacGregor for always looking over me and for their serendipitous interventions. I am profoundly indebted to my parents Sarbjit and Manjeet Mann, my sister Nikki Tonon, my brothers Sunny Mann and Kevin Tonon, and to Camillo, Dora, Ang, and Diana Cimino for supporting me in every imaginable way. Dana Dawson's constant friendship has sustained me.

I talk a lot. I have talked this book into existence over the last decade with my great mentor, John O'Neill, and with my partner, Frank Cimino, who always reminds me where I am going when I have felt lost.

This book ultimately belongs to my brother Gautam Mann, in whose spirit I read, write, learn, and teach.

Introduction

The Course of Recognitive *Phronēsis*: Ricoeur's Response to the Moralization of Inequality[1]

We are witnessing, in Canada and in the United States, the staggering stratification between rich and poor. Canada, historically known as the caring society, is home to 3.5 million people living in poverty, of whom almost 900,000 are children.[2] Where Canada has historically worked to mediate the relationship between rich and poor, its poverty rates are now comparable to the United States, where 3.7 million live in poverty.[3] This book examines how this kind of stratification reveals a growing "compassion gap" between rich and poor, between capability and disability.[4] Where the historical development of the caring or solicitous society—what François Ewald refers to as a society based upon solidarity—sought to *demoralize* the sociological and economic facts of inequality through the development of policy that decommodified public institutions of health, education, housing, and old age and disability pensions, today we seek to legitimize the withdrawal of the elite from the civic commons.[5] The result of this ahistorical deliberation on economic and social policy is the *moralization* of advantage and of disadvantage, of those who have it all and those who have nothing, or who have very little.

In this book, we will consider some of the dominant philosophical approaches to equality which have tended to divorce the ethical or the teleological conception of justice from the moral-deontological conceptions of justice and equality. The argument I will advance is that this divorce may itself be shown to actually reproduce the moralization of advantage and disadvantage. I shall advance and further develop Ricoeur's Aristotelian interpretation of the Rawlsian principles of justice, which demonstrates that the position of the "least advantaged" is to be understood in terms of the *tēlos* or the *aim* of *civic inclusion*—that is, that no-one is to be excluded from the distributive institutions of health, education, housing, and social transfers.[6] This principle of civic inclusion is embodied in the development of the interventionist state. Through the development of public institutions of health, education, housing, and social transfers, the social conditions of the development of moral selfhood is preserved against the onslaught of free range capitalism, which has always sought to tie persons' moral worth to their capabilities for participation in the market, and thus to moralize those disabilities that prevent persons' participation in the market, such as illiteracy, illness, homelessness, age, etc. The distributive figure of the least advantaged member has both an ethical and a moral significance, and in this way, serves to conjoin the teleological and deontological interpretations of selfhood and equality. What the shared figure of disadvantage teaches us is that disadvantage—and advantage—are not moral categories, but rather social categories: the sharing of advantage and disadvantage, of capability and disability, constitutes the historical development of public institutions of solicitude, of care, from which no-*one* is to be excluded. The distributive conception of disadvantage demoralizes disadvantage by configuring the solicitous society: any-one may become ill, become unemployed, be a single parent or care-giver; we will all age and we were all once children, and thus, the social costs associated with health, housing, and pensions are not to be treated as the *negative* costs of inequality and disadvantage but as the institutional articulation of solicitude which fosters any one's life story from childhood, youth, adulthood, and old age. Ricoeur's Aristotelian interpretation of Rawls's theory of distributive justice enables us to appreciate that the lexical ordering of the Rawlsian principles of justice articulating the distributive figure of the least advantaged citizen is done through this interpretation. Rawls's argument is that it is by sharing or distributing the position of the least advantaged member that the social, economic, and political institutions of society—what he refers to as the basic structure of society—develops. If the distribution of the disadvantage of poverty, illness, illiteracy and homelessness are themselves constitutive of the public institutions of society, then we cannot divide disadvantage from advantage without at the same time striking at the historical course of development of the social state, which has sought to distribute the inviolable status of moral personhood to everyone by distinguishing the moral worth of persons from their capability to sell their labor in the free market. It is through the inclusion of everyone in the solicitous institutions of health, educations, old age and disability pensions, and social transfers that we prevent the individualization of illness, illiteracy, old age, homelessness, and unemployment.

One-self as the singular, capable self, then, is not to be separated from *an-other* unemployed, single parent, disabled or homeless self. Thus Ricoeur's dialectic of *oneself as another* underwrites the *recognitive tēlos* of the redistributive institutions of a solicitous society which respects the dignity of another (the distributive self) *as* one-self (the capable self).[7] Where the distributive self underwrites the capable self, we are able to foster a *society of moral strangers*, that is, a society that moralizes neither wealth nor poverty.[8]

Ricoeur's Rawlsian Law of Inclusion

On Ricoeur's Aristotelian interpretation, the lexicographic ordering of the Rawlsian principles of justice demonstrates that the civic inclusion of citizens in the institutions of liberty and equality is the primary social good (or social "advantage") that underwrites all other social goods and advantages. That is, the social good of civic inclusion underwrites citizens' access to such diverse goods as health, education, personal fulfillment, creativity, and so on.

Without this foundational good of civic inclusion, the interrelationship between these advantages, and between advantage and disadvantage, becomes arbitrary at best and punitive at worst. Ricoeur's Rawlsian law of inclusion articulates the kind of mutual fitness that is required between polity and economy in a solicitous society. It is the lexicographic ordering of the political principles of justice over the difference principle that constitutes economic justice and grounds the Kantian *recognitive imperative* to treat persons never as means but always as ends in themselves. That is, it is this principle of economic justice that constitutes the modern welfare state's response to our *moral blindness* towards the social and economic well-being of our fellow citizens that rationalizes their civic exclusion from public institutions of care.

The lexicographic ordering of the Rawlsian principles of justice articulates a recognitive ordering of social goods. As Jean-Peirre Dupuy has argued, "the lexicographic subordination of the principle of difference, which is a principle of economic justice, to two principles of political justice of justice—equality of liberty and equality of opportunity—is an essential trait of *A Theory of Justice*."[9] Dupuy's argument is that the difference principle is only an expression of economic justice in its lexicographic relationship with the principles of political justice (the principles of equality). Ricoeur extends Dupuy's claim and argues that on its own, the difference principle, or maxi-min reasoning, would lose its ethical signification that provides it with the structure of an economic argument, and would regress into a kind of pseudo-economic argument that would itself become a justification for maxi-min reasoning in its utilitarian guise.[10] That is, *scrambling or violating the recognitive ordering between the political principles of inclusion (polity) and the difference principle (economy) leads to a legitimization of the sacrificial principle through the exclusion of our least advantaged citizens from the civic commons.* The principle of economic justice says that we *may not* permit those inequalities that would exclude citizens from civic-recognitive institutions for greater social or economic gain. Determining how inequalities are to be arranged so that they may be to everyone's advantage presupposes the *political* equalities constitutive of the basic respect owed to *each person.* This is the limit condition of the maxi-min principle insofar as it constitutes the reversal of the maxi-min principle from its utilitarian guise to its reformulation as a principle of social justice in which our least advantaged members are granted lexical priority in the development of the institution of citizenship.

Ricoeur and Rawls's Civic Imperative: The Law of Reciprocity

On Ricoeur's reading, the Rawlsian conception of the "least advantaged" member figurates the *tēlos* of civic inclusion, namely, to "*aim at the 'good life' with and for others, in just institutions.*" And at the same time, the figure of the least advantaged member has a moral signification. The law of reciprocity tells us that both advantage and disadvantage, capability and vulnerability, have a *distributive* structure. We recognize disadvantage not by locating it in the figure of the "chronically unemployed, the rough sleepers, the illiterate who dropped out of school very early, [or] those fourteen-year-old girls who become teenage mothers,"[11] but in terms of the *historical* development of public institutions that foster civic capabilities. The capabilities of persons to recognize themselves as moral agents, that is, as self-determining agents, only develop within the reciprocal or public institutions of the social state. We begin with a close reading of Ricoeur's essay in *The Just* (2000) in which he outlines a philosophical anthropology of the capable subject.[12] The question, "who is the subject of rights?", he argues is really a question of "who is capable of ethical and moral imputation," that is, it is a question of *recognition.*[13] Responses to the question "who?", to the question of recognition, in turn, are narratives of the capable subject. This narrative configuration of the capable subject precedes the juridical question—"who is the subject of rights?"—and on the other hand, the course of the configuration of oneself is at the same time a configuration of another: the capabilities of oneself for action, speech, narrative, and ethical and moral evaluation depend upon similar capabilities for another. The capabilities of oneself remain unintelligible and incomplete unless they are shared or distributed among everyone. The capabilities constitutive of the subject of rights are not to be located in myself or yourself, but in the *third party* institutions of language, education, health, law, and social policy. Herein lies Ricoeur's distinct contribution to capability justice scholarship, which has heretofore been overlooked by contemporary capability justice theorists: the capabilities of the subject of rights are civic or public capabilities, and are not to be found in, or *possessed* by, any particular individual.

When we assume that capabilities are possessed, and thus actualized, by persons as such, we are advancing what Ricoeur refers to as an "ultra-individualistic" conception of liberal thought, in which persons are regarded as being fully formed outside of their membership in the public culture of society. Ricoeur responds to this ultra-individualistic or neo-liberal conception of society with a plea in favor of a *civic* liberalism, in which the capabilities of the subject of rights are constitutive of our public institutions, and as such, extends the inviolability of personhood to every-*one*, rather than permitting the use of the principle of the non-violability of persons, which permits the flight of the elite from the civic commons in the name of autonomy, thereby moralizing and thus legitimizing the divide and even the opposition between advantage and disadvantage, between capability and disability. This civic interpretation of the Kantian principle of the inviolability of persons is to be found in John Rawls's theory of distributive justice. We shall develop Ricoeur's argument Rawls's proceduralist articulation of distributive justice is in fact a demonstration of the ethics of *oneself as another*. This may strike the reader as more than a little surprising, because in his proceduralist figuration of justice, Rawls argues that a truly just society is definite by virtue of its independence from ethical considerations of the good life; a truly just society can have no such *tēlos*. Rawls's deontological figuration of society, however, is a defense of justice as reciprocity. The figuration of the original position and the deliberations of the contracting parties therein demonstrates the ethics of *oneself as another*, of the distributive conception of selfhood, by translating Kant's principle of the inviolability of persons as the demand for *publicity*. Rawls gives the Kantian principle of the inviolability of persons a *social* interpretation: membership in society is to be configured such that the terms of cooperation I impose upon you I must also be willing to impose upon myself. I may not offer to sacrifice your status as a self-determining, autonomous person in exchange for greater social or economic gain for myself: the very conditions of the original position work to prevent such a sacrifice. And it is the reasonable conditions of the original position that represent the basic social, political, and economic background conditions of a just society. In short, on the plane of just institutions, the ethics of *oneself as another* is embodied in the publicity condition, which ensures that the inviolable status of moral personhood is extended to every-*one*.

Ricoeur's institutional-redistributive understanding of disadvantage works to *demoralize* vulnerability by refusing its separation from capability.[14] To locate disadvantage outside of the institutions of inclusion itself represents a violation of the anti-sacrificial law of justice. The recognitive ordering articulated by the sacrificial law tells us that *no-one* enjoys recognitive justice when some citizens are excluded from the civic commons because of poor health, disability, poverty, unemployment and old age. Herein lies the ethical significance of the lexicographic ordering of the Rawlsian principles of justice: We are all worse off when we moralize—or *individualize*—vulnerability.

In Chapter 2, we return to Ricoeur's "little ethics," which are articulated in each of the planes—the pursuit of the good life, with others, in just institutions—of the ethical intention. Our argument will be that each of the planes of the ethical intention represents a *socialization* of the Kantian principle of the inviolability of personhood. What this social or *reflexive* reading reveals that it is the norm of reciprocity that grounds the principle of the inviolability persons. That is, the autonomy of personhood is a *distributed* status, and in this way, is a *public* or *social* virtue.

In Chapter 3, having traversed Ricoeur's distributive figuration of each of the planes of the ethical intention, we return to Rawls' conception of *justice as reciprocity* and examine how it represents a procedural demonstration of the shared or the distributed character of the basic institutions of society which enables the development of fully autonomous citizens. That is, Rawls develops a proceduralist demonstration of Rawls's Aristotelian conception of distributive justice, which insists that there should be no division between the individual and society in a truly public society: this is the real meaning of distributive justice. We develop Rawls's Aristotelian defense of the rigorous requirements for a fully public society—a society which excludes no-*one* from development her capabilities for autonomous self-determination—through a critical examination of the charges of anti-communitarianism leveled at Rawls by major communitarian thinkers, such as Michael Sandel and Michael Walzer. Our argument will be that because of the anti-institutional character of Walzer's conception of communitarianism, his is not a genuinely public community, equipped with a civic *phronēsis* that prohibits the sacrifice of our least advantaged members. We shall go so far as to suggest that there is something profoundly anti-communitarian, and indeed elitist, about Sandel's conception of the constitutive community.[15]

In Chapter 4, we turn to examine the social and political implications of some of the contemporary pluralist-communitarian arguments against Rawls's proceduralist articulation of justice as fairness, which simultaneously draw on Walzer and Sandel on one hand, and to both Aristotle and Kant, on the other. I am thinking here of Martha Nussbaum's (2000) theory of capability justice.[16] Where we draw on Aristotle and Kant to develop a distributive conception of personhood, and in this way, configure the capability for autonomy through the public institutions of society, Nussbaum conjoins Aristotle's conception of capability—what persons are capable of doing and being—with Kant's principle of the inviolability of persons in a radically different way. Rather than interpreting the principle of the inviolability of persons through the Aristotelian emphasis on the capability of *oneself as another*, Nussbaum interprets the principle of the inviolability of persons as the *principle of each person's capability*. Drawing on the plural character of disadvantage of women living in poverty in India, a country which nevertheless possesses a robust constitutional regime, Nussbaum argues that Rawls' "resourcist" conception of justice, which she says, simply attempts to distribute material goods to everyone, and in this way cancels out their unique struggles to flourish. Nussbaum develops a list of what she calls "central" capabilities, which she says all persons must be able to develop in order to live a truly human life.[17] By defending the "essential" character of each of these capabilities, Nussbaum revitalizes the challenge to distributive justice posed by the pluralist-communitarian tradition.

We shall argue that Nussbaum's "resourcist" reading of Rawls depends upon her rejection of the lexical ordering of the principles of justice. Because Nussbaum rejects Rawls's distributive interpretation of the least advantaged member, she also inadvertently undermines the publicity requirement that underwrites the capabilities for autonomous personhood. But if capabilities are not publicly figured, from whence do they originate? If capabilities are not distributed, if they are not shared, to whom do they belong? If capabilities and disabilities to be located in each person as an end in herself, then do we not enter into a *possessive*, and thus individualized, comparison of advantage versus disadvantage?

Unless we understand disadvantage in terms of the *tēlos* of civic inclusion, we end up introducing a competitive logic into our deliberations on inequality as do Wolff and De-Shalit in their recent work, in which they credit the communitarian tradition of Walzer and Nussbaum, entitled *Disadvantage*.[18] In making their argument that government policy ought to prioritize the claims of the least advantaged in the crafting of social policy, Wolff and De-Shalit claim that we must first be able to develop a theory of disadvantage that would allow us to realistically identify what it means to be well-off and what it means to be badly off, and then to place "each member of society on a scale of relative advantage and disadvantage."[19] As the *tēlos* of civic inclusion, the figure of the least advantaged plays a normative role in the structuring of redistributive institutions and thus works to undermine the separation between advantage and disadvantage. Wolff and De-Shalit's approach is faced with the problem of trying to make sense of seemingly disparate advantages and disadvantages—satisfaction here, single motherhood there, education here, homelessness there. Wolff and De-Shalit know that they must try to make sense of these seemingly disparate advantages and disadvantages and following the complex or pluralist approach to equality,[20] refer to this problem as the problem of "clustering," where "for some reason, disadvantages cluster together."[21] Wolff and De-Shalit then propose the following approach to *declustering disadvantages*:

> To achieve [de-clustering], governments need to give special attention to the way patterns of disadvantage form and persist, and to take steps to break up such clusters. [. . .] If by improving the lives the least advantaged, governments can achieve a general declustering of disadvantage to the point where *we can no longer say who in society is worst off overall*, they have every reason to claim that they have moved society significantly in the direction of equality.[22]

The very problem of creating a scale of relative disadvantages and advantages reveals that Avnir and De-Shalit's conceptualization of the least advantaged *individualizes* disadvantage by separating and even opposing disadvantage to advantage. Disadvantage is here tied to particular individuals or groups, rather than informing an ethical-political response to *shared* vulnerability. In this respect, Ricoeur's argument is that when we justify the exclusion of some citizens from the institutions of redistributive justice, to borrow Kant's language, we treat them as means rather than as ends in themselves.[23] We fail to respect the dignity of persons when we hyper-moralize disadvantage or when we hyper-individualize disadvantage. We disable citizens' capacities for self-recognition as workers, caregivers, neighbors, and political agents by adopting a punitive response to unemployment, illness, and poverty; that is, by treating these disadvantages or inequalities as matters of individual responsibility rather than questions for social policy aimed at fostering a healthy, educated and ethical society.[24]

Where Wolff and De-Shalit argue that the objective of cultural or recognitive justice is to address the "hierarchical evils" of exploitation, exclusion, and repression, and consign the aim of distributive justice as locating and distributing the "currency" of justice, we argue that the cultural practices of distributive justice configure the solicitous relationship between rich and poor.[25] The "hierarchical evils" of civic exclusion, exploitation, and oppression represent a form of cultural or recognitive injustice insofar as they represent the individualization of vulnerability, that is, insofar as they articulate the weakening of a society's practices of sharing vulnerability in its distributive ethics of *oneself as another*. There can be no division between recognitive or redistributive justice, or between moral and economic justice. It is precisely when we begin to imagine such a divide that we begin to engage in a hierarchicalization of advantage against disadvantage. It is the hyper-individualization of citizens through their exclusion from civic institutions that leads to the "clustering" of disadvantage. A given society's sharing practices, or its *norms of reciprocity*, underwrite its redistributive and its recognitive justice practices, because these ethics of oneself as another configure the civic inclusion of citizens' civic life in public institutions of health, education and the provision of social transfers and which prevent citizens' exclusion from civic life in their neighborhoods, communities, work and families due to poor health, unemployment, illiteracy, and homelessness. These norms of reciprocity, these practices of sharing, then, work to prevent the *clustering of disadvantage*, or the build-up of "corrosive disadvantage," which characterizes the moralization of vulnerability in highly stratified neo-liberal societies.[26]

Recent comparative longitudinal studies on levels of health in Canada and the USA conducted by Siddiqi and Herztman have revealed that it is the slow historical development of *institutional redistributive practices* and public provisions afforded by society and not economic growth or direct health care spending as such, that have a significant impact on long-term population health.[27] Thus, the times during which Canadians' life expectancy has surpassed that of Americans, Canada exhibited higher rates of public expenditures on education, social programs and in the provision of a social safety net through progressive taxation.[28] Canada scored higher than the USA in indexes which measure what political economist Esping-Andersen refers to as "cross-class coalition building," or the distributive practices of society which foster interrelationships between capital and labor, such as unemployment insurance, progressive taxation, labor relations and the presence of political parties representing working-class interests.[29] Thus, Siddiqi and Hertzman's research shows that socio-economic gradients are steeper or more significant for population health outcomes in those societies with weak norms of institutionalized reciprocity. The historical development of institutions of distribution in Canada, such as old-age and disability pensions, education transfers, social transfers, national hospital, and unemployment insurance, and progressive labor laws has meant that between the early 1970s and the late 1990s income stratification did not increase in Canada and during the same period, each income quintile gained life expectancy at an equal rate. In contrast, the comparative weakening of American practices of reciprocity through, for example, reduced public spending, privatized health care and increasing income stratification between rich and poor has meant that at the same time that both rich and poor Canadians were gaining equally in health, the highest income quintile in America gained life expectancy at a faster rate than did the lowest quintiles. The relative weakening of American cross-class coalition building, and the resultant steepness of socio-economic gradients in population health (or the compounding of the disadvantage of poverty with the disadvantage of poor health), Siddiqi and Hertzman argue, must in turn be understood in light of the history of the New Deal, the post-war GI bills, the Great Society Programs and how the social and economic policies of the Reagan government worked to weaken these distributive norms.[30] A distributive understanding of disadvantage and advantage indexes in health and socio-economic status, then, is necessarily an *historical* understanding of the institutions that foster health through the provision of pensions, education and unemployment insurance. *In this way, a distributive-historical understanding of disadvantage or inequality works to de-cluster disadvantage by configuring vulnerability within our solicitous narratives of health, education, employment and social transfers.* Capabilities for health, education and work, then, are fostered through the *norm of reciprocity*, or the *anti-sacrificial* law that underwrites the ethical intention of "aiming at the 'good life' with and for others, in just institutions."[31]

The *civic imperative* that develops from the norm of reciprocity requires that the least advantaged member of society is to have *lexical* priority in all practices of wise deliberation (*phronēsis*) upon our institutions of citizenship. This is Ricoeur's principle of civic inclusion and it underwrites the course of recognition through which reflexive selfhood emerges. Ricoeur's Hegelian argument is that where reflexive selfhood is engendered through civic narratives of health, education, work, in short, through others, the "autoreflexive" (*autoréflexif*) subject is constituted by a kind of short-circuiting wherein she/he is spared these civic detours through others in her/his perfect self-identity.[32] Recognizing oneself is not reduced to self-identification; the mirrored or *reflected* consciousness of Desire must be sublimated into a *reflexive* consciousness.[33] It is Hegel, who, in his theory of the social state, gives an institutional account of the ethical intention to Rawlsian conception of the "least advantaged" member figurates the *tēlos* of civic inclusion, namely, to "aim at the 'good life' with and for others, in just institutions," from which moral autonomy develops, and in this way conjoins the teleological and the deontological traditions of justice. In Chapter 5, we turn to examine Hegel's theory of the social state, and we will pay particularly close attention to the historical implications of Hegel's ethical narrative of the reflexive development of the state in which public institutions are developed through the unrelenting investigation and uncovering of social and economic facts of inequality. We will appeal here to David MacGregor's (1996) argument that Hegel's theory of the social state anticipates the emergence of the modern interventionist state, which works to mediate the workings of free-range capitalism in order to preserve the autonomy and the well-being of worker-citizens. We will examine how Hegel's philosophical defense of the role of the social state in the preservation of moral selfhood underwrites Marx's celebration of the Factory Inspectorate's investigation of the social and economic conditions of the men, women, and children working in England's factories during industrialization. The process by which the state becomes objective to itself is not, as many commentators would have it, a totalizing one. Quite to the contrary, it represents the reflexive development of the state through the ethical interrelationships among the social institutions of the family, education, civic society, unions, and social transfers, which serve to foster and to preserve the development of autonomous personhood. We shall argue that the Kantian principle of the inviolability of persons is embodied in the relentless investigation of the social and economic facts of inequality in the social state, which in turn fosters civic deliberation and civic knowledge that actualizes the concept of freedom.

Ricoeur's distrust of the auto-reflexive self ("*Je me méfie du mot autoréflexive. . .*")[34] stems from its *moral blindness* towards the political, cultural, and economic facts of inequality. This is the civic tragedy involved in the compassion gap between the elite and the vulnerable poor. Moral blindness, the break in the dialectic between autonomy and vulnerability, perverts the Kantian conception of moral autonomy, which requires that we respect the otherness of the other.[35] It is this kind of reasoning that is deployed by Eric Nelson in his defense of the capability for moral choice-making.[36] Just as Wolff and De-Shalit presuppose a divorce between cultural practices of recognitive justice from the "currency" of distributive justice, Nelson argues that the principles of moral egalitarianism protect the individual's capabilities for moral choice-making, but the principle of economic egalitarianism violates this respect owed to the individual's capabilities for choice-making[37]:

> The Kantian idea of the person as an inviolable, autonomous chooser, which underwrites the first principle, is incompatible with the "embedded" view of human beings that justifies the difference principle (i.e., the notion that none of our attributes is, strictly speaking, "ours"). The former requires a respect for individual choices and for the distribution of assets that results from those choices; the latter allows for redistribution, but leaves us with no good reason to respect individual choice at all. Rawls, it turns out, cannot have both autonomy and redistribution, and the same applies to his disciples who have developed the capability approach.[38]

However, our argument is that *phronēsis*—wise moral reasoning—necessarily has an institutional-redistributive context, i.e., the *phronēsis* of the rational will must become adequate to a distributive understanding of capacity if we are to foster the health and well-being of *each* person. Just as Wolff and De-Shalit's scale of disadvantage presupposes the very opposition between capability and vulnerability that it seeks to address, and in this way individualizes vulnerability, Nelson understands recognitive justice as the exercise of individualist deliberation which stands in opposition to the society's historical deliberation on its distributive understanding of vulnerability. The divorce Nelson proposes between the principles of political justice and the principles of economic justice, then, represent a *regression* of the historical development of our civic capabilities, and it is for this reason that Nelson reduces moral equality to the capacity for individualist choice making. But Ricoeur's argument is that treating persons as ends in themselves, as moral agents capable of imputation, has only become possible with the development of those redistributive institutions which safeguard *every-one's* capabilities for self-recognition. The norm of reciprocity between the moral sphere (*Moralität*) and the institutional realm Ethical Life (*Sittlichkeit*) constitutes Ricoeur's Hegelian understanding of mutual recognition and engenders social science knowledge of the sociological and economic facts of inequality.

Phronēsis and the Slow Historical Development of Redistributive Institutions

Ricoeur's reading of the anti-sacrificial law of justice demonstrates that the pluralist requirement for recognitive justice is only satisfied where every-*one* has the capability to recognize himself or herself as parent, student, child, caregiver, neighbor, and as a member of his or her political community. These are needs we have on behalf of our others. The distributive conception of capability and selfhood developed by Ricoeur's Aristotelian reading of Rawls reminds us that the social costs entailed in the development and maintenance of public institutions of care underwrite a pluralist-recognitive conception of equality and thus are not to be regarded as the *negative* costs of vulnerability. Without a distributive understanding of capability and of vulnerability, our conception of justice itself remains elitist. We preserve citizens' capabilities for moral choice-making through the preservation of collective *phronēsis*, or moral deliberation, guided by the slow, historical development of institutionalized forms of care. This is so because the development of our practices of public provision *embodies* the history of civic *phronēsis*. In Chapter 6, we continue to flesh out Ricoeur and Rawls's philosophical account of the solicitous state by taking a closer look at the historical development of the principle of the inviolability of persons through the gradual inclusion of everyone in the public institutions of society. We shall consider how the *progressive enfranchisement* of women, persons of color, persons with psychiatric and intellectual disabilities, and most recently, the enfranchisement of prisoners, demonstrates the fundamentally distributed or shared character of the principle of autonomy. We will take as our point of analysis the reasoning of the majority in the constitutional challenge to Section 51(e) of *Canada's Elections Act*, which prohibited inmates serving two or more years in prison from the right to vote. In our analysis, we shall combine Ricoeur's remarkable analysis on the relationship between the capability for imputation and the concept of responsibility in his essays in *The Just* (2000) with historian T.H. Marshall's account of the development of social rights in the modern welfare state. By situating Ricoeur's analysis of the capability for imputation within Marshall's historical account of the development of social rights in the modern welfare state, we come to appreciate the *social* preconditions of the capability for self-recognition. The irrevocably social grounding of the capability for self-recognition and thus for autonomous self-determination has profound implications for the modern notion of autonomy: the exclusion of some one group or persons from the franchise represents a regression of the civic narrative of the progressive enfranchisement of every-*one* in the public institutions of society. Herein lies the two-fold meaning of *sanction*: in order for a punishment to be just, it cannot violate the public sanction that provides it with its legitimacy. Denying the right to vote to a discrete group of persons constitutes a violation of the public-social grounding of just punishment, and in this way constitutes an attack on the rights of every-one, embodied, to recall Ricoeur's fine phrase, in the third party. *Denying the right to vote to anyone entails the loss of liberty for every-one: such is the reasoning of the majority in Sauvé.* When we regress on the historical configuration of care, we endanger our capabilities for health, for education, for literacy, for work, for culture, and for political participation. Collective *phronēsis*, guided by the *tēlos* of civic inclusion, works to foster civic forms of recognition constitutive of a solicitous society.

Chapter 1

An Introduction to Ricoeur's Theory of Capability Justice

> We now encounter a form of passivity which I will call the self-actualization of everyone by everyone. By this I mean that we can only act through structures of interaction which are already there and which tend to unfold their own history that consists of inertias and innovations, which in turn themselves are sedimented in their turn. In other words, there can be no history of freedom or of freedoms without the mediation of a neuter or neutral term endowed with its own inertia; in short, if I may put it in these terms, a freedom in the third person which is actually the nonperson between persons (Ricoeur, 1978: 181).

Ricoeur's "philosophical anthropology" revolves around the development and the preservation of the capable subject. The juridical-legal-political question "who is the subject of rights?", Ricoeur argues, presupposes an anthropological question, namely, who is the subject capable of moral and ethical self-designation (Ricoeur, 1992: 2000)? That is, the question "who?" is a question of recognition. When we ask the anthropological question—the question of "who?"—the responses we yield are narratives of a capable subject. This configuration or narrative of the capable subject precedes and mediates the juridical question. The anthropological configuration of the capable subject, on the other hand, is only completed on the institutional plane of a political community. It is this two-fold movement between the political-institutional configuration of the subject of rights and the philosophical anthropology of the subject capable of self-recognition as the author of her speech, action, narrative, and thus capable of ethical and moral responsibilities that conjoin these capabilities of speech, action, and narrative to their author that constitutes Ricoeur's vision of liberal democratic politics.

Recognizing the subject of rights, then, implies the recognition of the capable subject. We recognize the capable subject by asking "who?". In answering the question "who?" the subject reflexively recognizes himself or herself as the capable agent. Four distinct capabilities can be identified in the course of recognition that is initiated when we ask "who?". The first, most primary capability is expressed in response to the question "who is speaking?" The subject must be capable of recognizing herself as the author, as the "focal point" of her many and diverse speech acts. The second recognitive question comes in the form "who is the author of an action?" The attribution of an action to author is often a difficult task, as attested to by the search for responsibility where the responsible agent will be required to compensate in some way the patient(s) of his action, and in the search for responsibility in historical conflicts. And yet, the importance of being able to recognize the author of an action cannot be emphasized enough in the designation of the subject of rights and duties. The third stage in the course of recognition underscores the *configurative status* of recognition. Questions about the authors of speech and of action lead us directly into the question of narrative identity, insofar as speech and action have a temporal quality, which is expressed in the narrative structure. Narrative identity is important too because it specifies what kind of recognition or identity we are seeking. We do not recognize persons or collectivities in the same way that we recognize unchanging structures, such as the genetic coding constitutive of the biological and chemical make-up of organisms. Rather, the narrative identity of the history of nations as well as of personal identity is configured, like all stories, by the emplotment of dramatic reversals of fortune, and this configuration confers meaning to the story of peoples and of actors. These contingencies, these reversals of fortune, give personal and collective identity a very different meaning than the identity of things or substances.

At the final stage of course of recognition, we recognize the capable subject through the application of moral and ethical evaluations. That is, we recognize the capable subject through the moral lens of obligation or the ethical lens of goodness. We see the political subject, to whom we impute rights and responsibilities, emerging very clearly at this stage of our recognitive investigation. It is the *reflexivity* of moral and ethical evaluations that make possible the recognition of the responsible subject: we are capable of recognizing ourselves as being worthy of esteem and respect because we are capable of recognizing our own actions and those of others as good or bad, just or forbidden. It should be noted that the ethical and moral predications of the capable subject is already presupposed in the capabilities for speech, action, and as the authors of our narratives. For we hold ourselves in esteem and respect ourselves insofar as we are capable of recognizing ourselves in our speech, action, and narration: "We esteem ourselves capable of esteeming our own actions, we respect ourselves in that we are capable of impartially judging our own actions. Self-esteem and self-respect are in this way reflexively addressed to a capable subject" (Ricoeur, 2000: 4). Taken together, then, the capability for ethical and moral predication constitutes the reflexive subject, capable of the imputation of social, political, economic and legal rights.

The subject's capacity to recognize herself as the author of her conception of the good life presupposes yet another detour in the return path to the self, in the development of genuine self-reflexivity. For in order to realize its capabilities, and thus to become genuinely capable of self-recognition, the subject requires the dialogical and institutional mediation. In short, genuine self-reflexivity presupposes the mediation of otherness. Ricoeur's argument is that there is a two-fold constitution to otherness itself: the dialogic plane, in which the other is a "you" and the institutional plane, in which the other is the third party (Ricoeur, 2000: 5). This dialogical and institutional mediation is an intrinsic part of Ricoeur's philosophical anthropology of the capable subject. It is Ricoeur's emphasis on the solicitous mediation of the capable of subject by virtue of the dialogic and institutional planes that will inform his Aristotelian interpretation of Rawls's distributive justice. By way of anticipation, we may say that the dialogical and the institutional mediation of the capable self is expressed by the *solicitous aim* of distributive justice. This solicitous aim of justice is characterized by the ethics of distribution, of sharing, because it is by virtue of this sharing that we establish the civic *trust* constitutive of the institution of language itself.

It is through language, at the most primitive stage of the anthropology of the capable subject, of speech, that we first encounter the mediation of dialogic and institutional otherness. In describing the capability for speech, we specifically emphasized the subject's capability to recognize her singular authorship in the utterances of her many and diverse speech acts. But in emphasizing the subject's capability for self-designation in this way, we ignored the context of interlocution that underwrites this self-designation. The singular speaker, the "I" presupposes a second person hearer, a "you". The interlocutory *positions* may here be reversed: when you designate yourself as "I," "I" hear "you," and when "I" hear "you," "you" are the "I" that is speaking. Everyone of course understands these basic rules of interlocution and "this mastery contributes in the following way to the emergence of the subject of rights: *like me* the other can designate himself as an *I* when he speaks. The expression 'like me' already announces the recognition of the other as my equal in terms of rights and duties" (Ricoeur, 2000: 6, original emphasis). While the interlocutory *positions* may be reversed, the subjects occupying these positions may not. At the same time, the *singularity* of the speaker and the listener itself depends upon the ethics of *similitude* governing our dialogic practices. In order to understand this, we need only appeal to our reliance on pronouns—even the direct appeal to "you," the listener, is impossible, without reference to the third expressed in the pronouns he/she/it. In appealing to these pronouns, we are appealing to everyone included within a linguistic culture, and thus to the institution of language itself. Interlocution depends upon not simply these rules of interlocution which designates one linguistic culture from another, but to what this linguistic culture constitutes, namely, an *ethics of sharing* through which each member of a linguist culture recognizes himself or herself as being part of, as sharing in, that culture:

> This recognition does not reduce to just the adoption of the same rules by everyone; it also requires the confidence each one of them places in the *rule of sincerity*, without which any linguistic exchange would be impossible. I expect that each will *mean what he or she says*. This confidence establishes public discourse on a basis of trust where the other appears as a third party and not just as a "you". In truth, this fiduciary base is more than an interpersonal relation, it is the institutional condition of every interpersonal relation. (Ricoeur, 2000: 6, original emphasis)

The ethics of sharing underwrites the *bond of trust* constitutive of the institution of language. Without the sense of sharing within a community of language, the development of the capability of speech would be impossible. Our appeal to the pronouns he/she/it is an appeal to this shared trust in a community of language by virtue of which our capability for speech is confirmed and realized.

It is through the configuration of trust, in which self-recognition unfolds, that underlies the realization of the capabilities for speech, action, and imputation. Thus, our capability to recognize ourselves as the authors of our actions unfolds from within "*inter-action*," in which my capabilities for action depends upon and unfolds within the context of my teachers, neighbors, friends, and ultimately, upon my political community. My personal initiatives are first recognized by others, and this interpersonal recognition is in turn mediated by educational, cultural, social, economic institutions within the democratic state by virtue of which my actions, undertaken in cooperation with others, may be extended to other communities and contexts, without being threatened by becoming limited to an overly personalized and thus overly moralized social community. On the plane of narrative self-recognition, the stories we tell in which we are the protagonists and in through which we hold ourselves in esteem are themselves intertwined with the stories of others, and in turn, in the societal practices of documentation or institutionalization in social time of the historical building up of cultures and institutions. These societal practices of documentation in turn support the vast detours through cultural, institutional, and historical processes and development genuine self-understanding must traverse. This triad of me/you/third person figurates self-esteem on the ethical plane as well. It is the other who first renders me responsible, and thus capable of self-esteem, by depending upon me: my very capability to recognize myself as worthy of esteem is itself grounded in the dependency of the other that I will, for instance, keep my word. My self-recognition as being capable of esteem develops within a context of *trust*. The legal-political signification of responsibility in the sense of the obligation to keep one's word in contractual obligations already indicates that the capability for self-esteem is supported by a bond of social trust that exceeds the face-to-face relation in promise-making. It is the ethical "principle that agreements should be kept" that underwrites the political-legal designation of the responsible subject, and this ethical principle of promise-keeping configures the recognitive capability of the subject in the face-to-face relation within the bond of fellowship (Ricoeur, 2000: 7). This ethical principle of promise-keeping, then, receives its formal legal-political articulation in the laws of the community, of the state, and ultimately, to humanity as a whole, where "the other is no longer 'you', but the third party designated in a noteworthy way by the pronoun 'everyone' [*chacun*], an impersonal but not anonymous pronoun" (Ricoeur, 2000: 8). The French chacun may also here be translated as "each," which in turn emphasizes the singularity in everyone.

The *each* in every-*one* signifies that it is to the *plurality* of persons that each of the capabilities—for speech, for action, for narration and for self-esteem—applies. In traversing the triadic figuration me/you/third person of each of the capabilities, we appreciate how the singularity of the listener and speaker, of the initiator of action, of the storyteller and of the promise-keeper is *actualized* and *preserved* through the *inclusion* of *each person* that the "face-to-face relation leaves out as a third party" (Ricoeur, 2000: 8). *The capabilities for speech, action, narration, and self-esteem must be extended to everyone in order to be actualized.* And we make the passage from the capability for selfhood to the actualization of selfhood through the ethical principle of plurality, expressed in the historical and social will of a people to live together in the historical and social commitment to extend the capabilities for personhood to *everyone*. This social and historical commitment to the inclusion of everyone in, to borrow Hannah Arendt's language, in the public sphere, is irreducible to the interpersonal or face-to-face relation, and thus the "political institution confers a distinct structure on this will to live together. . ." (Ricoeur, 2000: 8). Ricoeur names this collective or shared will to live together political power. Political power is an extension of the powers of the capable subject for speech, action, and narration, embodied in our institutionalized practices of sharing, political power bestows upon our practices an *historical perspective*, inscribing them upon social time. By virtue of this configuration, capabilities *endure*.

From Ricoeur to Rawls: Justice as the Neuter or the Third Party

This institutional configuration of this capability for political power has, as each of the other powers we have discussed, an ethical signification. The ethical signification of political institutions is *justice*. Here Ricoeur quotes John Rawls's opening lines from *A Theory of Justice*: "Justice is the first virtue of social institutions as truth is to systems of thought" (Ricoeur, 2000: 8). Justice, as the horizon of the capable subject, applies not to the personal subject, not to the "you," but to the third party, to "*every-one*." As the philosophical anthropology of the capable subject shows us, the capabilities of the *one*, of *you*, depend upon similar capabilities for an-*other*: my capabilities for self-recognition as a moral actor capable of speech, action, narration, and self-esteem remains truncated and thus incomprehensible outside of the reference to the third party, and it is by virtue of the reference to the third that my capabilities develop and endure: "The application to human interactions of the rule of justice presupposes that we can take society as a vast system of distribution, that is, of the sharing of roles, burdens, tasks, well beyond the distribution that takes place on the economic plane of market values" (Ricoeur, 2000: 8–9). *On the ethical-political plane of just institutions, distribution refers to the historical commitment—constitutive of political power—to act and live together, by virtue of the extension of the capabilities of selfhood to every-one.*

Each side of this two-fold movement between the philosophical anthropology of the capable subject—distinguished by the question who?—and the realization of these capabilities by virtue of their mediation by historical and political institutions reflects two distinct traditions in liberal thought. The liberal tradition that emphasizes the capabilities constitutive of selfhood as such, that is, independently of political membership, correctly underscores the rights of humanity itself, and this tradition underwrites the philosophical anthropology of the capable subject. This respect owed to the rights of humanity as such, it is true, informs the positive rights of the subject. On the other hand, this tradition of liberal thought is governed by a serious misconception of the philosophical anthropology upon which it relies: it confuses our *capabilities* for action, speech, narration, and for self-esteem for the "*accomplishments*" of individuals (Ricoeur, 2000: 9). The anthropological response to the question "who is the subject of rights?" emphasizes the subject capable of recognizing herself as worthy of self-respect, corresponds to a tradition of liberal thought in which the autonomy of the individual precedes her membership in the state. The rights and liberties owed to persons capable of action, speech, narrative, and imputation is constitutive of the rights of humanity as such, of persons as ends in themselves. This is the "ultra-individualistic" tradition of social contractualism, in which the individual is the fully actualized subject of rights *prior* to entering into the social contract; she wagers these real rights, or what we refer to as natural rights, in exchange for social rights, characterized as the right to security in Hobbes or the right to citizenship or civil status in Rousseau and in Kant. The significance of this individualist interpretation of liberalism, represented by social contractualism, is that the subject's relationship to other individuals is at best contingent and at worse revocable. In this way, the individualist interpretation threatens public institutions, which embody the ethics and the history of our practices of sharing.

There is another tradition in liberal thought, what we may call the *civic tradition* in liberal thought and to which we may appeal in answering the question "who is the subject of rights?" It is this civic tradition in liberal thought that configures the two-fold movement between the *capabilities* of selfhood and the *actualization* of selfhood, and it is to this civic liberalism that Ricoeur dedicates the essays in *The Just*, and in his work as a whole. What distinguishes the civic tradition from the "ultra-individualistic" tradition in liberal thought is its figuration of the capabilities for selfhood in the third party, that is, in the public culture of society—the fiduciary base—which funds every-*one*'s capabilities to recognize herself as an autonomous, self-determining moral agent:

> Without institutional mediation, individuals are only the initial drafts of human persons. Their belonging to a political body is necessary for their flourishing as human beings, and in this sense, this mediation cannot be

> revoked. On the contrary, the citizens who issue from this institutional mediation can only wish that every human being should, like them, enjoy such political mediation, which when added to the necessary conditions stemming from a philosophical anthropology becomes a sufficient condition for the transition from the capable human being to the real citizen. (Ricoeur, 2000: 10)

The inviolable rights of humanity, of persons as ends in themselves, emphasized by neoliberalism are, by virtue of justice, rights that are distributed—shared—by everyone. The very principle of the inviolability of personhood—of the respect owed to persons as ends in themselves—is threatened and indeed becomes disfigured in its elitism—when its historical preservation in the solicitous mediation by the mediation of political membership is forgotten or repressed.

John Rawls: A Proceduralist Defense of the Civic Tradition in Liberal Thought

We find an articulation of the civic tradition of liberal thought in the work of John Rawls. It might strike the reader as more than a little strange that we appeal to Rawls at this juncture—whose social contractualism situates his theory of justice soundly within the deontological tradition—and conjoin him to the ethical tradition that characterizes Ricoeur's Aristotelian philosophical anthropology, which emphasizes as we have seen the ethics of reciprocity, of sharing, in the development of the capable subject. However, my argument will be that Rawls's proceduralism articulates the *ethical aim* of Rawls's principles of justice, expressed by Ricoeur's distributive ethics of *oneself as another*, namely, the intention to "aim at the good, with and for others, in just institutions" (Riceour, 1992: 172). Rawls's proceduralism is a demonstration of the way in which the subject—capable of self-recognition as the author of her actions—is configured by the norms of reciprocity constitutive of the basic structure of society. In so doing, I appeal to Ricoeur's argument that the procedural character of Rawls's deontological theory of justice itself works to support the ethical foundations upon which it ultimately rests.[1] Unless we are able to understand the significance of the ethics of reciprocity articulated by Rawls's proceduralist explication of the principles of justice, we are in danger, I shall argue, of badly misunderstanding the relationship between his proceduralism and his critique of arbitrary inequality.

If we are to understand in what way Rawls's proceduralist theory of justice as an articulation of the civic tradition in liberal thought, in which the capabilities of selfhood are realized from within the institutional configuration of society, we must first develop a full account of what it is that the contractualist exercise, represented by the original position, is supposed to demonstrate. For it is possible, and indeed quite common, to provide only a partial reading of the Rawlsian contractualist exercise. This partial reading consists in aligning Rawls with what Ricoeur has referred to as the "ultra-individualist" version liberalism, which rests on the idea of the fully formed individual, equipped with a schedule of natural rights, and who exists prior to the mediation of the institutions of society.[2] I call this a partial reading of Rawls's proceduralist account of justice, because it captures only half of Rawls's two-fold, or dialectical, conception of justice. The grounds for this individualist interpretation may be found in the second part of Rawls's articulation of the subject of justice, found in the opening lines of *A Theory of Justice* (1971): "Each person possesses an inviolability founded on justice that even the welfare of society as a whole cannot override. For this reason justice denies the loss of freedom for some made right by the greater good shared by others" (Rawls, 1971: 3). If we attempt to derive Rawls's proceduralist exercise solely from his articulation of the inviolability of persons, we invariably arrive at an individualist interpretation of Rawls's liberalism, for on this reading, the Kantian principle of the inviolability of persons—the freedom of persons as ends in themselves—precedes society. Society, in turn, represents a threat to this principle of autonomy. But the principle of the inviolability of persons follows the first part of Rawls's articulation of the subject of justice, namely the social institutions constitutive of the basic structure of society: "Justice is the first virtue of social institutions, as truth is to systems of thought. A theory however elegant and economical must be rejected or revised if it is untrue; likewise laws and institutions no matter how efficient and well-arranged must be reformed or abolished if they are unjust" (Rawls, 1971: 3). Taken together, Rawls's opening declarations tell us what his proceduralist account of justice will defend: It is the task of the institutions of society to preserve the inviolability of persons as ends in themselves. Read in the other direction, this means: the autonomy of persons—each person's capability to recognize herself as the author of her conception of the good—depends upon just institutions. The significance of the dialectic between just institutions and the justice that funds the inviolability of persons consists in Rawls's overarching argument that the inviolability of persons is preserved when the status of moral personhood is extended to everyone in the political community: the recognitive capabilities of *oneself* depend upon the distribution of these recognitive capabilities to *everyone. Unless we are able to preserve this distributive interpretation of the recognitive capabilities constitutive of moral selfhood, the capabilities for moral personhood are threatened, not just for our least advantaged citizens, but for everyone.* But I am getting ahead of myself: we must work our way through Rawls's contractualist exercise in order to see how this exercise itself is demonstration of the norms of reciprocity. By drawing out the relationship between Rawls's two-fold declaration of the subject of justice, namely, the dialectic between the basic structure of society and the inviolability of persons, my aim is simply to avoid the typical reduction of Rawls's analytic theory to the principle of the inviolability of persons, by paying close attention to the how the very proceduralist character of Rawls's theory is aimed towards a defense of the social institutions that underwrite the autonomy of persons. Allow me one more prediction: If our argument that Rawls's proceduralism is a demonstration of an ethics of reciprocity, then we will also be able to discern a Rawlsian theory of capability justice.

Rawls makes it clear that the conception of justice he develops is not meant as an account of the good society, nor even of the principles of right, though the principles of justice constitute a part of the conception of the good society and of the right. Rather, Rawls draws on the "usual sense of justice," which, drawing from both traditions of the good and the right, defines the tasks of justice as the elimination of injustice of arbitrary inequality articulates the sense of justice. The aim of our sense of justice recalls Aristotle's concern with the search for proportionate equality pursued by justice is fairness:

> I shall focus attention, then, on the usual sense of justice in which it means essentially the elimination of arbitrary distinctions, and the establishment within the structure of a practice of a proper share, balance, or equilibrium between competing claims. The principles of justice serve to specify the application of "arbitrary" and "proper", and they do this by formulating restrictions as to how practices may define positions and offices, and assign powers and liabilities, rights and duties. (Rawls, 1999: 191)

We cannot emphasize enough the significance of the vice of arbitrary inequality for Rawls's conception of justice: it is the amelioration of arbitrary inequality that conjoins the social institutions of society with the principle of the inviolability of persons. For it is the vice of arbitrary inequality that violates the principle of the inviolability of persons, by virtue of which each person possess an original claim to equality, to inclusion in the fraternity of moral personhood. This sense of justice, in turn, configures justice, not social or economic efficiency as the first virtue of social institutions. The principles of justice, in designing the basic structure of society, distinguish between arbitrary inequality by furnishing the institutions of equality, and thereby identify legitimate inequalities, by virtue of which each citizen designates herself as the author of her conception of the good—or, to use Rawls's language, each citizen can be said to have *merited* her conception of the good.

Justice as Reciprocity: The Golden Rule as the Basic Structure of Society

It is the task—and what I will argue following Ricoeur, the ethical task—of the elimination of arbitrary inequality that governs the Rawlsian version contractualist exercise, and which distinguishes it from the social contract tradition from which it derives. Rawls's conception of justice carries to a higher level of abstraction the social contractualism of Locke, Rousseau, and Kant, in which the original position generates the conditions under which individuals possessing natural rights negotiate the terms under which they concede to membership within a particular society, or by virtue of which they design a governing body. In abstracting from this conception of the original position, Rawls's conception of justice seeks not to specify the conditions of individual members' concession to membership in a political community, but rather to *specify the conditions of mutuality*.

It is important that we understand what Rawls means when he says that his conception of the social contract as conceived by Locke, Rousseau, and Kant (Rawls, 1971: 11). For what he is saying is that the original parties, by participating in the deliberations in the original position, are not contracting into a *particular* society, nor to a *particular* form of government. Rather, the original contract, or what Rawls refers to as the original position, applies to the principles of justice constitutive of the basic structure of society, of the public figuration of the principles of cooperation among free and equal persons in the public institutions of society. By entering into the original position, mutually self-interested, rational, and similarly situated persons, set about defining not the particular claims they want to make against one another; the object, rather, is to articulate a system for the fair adjudication of such claims. A system of adjudication is fair when everyone can agree to it: thus, the principles of justice must be publicly acclaimed. It is the public character of the basic structure of society, articulated by the principles of justice, that distinguish justice as fairness from other conceptions of justice, such as justice as efficiency, as it is articulated by the utilitarian tradition.

The circumstances of justice, namely, the requirement for a fair system of self-interested persons who nevertheless are similarly situated in terms of their needs and capacities, wish to press their respective claims against one another. We say that persons are self-interested insofar as they seek their own advantage in any cooperative venture they undertake. But even at this stage of analysis, Rawls's conception of the self-interested individual is not as narrow as Hobbes's: what strikes us as artificial in Hobbes' characterization of self-interest is that it cannot account for our experience of loyalty and devotion, which we experience within our familial, religious, and other social associations, and which lead us to behave in ways that exceed the confines of narrow self-interest. We arrive at a more realistic account of the self-interested personality by interpreting the "person" along the lines of self-interested families or associations (Rawls, 1999: 199). Mutually self-interested persons are also rational: they are able to accurately assess what their interests are, and are able to choose among conflicting interests. When choosing between conflicting ends, persons are able to determine which short-term interests may be sacrificed for long-term gains. Having engaged in this cost–benefit analysis, they are able to adhere to their chosen course of action and resist the temptations posed by short-term gains. Rawls adds one more aspect to this definition of rationality, found in price theory: rational persons do not experience envy at the very perception of differences between their relative positions. Envy or resentment arises only when these differences are explained by reference to the workings of unjust institutions or to the workings of arbitrary luck (Rawls, 1999: 199). Finally, these mutually self-interested and rational persons have similar, or at least complementary, interests and capabilities, such that cooperation among them is possible. They are also more or less equal in terms of power, preventing any-*one* from dominating an-*other*.

The rational pursuit of self-interest leads persons to press their claims upon one another. It is here, Rawls argues, that questions of justice arise. But if the rational pursuit of self-interest represents the "circumstances in which questions of justice arise," it is the remaining feature of personhood—what Rawls refers to as the constraint of having a morality—that represents the procedure by which principles of justice are chosen and affirmed. Recall that these principles of justice will serve to adjudicate among the competing claims generated by the rational pursuit of self-interest. Having a morality implies that the principles of justice—and thus the basic institutional make-up of society—must be affirmed by one-self *as* an-other. That is, each person must act not only rationally, but reasonably as well; moral persons must act not merely rationally, but also reasonably, by acknowledging the limits of one-self, thereby acknowledging the limits of an-*other*:

> Once the procedure is adopted and carried through, each person is committed to acknowledging principles as impartially applying to his own conduct and claims as well as to another's, and he is committed moreover to principles which may constitute a constraint, or limitation, on the pursuit of his own interests. Now having a morality is analogous to having made a firm commitment *in advance* to acknowledge principles having these consequences for one's own conduct. (Rawls, 1999: 202)

It is in this way that the pursuit of self-advantage becomes, in the sense of justice, the pursuit of common advantage, "for non is willing to sacrifice anything for the others" (Rawls, 1999: 203).

Taken together, the circumstances in which questions of justice arise and the constraints of having a morality give rise to two serially ordered principles of justice. The first principle, which is lexically prior to the second principle, states that all persons are to enjoy equal access to a suite of political liberties. That persons are equal is represented in the conditions that give rise to questions of justice, namely, that persons are similarly situated in terms of their needs, powers, and capabilities, and that all pursue their rational interests in a mutually self-interested manner. But it is this very equality in liberty that gives rise to the second principle, which states that liberties may be maximized by permitting certain inequalities, so long as the first principle of equality of liberty is not sacrificed. It is here that the constraints of having a morality configure the circumstances in which questions of justice arise, by ensuring that no-one's liberty is sacrificed for greater social or economic gain. Later on, we shall consider how Rawls refers to the configuration of the circumstances in which questions of justice arise by the constraints of having a morality as the configuration of "rational autonomy" by "reasonable" or "full autonomy." Inequalities will be arbitrary from a moral point of view, unless they can be shown to be to everyone's advantage, that is, unless they maximize everyone's capability for moral authorship, for liberty. Furthermore, the offices or positions from which differences in liberties flow must be open to all. Taken together, "[T] these principles express justice a s a complex of three ideas: liberty, equality, and reward for services contributing to the common good" (Rawls, 1999: 193). From a Kantian constructivist point of view, the autonomy of rational agents is only realized from within the constraints of the full publicity requirement embodied in the social institutions of the basic structure of society. In Hegelian fashion, we may say that persons' capabilities for rational autonomy are only realized from within the reasonable or fully autonomy embodied in the social institutions of the state. It is the conflation of rational autonomy with full autonomy that permits the separation of the principle of autonomy from the principle of equality.

Our "sense of justice" teaches us that there is something unjust about arbitrary distinctions. But the question here is, what is it about the arbitrary distinctions between persons that renders them unjust? Another way of asking this question is, what is the origin of our sense of justice? Rawls refers to the procedure by which he arrives at the principles of justice which will "serve to specify the application of 'arbitrary' and 'proper' distinctions between persons as a 'Kantian constructivism,' and will thereby appeal to Kant's conception of practical reason. But Rawls applies Kant's practical reasoning not to the individual moral person as such, but rather to the *social* conditions by virtue of which person's capabilities for autonomous authorship, for imputation, develop. That is, the subject of Kantian constructivism is the basic structure of society. It is the way the basic social, economic, and political structure of society makes use of the arbitrary or the natural distinctions between persons "and permits them to affect the social fortune of citizens, their opportunities in life, and the actual terms of cooperation between them" that is the subject of Rawls's Kantian constructivism (Rawls, 1999: 337).[3] The natural distinctions between persons—those advantages and disadvantages that flow from the socio-economic, educational, health starting places for children, are, morally speaking, arbitrary. What makes the distinctions between persons morally relevant is the way in which societies share or distribute these natural contingencies in its basic structure:

> A further essential distinction is between the unequal distribution of natural assets, which is simply a natural fact and neither just or unjust, and the way the basic structure of society makes use of these natural differences and permits them to affect the social fortune of citizens, their opportunities in life, and the actual terms of cooperation between them. *Plainly it is the way that social institutions use natural differences, and allow accident and chance to operate, which defines the problem of social justice.* (Rawls, 199: 337–338, my emphasis)

Distinctions between persons gain their properly moral tenor from within societal practices of distribution and sharing. The inviolability of personhood established by virtue of the just distinction between persons, is itself grounded in the *norm of reciprocity* embodied in the institutionalized practices of giving and receiving. The very status of moral personhood is a distributed or a *shared* status. Rawls, in emphasizing, and indeed in developing, the social role of morality, conjoins the Judaeo-Christian of the Golden Rule, which taught us that the preservation of *one*-self may not come at the expense of an-other: the norm of reciprocity prohibits this sacrificial calculation in favor of the public deliberation of oneself *as* another. Thus while in Kant's moral philosophy, each individual moral actor, in proposing a maxim, is to engage in a comparison of social worlds, i.e., the social worlds that would result from the enactment of a given maxim, this comparison of social worlds is nevertheless undertaken by the individual moral actor in order to test a given moral principle:

> Thus Kant proceeds from the particular, even personal, case of everyday life, he assumed that this process carried out correctly would yield a coherent and sufficiently complete system of principles, including principles of social justice. *Justice as fairness moves in quite the reverse direction: its construction starts from a unanimous collective agreement regulating the basic structure of society within which all personal and associational decisions are to be made in conformity with this prior undertaking.* (Rawls, 1999: 339)

On Rawls's account, Kantian practical reason applies not to the capability of the individual agent to universalize her moral maxim, and to thereby recognize herself as the autonomous author of her action and speech, but rather to the way in which the social, political, and economic institutions engender every-one's capabilities for moral autonomy. The Kantian emphasis on the universal—which requires that we treat every-one not merely as a means, but as an end in herself—is realized not in the reasoning of the autonomous moral agent, but rather in the fully public culture of a society articulated by the principles of justice, embodied in the social, political, and economic institutions of society. We pursue our personal and associational commitments from within this public culture, which prohibits the sacrifice of one-self for greater social and economic benefits of an-other, or more accurately, prohibits the pitting of the disadvantages of one-self against the advantages of an-other. Justice does not develop from the immediacy of the I–you relation, and thus outside of the neutral term, to borrow Ricoeur's language. The "I–you" relation already presupposes the public culture of "we" and the "they" embodied in public institutions. Thus, the neutral term or the third party—"the nonperson between persons"—constitutes the heart of the human bond:

> What is more, just a very small part of the human bond may be personalized, and this personalization proceeds from our continuing effort to internalize more of a bond that is first of all a neuter bond. The greatest part of our social life consists in coordinating roles, services, labours and works which are only slightly personalized. (Ricoeur, 1978: 181)[4]

It is the development of the neutral term, Ricoeur argues, that is configured by Hegel's account of "objective spirit." Freedom requires for its actualization the mediation of the institutions of family, law, economy, and social and political life: "We may well undertake to internalize these objective relations and to make them more intimate, but we cannot engender them as objective in terms of this project toward intimacy" (Ricoeur, 1978: 181–182).[5] It is in the objectification of the neuter bond that the history of the development of public life is to be found, and this historical development of the public culture of a society plays an educative role in the development of citizens' capabilities for moral authorship. The capability for moral authorship is not given a priori, as a fact of reason, but is engendered by the historical development of the public culture of society:

> Once this condition [of full publicity] is imposed, a moral conception assumes a wide role as a part of public culture. Not only are its first principles embodied in political and social institutions and the public traditions of their interpretation, but the derivation of citizens' rights, liberties, and opportunities, invokes a certain conception of their person. In this way citizens are made aware of and educated to this conception. They are presented with a way of regarding themselves that otherwise they would most likely never be able to entertain. Thus the realization of the full publicity condition provides the social milieu within which the notion of full autonomy can be understood and within which its ideal of the person can elicit an effective desire to be that kind of person. (Rawls, 1999: 339–340)

There can be no strict division between the individual and society, and when we attempt to erect such a wall, we endanger everyone's capability for full autonomy: this is the message of Rawls's theory of distributive justice. Full autonomy is a social, and a merely an individual, virtue: it is realized by the background social conditions constitutive of a public society. [6]

The Ethical Aim of the Subject of Justice

If the subject of justice is the way in which the basic structure of society works to share naturally occurring disadvantages and advantages—thereby rendering the distinctions between persons morally significant—and if this sharing, this distribution, is embodied in the historical development of the public institutions of society, then the deontological conception of justice is not only not opposed to the ethical tradition expressed by the norm of reciprocity (the Golden Rule), *but is invaluable to its anti-sacrificial aim.* For the sharing of advantage and disadvantage, ability and disability, expresses the ethical figuration of *oneself as another*: I may be said to have authored or merited my education, my health, and my well-being so far as you, too, have the capabilities for education, health, and well-being. Ricoeur notes that while much has been made of Rawls's criticism of the teleological tradition expressed in the utilitarian tradition, in which the well-being of some may be sacrificed in return for the maximization of the advantage for the many. But what is overlooked, Ricoeur teaches us, is that it is Rawls's social figuration of practical reason—justice as reciprocity—that responds to the ethics of utilitarianism.

The original position represents the condition of mutuality by virtue of which free and rational persons define the principles of justice which will govern their association. The purely hypothetical character of the original position, then, far from endorsing an individualistic pact which outlines the terms of cooperation according to which persons concede to social cooperation, configures the autonomy of moral personhood in terms of principles of mutuality governing the basic structure of society.

From this higher level of abstraction, then, the contractualist exercise applies not to the individuals entering into the contract as such, but rather to the way in which the basic structure of society—its major political, economic, and social institutions taken together—*distributes* the benefits and burdens and the rights and duties amongst members of a political community engaged in—and committed to—the project of social cooperation. The moral relevance of the basic structure of society consists, in turn, in the way in which the distributive configuration of the social institutions determine the life prospects of the individuals to take part in this cooperative venture. It is for this reason that Rawls identifies the basic structure of society and the role it plays in determining the life prospects and moral capabilities of its members, as the basic structure of society. We know intuitively Rawls says that when citizens are excluded from the public institutions of society, their moral capabilities to recognize themselves as the authors of speech, of their actions and of their life plans and thus as autonomous agents, is undermined. Members of a political community are born into unequal starting positions within the basic structure of society, and this inequality—this civic exclusion—has punitive consequences for our least advantaged members:

> In this way the institutions of society favour certain starting places over others. These are especially deep inequalities. Not only are they pervasive, but they affect men's initial chances in life; yet they cannot possibly be justified by an appeal to notions of merit or desert. It is these inequalities, presumably inevitable in the basic structure of any society, to which the principles of social justice must in the first instance apply. (Rawls, 1971: 7)

The effects of arbitrary inequality on persons' moral capabilities are vast. When a society endorses arbitrary inequalities, that is, attributes moral authorship to some for their advantages in, say, wealth, health, employment, housing, and education and others for disadvantages such as poverty, unemployment, illiteracy, and poor health, it is endorsing *divisions* between its capable citizens and its vulnerable citizens. What Rawls is describing here is the stratified neo-liberal society, which *moralizes* the circumstances of both advantage and disadvantage, which neither the capable subject nor the disabled subject can be said to have authored. And while we come to accept these arbitrary inequalities, inequalities that legitimate the growing divisions within society, before we attribute to persons their moral circumstances which they cannot have merited, we must be able to determine whether persons would freely contract into these arbitrary inequalities and if we determine, as we very likely would, that autonomous persons would not agree to be distinguished from one another on the basis of arbitrary inequalities, we need to determine the fair or just grounds upon which free persons would *mutually* agree to from which each person is able to distinguish herself in terms of her capabilities for moral authorship and thus of moral status. It is by eliminating arbitrary inequality that we preserve the inviolability of persons, or the capability of the person to recognize herself as the genuine author of her advantages or her disadvantages.

In Rawls's version of social contractualism, it is the original position that represents a situation of fairness from which *just* as opposed to *arbitrary* distinctions between moral persons can be mutually agreed upon. The social contract is best understood by the more specific idea of *proceduralism*, because the original position itself enacts the fairness that the principles of justice will articulate. Indeed, it is from the original position of fairness that Rawls's theory as a whole derives its name—justice as fairness. The original position is designed so as to represent the equality that governs moral persons. The contracting parties in the original position are mutually self-interested thus each person is assumed to be rational, i.e., interested in her self-preservation, not only in the long run, but also considered in terms of her long-term life prospects. In this way, persons in the original position relate to one another from within a position of equality, and from this standpoint of equality, the contracting parties arrive upon a mutual agreement on the principles of justice that will define the terms of their cooperation and to which they can appeal when conflicts arise over the distribution of benefits and burdens of living together (Rawls, 1971, 11). When we begin to think about which principles similarly situated persons who enjoy equal moral status would choose, we are necessarily asking a question about the *conditions of mutuality* or perhaps more precisely, the *law of mutuality*, because as we will see it is by virtue of the norm of mutuality that the autonomy or the inviolability of moral persons is preserved. The original position, then, is a demonstration of justice as fairness insofar as it is a demonstration of the norm of reciprocity. And this norm of reciprocity is expressed by the principles of justice that will configure the basic structure of society from which the capable self emerges:

> In the sense in which I shall use this concept, the question of reciprocity arises when free persons, who have no moral authority over one another and who are engaging in or find themselves participating in a joint activity, are among themselves settling upon or acknowledging the rules which define it and which determine their respective shares in its benefits and burdens. *The principle of reciprocity requires of a practice that it satisfy those principles which the persons who participate in it could reasonably propose for mutual acceptance under the circumstances and conditions of the hypothetical account* (Rawls, 1999: 208, my emphasis)

The principles of justice that anyone from within the original position might endorse, then, are those that any other would similarly endorse. We must bear in mind that the contracting parties come together to contract into the principles of justice that will specify their terms of cooperation and according to which they will address their claims against one another. For the basic structure of society, articulated by the principles of distributive justice, is constituted by persons who both *share in* this cooperative venture, and who *have a share* in this cooperative venture.

This description of the original position—governed by the norm of reciprocity—presupposes another constraining feature which contributes to the generation of the principles of justice, namely, the veil of ignorance. The original position of fairness is itself enacted through the veil of ignorance, which works to remove from consideration in the choosing of the principles of justice, information irrelevant from the standpoint of justice, or indeed, that which we normally consider to stand in opposition to considerations of justice. We tend to think, for example, that the choosing of the principles of justice should not be affected by natural advantages in fortune or in social position and nor do we think that person's particular conceptions of the good are particularly relevant to the principles to be chosen. The aim of the original position is to rule out those principles which it would be rational for persons to choose, if they had access to certain kinds information about their particular position in society, but which are nonetheless irrelevant from the standpoint of justice. Thus a wealthy person would rationally favor principles that would make taxation of the wealthy unjust; conversely, a poor person would argue for principles that oppose this principle:

> To represent the desired restrictions one imagines a situation in which everyone is deprived of this sort of information. One excludes the knowledge of those contingencies which sets men at odds and allows them to be guided by their prejudices. In this manner the veil of ignorance is arrived at in a natural way. (Rawls, 1971: 19)

Those aspects of self-knowledge that are to be excluded within the original situation of fairness, then, are precisely the *contingent* aspects of self-knowledge that work to divide men from one another. This contingent self-knowledge is excluded because it is irrelevant from the standpoint of justice: it works by reinforcing arbitrary inequalities between persons. Thus, contingent or arbitrary self-knowledge that is excluded from within the original position of fairness includes *socio-economic status, class status, personal psychology, conceptions of the good life, etc.* What justice seeks—through the preservation of persons as ends in themselves—is the capability for each person to recognize herself as the author of her conception of the good, and this capability for self-recognition is not possible unless others also have similar capabilities for self-recognition. It is this shared quality of the capabilities for self-recognition that become truncated when societies become divided on the basis of arbitrary inequality, wherein capabilities and disabilities are ascribed to persons who cannot be said to have authored or merited them.

The principle of justice holds, first, that all persons ought to be recognized as being equal in liberty and then holds that inequalities in liberty are only legitimate where they can be shown to be to the benefit of the least advantaged member. Differences between citizens in income, responsibility and wealth are only legitimate when they work to extend the principle of equality to include all persons. What this means is that natural or contingent abilities and disabilities are to be *shared* or *distributed*. That is, we satisfy the first principle of equality when we preserve all persons' capabilities to recognize themselves as moral agents, by including every-*one*—the propertied, the educated, the homeless, the illiterate, the healthy, the chronically ill, the able-bodied and the disabled—within our public institutions constitutive of equality, liberty and equality of opportunity. It is by virtue of this *principle of inclusion* that we assure the capability for self-recognition to every-*one*, and thereby preserve the distinctions between persons, from within a cooperative scheme.

From within the original position of fairness, *all claims* are to be understood in terms of the requirement for mutual recognition of the principles of justice. Claims that cannot be adjudicated from within this position of mutuality *cannot* be considered from within the social contract, for they do not meet the criteria of reciprocity. This is what Rawls expresses with the publicity requirement—the principles of justice and their requirements of contracting parties are to be publicly known and acknowledged. And it is this condition of publicity that is modeled by the social contract together with the veil of ignorance: the social, economic and political institutions comprising the basic structure of society so as to meet the criteria of publicity, that is, the capabilities for self-recognition, for *one*-self, are to be distributed, to be understood as the capabilities for an-*other*. It this distributive interpretation of capability, modeled by the original condition of fairness, that is articulated by the principles of justice which are to underwrite the basic structure of society.

It is in this way, Rawls argues, that the social contract tradition constitutes a reply to the *sacrificial* ethics of the utilitarian tradition, that is, it is the norm of reciprocity that configures the position of the least advantaged member. This is what Rawls means when he says that the position of the least advantaged member is not located in an *individual* as such, but rather expresses a representative position from within the original position, *and in this way the representative position of the least advantaged member is shared by everyone*. The advantages and disadvantages of adopting any particular conception of justice, then, may only be understood from within the norm of mutuality enacted by the social contract. When we argue that the principles of justice articulated the norm of mutuality modeled by the social contract, we are not arguing that the principles of justice, either taken as a whole, or even the difference principle in particular, aim towards some ideal of social welfare as such. For we can read the difference principle as a principle of redress, and make the argument that because inequalities at birth in terms of native endowments and inherited social inequalities, cannot be said to have been earned or merited, we must devote more attention and resources into redressing this arbitrary inequalities in order to make possible genuine equality of opportunity: "The idea is to redress the bias of contingencies in the direction of equality" (Rawls, 1971: 100–101). Thus, the principle of redress may require that we devote more resources to the education of less intelligent than to the more intelligent. While the difference principle shares with the principle of redress that unmerited inequalities are unjust, it does not seek to resolve these inequalities by, for example, taking resources for literacy for the more intelligent and giving them to the less intelligent. Rather, the difference principle seeks to preserve every-*one's capabilities* for literacy by *distributing* natural capabilities and disabilities, such that the least advantaged member's long-term expectations are raised. Thus, the difference principle holds that, in this example, if it is the case that by providing more resources for literacy to the more intelligent would improve the long-term expectations of the least advantaged members, then such an allocation would be permissible, and if providing more resources to the education of the more intelligent does not achieve this aim, then it is not permissible, according to the standards of justice. It is by distributing natural advantages—and not merely by exchanging advantages for disadvantages—that we prevent considerations of social or economic efficiency from overriding our consideration of the capability of our least advantaged member, by becoming literate, to take part in the social, cultural and political aspects of the society in which he lives.

> We see then that the difference principle represents, in effect, *an agreement to regard the distribution of natural talents as a common asset* and to share in the benefits of this distribution whatever it turns out to be. Those who have been favoured by nature, whoever they are may gain from their good fortune only on terms that improve the situation of those who have lost out. (Rawls, 1971: 101, my emphasis)

In this way, we preserve the meaningful distinction between citizens that they may be said to have earned; this is the first sense in which the principle of the inviolability of persons is endorsed by the norm of reciprocity articulated by the principles of justice. But we also configure the principle of the inviolability of persons by ensuring that this moral status is extended to our least advantaged members. For the moral truth expressed by the principle of the inviolability of persons is endangered when we do not extend its application to all moral persons. The subject of justice, then, is this very interrelationship between the moral authorship of persons and the important distinctions by virtue of which each man is capable of self-recognition, and the basic structure of society that preserves this moral capability for self-recognition by extending it to all persons of a political community. Neither the inviolability of persons nor the basic structure of society may be understood outside of their interrelationship. It is impossible, then, to entertain "any tabulation of advantages and disadvantages" that does not meet criteria of mutuality (Rawls, 1999: 221). In other words, because the *representative positions of the least advantaged member and the position of the most advantaged member are shared* behind the veil of ignorance, the contracting parties to do not oppose themselves to one another through *possessive* understanding of advantage and disadvantage: this is precisely what is prohibited by the veil of ignorance. We must keep in mind that the social contract in itself expresses "an essential part of the concept of justice" by generating principles of justice that will be constitutive of the basic structure of society—of its social, economic, and political institutions taken together—and in which the moral status of each person will be engendered and preserved (Rawls, 1999: 221).

It is this possessive interpretation of advantage and of disadvantage and their consequent opposition that characterizes the utilitarian conceptualization of the just society as the most efficient society. Rawls is able to draw out the features of the norm of reciprocity governing the social contract and its articulation in the principles of justice by comparing it to the model of justice as efficiency endorsed by the utilitarian tradition advanced by Bentham (1962) and Sidgwick (1962). This possessive interpretation of advantage and disadvantage in turn may only succeed where the principle of mutuality—expressed by the publicity requirement in the original position of fairness—is denied. In response to the utilitarian view of justice, Rawls begins by noting that in its application, claims that run contrary to the conception of justice as fairness do not have any moral force. In violating the norm of reciprocity—and thus of community—one who presses a claim against another, which she at the same time would be unwilling to submit, has no moral grounds from which she may protest when such a claim is denied. But on the utilitarian view, anti-social claims are able to proceed because utilitarianism is concerned with designing the basic structure of society so as to promote general welfare of society, and on this view, "justice is a kind of efficiency" (Rawls, 1999: 215). Justice as efficiency is modeled by an administrative figure of the legislator who surveys the urgency of each of the different individual desires in society and the benefits and burdens accruing from these desires are distributed so as to maximize the overall advantages over disadvantages. Decisions on the distribution between benefits and burdens are made, from this administrative view, on the basis of the intrinsic worth of the individualized desire, without regard for the moral relations that bind individuals to one another.

> Moreover, the individuals receiving these benefits are not conceived as being related in any way: they present so many different directions in which limited resources may be allocated. The value of assigning resources to one direction rather than another depends solely on the preferences and interests of individuals as individuals. *The satisfaction of desire has its value of irrespective of the moral relations between persons, say as members of a joint undertaking, and of the claims which, in the name of these interests, they are prepared to make on another. . .* (Rawls, 1999: 217, my emphasis)

The problem with the utilitarian's administrative view of society is that lies in its focus on organizing institutions so as to maximize advantages, which are regarded as being intrinsically valuable, is that such a view does not consider the ethics of cooperation between members of society, which it nonetheless presupposes its pursuit of the design of an efficient society. On the utilitarian view of society, then, cooperation is grounded not in the norm of reciprocity, which demands that each person within the scheme of cooperation, and indeed by virtue of the terms of cooperation itself, be regarded as ends in themselves, but rather in terms of a coerced cooperation, which rather than preserving the moral status of persons, implies their sacrifice. And because it is willing to sacrifice some members of society so as to maximize the advantages accrued by the others, the utilitarian design of an efficient society fails the test of publicity modeled by the social contract—that is, advantages and disadvantages are not interpreted as *shared* or *distributed* in the design of social institutions.

The failure of utilitarianism to meet the requirements of publicity, of mutuality, is illustrated by Rawls in his illustration of the implication of the efficient treatment slavery. Utilitarianism permits the consideration of the advantages accrued by the slaveholder, by declaring the practice of slavery as unjust insofar as it does not counterbalance the disadvantages accrued by the slave, and its overall inefficiency as an institution of labor.

But viewed from the perspective of justice as reciprocity, the *advantages accrued by the slave holder would not be considered at all*: those claims that could not be mutually—that is, publicly—acknowledged by all as defining the terms of their cooperation has no moral purchase. Thus, any advantage that may accrue to the slaveholder from the practice of slavery is irrelevant to the injustice of slavery: "Where the conception of justice as reciprocity applies, slavery is always unjust" (Rawls, 1999: 219). Rawls, of course, is not claiming that classical utilitarians endorsed slavery. His argument is much more fundamental than that: Rawls is "rejecting a type of argument" that endorses the *division* between advantages and disadvantages, because it is this very argument for the division between considerations of the advantages to be accrued by an individual on one hand and the disadvantages to be accrued by an individual or a group of individuals on the other—represented by the figure of the ideal legislator who seeks to maximize the overall advantages that underwrites the profound *individualism* of the utilitarian calculation of advantage versus disadvantage:

> Occasionally persons do stand to one another; but this is not the general case, nor, more importantly, is it the case when it is a matter of the justice of practices themselves in which participants stand in various relations to be appraised in accordance with standards which they may be expected to acknowledge before one another. Thus, however mistaken the notion of the social contract may be as history, however far it may reach itself as a general theory of social and political obligation, it does express, suitably interpreted, an essential part of the concept of justice. (Rawls, 1999: 223)

The principle of tallying up of advantages and disadvantages—in the name of maximizing overall social or economic advantages—cannot, then, underwrite the common practices constitutive of cooperative society, because it succeeds by denying the very norms of reciprocity that persons seeking to define their terms of cooperation seek to articulate, while meeting existing individual interests more effectively. The original position of fairness models the norm of reciprocity by virtue of which persons—representing unequal representative positions—acknowledge one another, thereby prohibiting the sacrifice any-*one* for greater social or economic gain.

In modeling the norm of reciprocity from which persons define the principles of justice that the mutually acknowledge as defining the terms of their cooperation, the social contract represents a radical departure from the classical tradition of utilitarianism. This is so because the requirement for mutuality governing the social contract prohibits the selection of the principle that could not be publicly acknowledged by each representative man occupying a different position or office within the basic structure of society, would not acknowledge in front of each of the other representatives. The idea here, expressed by the difference principle, is that any inequalities in the income, wealth, and responsibility attaching to offices and positions, open to all, would not receive public acknowledgment from the representatives unless each was convinced that her position is thereby improved. This *maximization of the minimum share articulates the anti-sacrificial ethics* of Rawls's conception of justice as reciprocity. What Rawls's anti-sacrificial ethics adds to traditional conceptions of justice is that the social, economic and political institutions of society are public when are configured by the sharing of advantage and disadvantage, that is, when no-one is excluded by virtue of illness, disability, poverty, single parenthood, unemployment, illiteracy or by virtue of wealth, education, naturally good health. This principle of maxi-min, then, underwrites the recognitive capabilities of everyone by virtue of the norm of mutuality that it articulates as the just grounds for the design of the basic structure of society.

Having traversed the demonstrative role of Rawls's social contract, we may now appreciate its deontological character. That is to say, the social contract exercise models the relationship between the basic structure of society and its role in the preservation of the inviolability of persons. In this way, the original position, or to the kind of teleological conception of justice against which it is aimed. Rawls's deontological conception of justice is aimed specifically against classical utilitarianism's aim to maximize the greatest sum of satisfactions in society. It is the lexical ordering of the principles that assures the relationship between the basic structure of society, comprised of its social, political, and economic institutions, and the preservation of the moral status of each person. It is when the institutional make-up of a society underwrites the inviolability of persons that a society may be said to be just. It is important to recognize that it is this interrelationship that is modeled by the social contract, because it is by demonstrating the distributive character of the capabilities for self-recognition, for moral status, that the social contract opposes itself to a particular version of teleological conception of justice, namely, classical utilitarianism. Rawls's key observation—enacted through his proceduralist account of the original position—is that in the utilitarian conception of justice, the individual *precedes society*. And it is this against the individualism of the utilitarian conception of justice, and the sacrificial practices that this individualism underwrites, that the procedure is aimed. That is to say, the aim of the social contract—by demonstrating the distributive (the institutional) configuration of the capable subject—is at the same time a demonstration of what, following Jean-Pierre Dupuy, Ricoeur refers to as the *anti-sacrificial ethics* of the principles of justice.

In order to appreciate the anti-sacrificial ethics articulated by the principles of justice, we must first understand the significance of the *lexicographical* ordering of the principles of justice. The second principle, also known as the difference principle, requires that inequalities in income, responsibility and wealth are only permissible if they are to everyone's advantage and is thus a principle of economic justice. However, this principle of economic justice remains unintelligible outside of its subordinate positioning vis-à-vis the principles of political justice, namely, equality of liberty and equality of opportunity. The inclusion of each member of society within the institutions of political justice is prior to, and thus cannot be violated by, differences in income, responsibility, and wealth. That is to say, differences in income, wealth and responsibility *cannot justify the exclusion of citizens from the institutions of political justice.* Rather, such differences are only permissible when the principles of political justice are satisfied. Unless differences in income, responsibility, and wealth are configured from *within the distributive institutions of society*, they will be regarded as being unjust, and these differences will work to polarize members, opposing them to one another. This is what utilitarianism risks when it prioritizes the sum of social or economic advantage over the distribution of both advantage and disadvantage through the *institutionalization of mutuality*.[7] It is by virtue of the institutionalization of mutuality that we are to understand Rawls's radical reversal of the utilitarian conception of maximizing the minimum share: understood from the perspective of individualism, the maxi-min principle regards each individual's claim to an advantage as being legitimate, irrespective of the individual's interrelationship with others, but when we interpret the maxi-min principle from within the norm of reciprocity, from within the position of oneself as another, we seek to raise the position of the least advantaged member, because we realize that our own capabilities for self-recognition as the individual authors of our conceptions of the good depends upon similar capabilities for our others. For it can be argued that the maxi-min principle is akin to a risk-aversion principle utilized by players in a game. A poker player will not risk becoming the slave to another, if given the opportunity to become king. But knowledge of individual psychology is not available to the contracting parties behind the veil of ignorance. That the maxi-min principle cannot be interpreted possessively is revealed by the very task that the contracting parties set themselves: since they are similarly situated (behind the veil of ignorance), they understand themselves as being *mutually* self-interested, and from this perspective of mutual self-interest, they are to propose—and ultimately agree upon—principles of justice by virtue of which they will be able to define the terms of their cooperation, and which will enable them to press *legitimate* claims against one another. That is to say, the contracting parties seek to establish a cooperative scheme, fitted by the appropriate social, economic, and political institutions, and their *membership* within this cooperative scheme will in turn underwrite the legitimate differences in income, responsibility and wealth, which distinguish—and indeed recognize—the individuals who take part in the cooperative life of society. The recognitive basis of selfhood, then, is thoroughly public, thoroughly shared. And it is because the recognitive basis of selfhood is distributed through the social, political and economic institutions of society that no-one's capability for moral selfhood is sacrificed: this is what the social contract models. Contrary to modeling decision-making in a situation of uncertainty, or modeling risk aversion, both of which would imply that the members of the social contract deliberate in isolation, the social contract models an ethics for *collective deliberation*.[8]

The demonstration of the norm of reciprocity by the social contract's configuration of public or civic deliberation represents Rawls's response to the problem of arbitrary inequality. Thus, societies which separate and thus oppose advantaged to disadvantage sacrifice their least advantaged citizens through the legitimation of the elite withdrawal from the public institutions through which capabilities and disabilities, advantages and disadvantages, are shared. Here Ricoeur notes that while Rawls's deontological figuration of the moral status of persons within a distributive scheme, governed by the norm of reciprocity, is aimed against the sacrificial impulse of the utilitarian version of teleological ethics, it is nonetheless a *demonstration* of a sense of justice, expressed in the considered conviction that arbitrary inequalities, which punish or reward persons for disabilities or abilities which they cannot be said to have merited, are unjust. This sense of justice, which opens Rawls's *A Theory of Justice*, is first expressed by the Golden Rule, which says, "Do not do unto others what you would not have them do unto you." Is not the prohibition against the exclusion of our least advantaged members from the institutions of political justice, of equality, through the demonstration of mutuality, publicity, and reciprocity by the social contract, and expression of our considered convictions "ultimately rooted in the sense of justice equivalent to the Golden Rule applied to institutions and no longer to individuals in a face-to-face relation, and moreover to institutions considered from the point of view of their distributive function?" (Ricoeur, 2000: 55). And while our considered convictions, grounded in the Golden Rule, articulate the injustice of the victim of the sacrifice, of the injustice that is done to our least advantaged members when we exclude them societal membership, we need a way of clarifying how to ameliorate this injustice. *Implied here is the necessary task of determine a just—as opposed to punitive—distribution of income, responsibility, and wealth.* It is in clarifying, to borrow Aristotle's language, the requirements of proportional equality, that we require the aid of rational arguments. However, these rational requirements cannot take the place of the ethical foundation of the norm of reciprocity—of sharing—articulated by the Golden Rule.

Chapter 2

The Redistribution–Recognition Debate Revisited: The Ethical Intention in Redistributive Justice

A major approach to understanding the growing stratification between rich and poor characterizing modern neoliberal states has emerged in the form of a debate between arguments between proponents of redistributive justice and proponents of recognition justice. On one hand, recognition theorists assert that injustice results from cultural, political, gendered, and racialized forms of misrecognition of society's vulnerable and marginalized members. On this reading, economic injustice or maldistribution is itself an expression of the politics of misrecognition, in which the victims of maldistribution share in the normative experience of characterizing misrecognition share in the normative experience characterizing misrecognition, namely, humiliation, and disrespect.[1] And this is not all. As Charles Taylor has pointed out, the problem of misrecognition is a distinctively modern problem: its development may be traced through the historical, political, and economic development of the "inwardly generating self," of the "authentic" or individual identity, as distinguished from social forms of identity and recognition that prevailed in premodern times.[2] This idea of an authentic identity has been extended and applied to cultures and culture-baring persons' struggle for recognition, for equal respect, from the legal, political, cultural, and economic institutions of modern liberal societies. On the other hand, redistributive justice theorists argue that such cultural forms of misrecognition as sexism, ableism, and ageism cannot be fully understood apart from a class analysis of the maldistribution of income, social transfers, old age and disability pensions, as well as the exclusion of vulnerable members of society from public institutions of health, education, and employment.[3]

But the redistribution–recognition debate and the relations of inequality it seeks to articulate may themselves be traced back to the relationship between liberty and equality in the history of democratic thought.[4] This history reveals a—growing—opposition between the capability to recognize oneself as culture-bearing, as mothers, as care-givers, as workers, as literate, as propertied and as healthy, and the disabling of this capability for self-recognition through chronic illness, disability, illiteracy, homelessness, and unemployment. That is, the capabilities for self-recognition underwrite the autonomy of persons to author their conception of the good, poor health, illiteracy, unemployment, and homelessness disable person's capabilities for self-recognition, and thus for autonomy. There is, in short an increasing division between the capabilities of *one*-self and the disabilities of an-*other*. A *possessive* logic underwrites this division between capability and disability, between autonomy and vulnerability. The capabilities of oneself for self-recognition are regarded as being constitutive of oneself: I possess my capabilities for literacy, housing, good health, and the disabilities of poor education, poverty and illness are similarly regarded as being constitutive of another. To frame the problem in terms of the redistribution–recognition debate, the recognitive capabilities of one-self are becoming increasingly indifferent to the recognitive capabilities of another; that is, we are losing sight of the *redistributive*, or the shared, grounding of self-recognition, of autonomy.

In this book, I want to suggest that it is the possessive conceptualization of the capabilities for selfhood that informs the growing socio-economic inequalities in modern society. It is to the reversal of this possessive individualism—of oneself *contra* another—that public deliberation on our divided society must address itself. Civic *phronēsis*, to borrow Aristotle's language, itself embodies the translation of oneself *as* another.

It is in the political philosophy of Paul Ricoeur that we find a model for civic *phronēsis* on the recovery of our collective "desire to live well, with and for others, in just institutions," that is, of the shared grounds of our capabilities for selfhood (Ricoeur, 1992: 239). Ricoeur designates our collective desire to live together as an *ethical intention* (*telos*), and thereby designates the *collective* or *redistributive* grounding of the capabilities for self-recognition, for autonomy, in the Aristotelian heritage. Ricoeur's Aristotelian interpretation of redistributive justice may strike the reader as more than a little surprising, and indeed represents a rather striking departure from the widely agreed upon characterization of redistributive justice in the Kantian deontological tradition. The major deontological articulation of justice is of course John Rawls's conception of justice as fairness. But Ricoeur's teleological interpretation of Rawls's conception of justice as fairness, in which the aim of justice is the equitable (as distinguished from egalitarian) distribution of basic social goods required by citizens to live a free life, is not meant to simply supplant the Kantian deontological tradition with the Aristotelian teleological tradition (Ricoeur, 1992: 170). In interpreting justice as fairness in light of our ethical intention to live together, Ricoeur is also giving this ethical intention a distributive figuration: it is by discerning the *norm of reciprocity* that mediates the imperative of recognition that is owed to persons as ends in themselves (reflected in the solicitous care of persons in their singularity) and the imperative of redistributive justice (which extends the ethics of equality articulated by the solicitous care for the otherness of the other to all members of the political community), that enables Ricoeur to develop a political theory that is grounded in Rawls's theory of *distributive capability*.[5] This distributive interpretation of capability is the result of reading together the teleological and the deontological conception of justice, which have typically been regarded as being *opposed* to one another.

The distributive interpretation of capability that results from Ricoeur's interpretation of Rawls's theory of justice as fairness as an affirmation of our collective will to live together is a novel approach to understanding equality and capability justice. It is this distributive conception of the capabilities for selfhood that will permit us to overcome the false antinomy between capability and disability, between advantage and disadvantage, between liberty and equality, between oneself and another.

Civic *Phronēsis*: Ricoeur's Aristotelian Phenomenology of the Norm(s) of Reciprocity

"Aiming at the good life . . ."

The ethical aim of the good life "belongs to the Aristotelian heritage, where ethics is characterized by its teleological perspective" (Ricoeur, 1992: 170). Ricoeur interprets our capabilities for moral dignity from within Aristotle's ethical telos of the good society, which Ricoeur defines as "*aiming at the good life, with and for others, in just institutions*" (Ricoeur, 1992: 172, original emphasis). In developing Ricoeur's civic interpretation of *phronēsis* or deliberation, I argue that the Rawlsian figuration of *phronēsis* is guided by the Aristotelian ethical aim for the civic inclusion of our most vulnerable citizens. In this Aristotelian interpretation, the Rawlsian figuration of *phronēsis* figures a civic methodology for responding to individualist models of deliveration, which serve to attack our shared or distributive narratives on human vulnerability and capability. The Aristotelian ethical aim is constituted by our *practices of sharing* which configure a *solicitous* response to relations of inequality that inform persons' pursuit of the good life. We will recall that for Aristotle, all human action aims at some good, and that the highest good achievable by human action is happiness, or well-being (*eudemonia*). Aristotle will specify this and admittedly abstract conception of the human good by clarifying the *function* of man. The function of man, Aristotle argues, is to act and deliberate well, in accordance with virtue (Aristotle, 1097, §1–§16, pp. 7–9). This aim may be interpreted as the development of the capability to determine the course of one's life, to specify one's "life plan," to borrow Ricoeur's language, so as to be able to recognize oneself as the author of that life plan. The function of man, in short, may be understood as the capability for *imputation*.[6]

For his part, Rawls will emphasize with Aristotle the integral role that the capability to revise and to reformulate one's conception of the good, as well as the practices by virtue of which citizens pursue their conceptions of the good, constitutes the *reflexive* aspect of selfhood that grounds the self's capability for imputation, for self-recognition. Aristotle's teleological characterization of human practice invites an hermeneutics of the capability for self-recognition. While there has been some debate on whether the horizon of Aristotle's teleological conception of action rests with the determination of the practice itself, that is, or whether deliberation consists in the revision of practice in light of the aim of the good, and if it does, then the question arises whether the aim itself can be revised. Thus, for example, Aristotle argues that the doctor does not deliberate about whether or not to heal, or the politician whether or not to promote social cooperation. In sum, an expert in any field does not deliberate about the ends to which her science aims (Aristotle, 1112b, §11, p. 35). Ricoeur extends Aristotle's teleological conception of praxis by arguing that there need not be a contradiction between the decisions we make about the practices constitutive of our life, and the idea of the good governing our life as a whole. The teleological relationship between our practices and the aim of our life taken as a whole invites a "back-and-forth" hermeneutical movement between the modes of deliberation appropriate to the scale of intermediate practices, which must nonetheless maintain a level of self-sufficiency in order to be carried out, and our global-level deliberations about the conception of the good that defines our life as a whole (Ricoeur, 1992: 179). This interpretive back-and-forth between practices and life plans underwrites, to borrow Alasdair MacInytre's language, a "narrative unity of a life," by virtue of which we may identify with confidence the author of the life plan.[7] Even more significantly, for Ricoeur, the narrative confirmation of a life underwrites the extension of the evaluative judgments we make of a given action to the actor himself, thereby extending the narrative identity of character to the ethical identity of the subject. And yet, because the ethical identity of the subject retains its narrative structure, the fully autonomous or voluntary character of a life plan is itself contextualized in terms of luck, reversals of fortune and the tragedy characteristic of all stories. The ethical subject is not fully autonomous; she "appears from the outset as suffering as well as acting" (Ricoeur, 1992: 178). She is both an agent and a patient of social luck, of arbitrary inequality, to anticipate Rawls.

". . . with and for others . . ."

The very status of the self as both acting and suffering points to its figuration by others in the pursuit of the good life, to which Ricoeur gives the name of *solicitude*: all of the capabilities implied in the self's pursuit of the good life, all of the ethical experiences of the "I can," presuppose the mediating role of others. It is this mediating role of others, Ricoeur argues, that is celebrated by Aristotle in his treatise on friendship. The solicitous regard conferred to the self in friendship serves as a transition between the apparently solitary pursuit of the good, and the fully social or public virtue of justice on the political plane. Friendship, like the pursuit of happiness, is an activity, and thus belongs in the realm of ethics. Furthermore, although Aristotle's treatise on friendship may be read as a deliberation on self-love (*philautia*), the friendship of the self to itself—the reflexivity of the self—is from the outset enabled by the *mutuality* of friendship, for "the excellent person is related to his friend in the same way as he is related to himself, since a friend is another himself" (Aristotle, 11706, §10, p. 150). The mutuality of friendship preserves the plurality of personhood. This becomes clear when we ask about the object of friendship. Where friendship based on utility or pleasure is merely conditional, because the friend is only valued for the sake of some perceived advantage, complete friendship preserves the good of each friend:

> But complete friendship is the friendship of good people similar in virtue; for they wish goods in the same way to each other insofar as they are good, and they are good in their own right. [Hence they wish goods to each other for each other's own sake]. Now those who wish goods to their friend for the friend's own sake are friends most of all, for they have this attitude because of the friend himself not coincidentally. (Aristotle, 1156a, §, p. 122)

It is of course true that, for Aristotle, what each friend loves most in the other in complete friendship, is the thinking and deliberating part, and as such, the very mutuality that governs friendship at the same time seems to reinforce the "self-sufficiency" of the excellent person, who, way may recall, may not need friends at all. But we immediately discern that the very self-sufficiency of the happy man presupposes friends. Friendship, like the capability for deliberation constitutive of the happy man, is an activity. Activity "comes into being, and does not belong to someone all the time], as a *possession* does" (Aristotle, 1169b, §5, p. 149, my emphasis). Thus, happiness is an activity, and not a possession, and the activity of the good person is excellent and pleasurable because it is an end in itself. We are better able to observe the excellent activity of our "neighbors," and we find them to be "naturally" pleasant, for they are both good, and are our own. For in perceiving the activity of our excellent friends, we perceive that we are, and this is pleasant in itself: "The blessed person, therefore, will need virtuous friends, given that he decides to observe virtuous actions that are his own, and the actions of a virtues friend are of this sort" (Aristotle, 1169b, §149). Ricoeur here notes that the very desire the happy man has for what is his own is inseparable from his need for friends, and in turn, the very pleasure that is derived from perceiving what is one's own works to undermine the self-sufficiency of Aristotle's intellectualist conception of friendship: "In this way, lack dwells at the heart of the most solid friendship" (Ricoeur, 1992: 187, original emphasis).

It may here be objected that Aristotle's conception of friendship remains incomplete, because Aristotle does not develop the role or even the significance of otherness. Ricoeur responds to this question by looking beyond the historical context of Aristotle's conception of friendship, which is exclusionary, to the phenomenology of mutuality that grounds friendship:

> Friendship, even when it is released from the socio-cultural limitations of *philia*, appears to me to constitute a fragile balance in which giving and receiving are equal, hypothetically. In truth, it is this equality that Aristotle has in mind when he defines the *mutual* character of friendship. Now this balance can be considered as the midpoint of a spectrum, in which the end points are marked by inverse disparities between giving and receiving, depending on whether the pole of the self or that of the other predominates in the initiative of the exchange. (Ricoeur, 1992: 188, original emphasis)

It is configuring this balance between giving and receiving that will carry us from the interpersonal to the institutional plane, and back again to the self that is capable of perceiving its own goodness. For the self does not possess its self-esteem, but rather shares its capability for self-esteem, and thus for self-recognition, with others. The capability for self-recognition, then, presupposes the solicitude of mutuality, where solicitude is extended to every-one, and becomes, on the plane of justice, equality. We recall here the reflexivity of the self, the self's very recognition of itself in its pursuit of the good belies the *need* for friends. In this self-recognition, enabled by the solicitude of friendship, "*the self perceives itself as another among others*" (my emphasis). This is the sense of Aristotle's 'each other' (*allelous*), which makes friendship *mutual*" (original emphasis) (Ricoeur, 1992: 192). The ultimate gift of solicitude is its objectification of the capability for self-recognition in the *third party* on the institutional plane through the distribution of the status of "other" to *each* member of the political community. We will wait to fully explicate the distributive status of selfhood until chapter four where we will develop the political implications of Ricoeur's Aristotelian apperception of mutuality, which will be composed of three moments: reversibility, non-substitutability, with similitude governing the ideas of reversibility and substitutability.

". . . in just institutions . . ."

The phenomenology of solicitude reveals that *similitude* governs the capability of persons to recognize themselves as the autonomous authors of their conception of the good:

> I am that being who can evaluate his actions and, in assessing the goals of some of them to be good, is capable of evaluating himself and judging himself to be good. The discourse of "I can" is, to be sure, a discourse in "I." But the main emphasis is to be placed on the verb, on being-able-to-do, to which responds on the ethical plane, being-able-to-judge. (Ricoeur, 1992: 181)

If it is similitude that governs the solicitude of friendship, it is justice that preserves moral authorship on the institutional plane. For the *other* that preserves my capabilities for moral authorship includes the other-than-you, it extends beyond the face-to-face friendship dyad. That is, well-being, understood as the realization of the capability for autonomous self-determination, presupposes not only friendship, but life in shared institutions. Just as similitude preserved the solicitude characterizing the interpersonal plane, so justice will preserve equality on the institutional plane.

When we say that the institutional plane of the ethical intention has a distributive structure, we mean that the institution articulates our collective wish to live together in such a way as to extend the solicitous regard for *one*-self, for a friend, to an-*other*, that is, to each person that is excluded from the "I"–"thou" dyad. The institution is, in other words, the third part that underwrites the recognitive capabilities of the I–you dyad:

> The third party, however, is straightaway, and no pun intended, *the inclusive middle term* (*tier inclus*) within the plurality that constitutes power. In this way, there is a limit imposed on every effort to reconstruct the social bond on the sol basis of a strictly diadic dialogic relation. The plurality includes third parties who will never be faces. A plea for the anonymous in the literal sense of the terms I therefore included in the fullest aim of the true life." (Ricoeur, 1992: 195, original emphasis)

Traveling backwards, now, along the path of the ethical intention that we have been tracing, it is the third party, the moral stranger, to borrow Michael Ignatieff's fine phrase, that the collective will to live together configures.[8] The ethical experience of mutuality is, to borrow Hegel's language, made objective to itself in the figuration of the moral stranger on the institutional plane.

It is the institutionalization of the capabilities of the third party, from which the recognitive capabilities of the "I" and the "you" emerge, that permit the intersection of the deontological and the teleological traditions on the institutional plane. For the institutionalization of the capabilities of the third party has a moral and an ethical significance: it represents a distributive or shared interpretation of capability justice, thereby expressing our collective belief that the capabilities for moral personhood belong to no-*one*, but rather to every-*one*. We shall say later how Rawls's deontological conception of justice is itself a demonstration of this *social* view of moral personhood. The question then will not be whether Rawls's proceduralism is aimed against the teleological tradition of utilitarianism, but whether the very social character of justice—expressed by the opening lines of Rawls's *A Theory of Justice*—"Justice is the first virtue of social institutions, as truth is to systems of thought"—does not invite us to place justice at the summit of the Aristotelian conception of the collective pursuit of the good life. But while Rawls conceives of justice as the social virtue of institutions, Aristotle seems to apply justice to the regulation of relations between persons, and so the argument can be made that even if Aristotle did conceive of justice as a virtue, thus placing justice within the ethical pursuit of the good life, justice remains for Aristotle an interpersonal virtue, and applies to relations of giving and receiving between individuals. In assigning justice a place among the virtues, Aristotle seeks to define justice as an intermediate, as the "mesotes" or the just measure between two extremes. But Aristotle's figuration of justice as the intermediate does not necessarily give it an institutional significance, because each of the Aristotleian virtues are understood as expressions of the intermediate, including the private virtues. And yet, Ricoeur notes, the very way in which Aristotle defines justice as the intermediate carries the virtue of justice from the interpersonal to the institutional plane.

Our first clue regarding the two-fold character of justice is the distinction—and the relation—Aristotle observes between the legal-institutional plane and justice. The laws of the polity, which aim to bring about and preserve the well-being of society, constitute the institutional plane proper (Aristotle: 1129a25, §13, p. 68). The primary form of justice, what Aristotle refers to as justice as fairness, forms a part of this institutional plane of law. The very fact that justice as fairness forms a special part of the institutional plane of law reveals the significance of justice as fairness, especially when we consider Aristotle's characterization of the legal-institutional plane of society as "complete virtue" (Aristotle: 1129b, §15, p. 69). Aristotle designates the legal-institutional realm of justice as complete virtue, because the good laws of society can be said to underwrite all the other virtues, which in turn underscores the ethical role of the virtues themselves, namely, that they are to be directed towards the well-being of others, of fellow citizens. If justice as fairness forms a part of complete justice, it, too has an important role to play in preserving the well-being of the polity through its particular figuration of the relationships between citizens who make up the polity: "The 'partial' virtue to which Aristotle confines himself can, as a result, be no less ethico-political than the complete virtue that encompasses it" (Ricoeur, 1992: 199).

How, then, does this "partial justice"—justice as fairness—govern the relations between citizens, thereby forming an important aspect of the institutional life of the polity? Justice as fairness fulfills its institutional role through its *distributive function*, through its mediation of the sharing of the benefits and burdens constitutive of the intention to live together:

> Equality for the people involved will be the same as for the things involved, since [in a just arrangement] the relation between the people will be the same as the relation between the things involved. For if the people involved are not equality, they will not [justly] receive equal

> shares; indeed, whenever equals receive unequal shares, or unequal's equal shares, in a distribution, that is the source of quarrels and accusations. (Aristotle: 1130b, §6, p. 71)

What strikes us right away in Aristotle's description of justice in its distributive role, is that distribution is here irreducible to the economic sphere, to the *equalized* sharing of material goods, which have the effect of blurring the line between society and economy. The Aristotelian interpretation of distributive justice works to sharpen *both* sides of the ethical intention to live together—the wish to be included in the institution on one hand and the distinction that is accorded by this civic membership on the other. That is, it is the capabilities for civic membership—roles, tasks, advantages, disadvantages—that are apportioned amongst members of a community. The social practice of "apportion," then, coordinates civic membership by including every-*one* in civic institutions and thereby conferring the distinction of having a share to *each* member of a community: "And the two things go together. For it is to the extent that shares distributed are coordinated among themselves that those who have a share can be said to participate in a society that may be considered, to borrow Rawls's expression, to be a cooperative enterprise (Ricoeur, 1992: 200). This distributive interpretation services to undermine the false divide between individual and society. The *distinctions* afforded by membership cannot be separated from the grounds of this membership.

Just apportionment, just distribution, articulates the twofold ethical aim of preserving the inviolable distinction of having a share in a political community and the inviolable right of persons to be included in political membership. For this reason, Aristotle defines special task of distributive justice as determining the fair apportionment between the inequalities of distinction and the equality of membership, both of which are necessary for the health and well-being of the political community:

> Special justice, however, and the corresponding way of being just have one species that is found in the distribution of honours or wealth or anything else that can be divided among members of a community who share in a political system; for here it is possible for one member to have a share equal or unequal to another's. (Aristotle, 1130b, §12, p. 71).

While the distinctions afforded by membership may be unequal, due to differences in training, responsibility and the esteem they afford, these inequalities themselves must be justifiable on the public grounds of equality in membership. The unfair (and thus unjust) person is he who, in seeking to possess for himself a greater share of advantages accrued by political membership, and chooses less of the burdens of sharing in this membership. The injustice of the "overreacher" lies in his retreat from shared life with fellow citizens, whilst insisting, blindly, on the advantages membership accrues (Aristotle, 1129a25, §8, p. 68). That is, the overreacher violates the grounds of equality from which unequal distinctions are to be justified. And at the same time, strict equality is not sufficient for justice, because our practices of sharing must take into account differences in merit between persons engaged in the sharing, without which cooperative sharing among members would not be possible: "For if the people involved are not equal, they will not *justly* receive equal shares, indeed, whenever equals receive unequal shares, or unequal equal shares, in a distribution, that is a source of quarrels and accusations" (Aristotle, 1130b, §6, p. 71). Justice as fairness—as the intermediate—seeks to achieve equality. But this equality is of a very particular kind, because it must equalize the relationships between in each case, person and merit: "Hence the just (since it requires equal shares for equal people) is in some way proportionate" (Aristotle, 1130b, §8, p. 71). The Aristotelian conception of the virtue of justice, then, conjoins equality with the pursuit of recognition of the distinction between persons. In this way, Aristotle defined the aim of justice as the pursuit of proportional equality, rather than strict egalitarianism, a pursuit that is taken up by Rawls in his vision of a cooperative society that extends the inviolability of moral personhood from the self-recognition of the singular, practiced, capable person as the author of her conception of the good, a recognition reinforced by her constitutive community that holds her in solicitous regard, to every-*one* in a political community:

> Aristotle thus posed the formidable problem, which Rawls will take up again, of justifying a certain idea of equality without crediting egalitarianism . . . *Equality*, however it is modulated, *is to life in institutions what solicitude is to interpersonal relations.* Solicitude provides to the self another who is a face, in the strong sense Emmanuel Lévinas has taught us to recognize. Equality provides to the self another who is an *each.* (Ricouer, 1992: 202, original emphasis)

The solicitude which characterizes the interpersonal plane is extended to the good society on the institutional plane. But where solicitude gives the self *another* singular self, the solicitous society, in the name of equality, configures a morally distant, a de-moralized self. In short, justice provides the self with the third party. We may not recognize, on the institutional plane, the third party by virtue of her capabilities or her disabilities, we may not *identify* this other with her capabilities or her disabilities, because the capabilities and disabilities of the third party are not *individualized*, but rather *shared* in the form of *public institutions*. This is what we mean when we say that public institutions are to be interpreted distributively. Society owes its historical development to the progressive inclusion of both capabilities—for literacy, for education, for housing, for mental and physical health, for parenthood, work, and for political participation—and for disabilities such as mental and physical illness, unemployment, and homelessness—into our public, shared institutions. Ricoeur refers to his conceptualization of the distributive character of the capabilities and disabilities of personhood to Rawls's argument that it is mutuality that grounds our disinterest in the interest of others. It is here that the deontological and teleological traditions intersect in remarkable ways; for both the *social* point of view that is expressed by the Kantian defense of persons as ends in themselves. On Ricoeur—and Rawls's—respective sociologization of Kant's moral philosophy, the Kantian emphasis on the inviolability of persons, and thus the fundamental and irreducible *plurality* of personhood, is itself the expression of what Rawls will refer to as the "fully social nature of human relationships" (Rawls, 1977: 159). As such, moral autonomy is only fully realized on the institutional plane of the public commitment to live together.

Ricoeur and Rawls's Sociologization of Kant's Moral Philosophy

As we turn now to examine Ricoeur and Rawls's sociological renderings of Kant's moral philosophy, it is essential that we not lose sight of our placement, with Ricoeur, of distributive justice within the Aristotelian tradition. For it is by virtue of this ethical-social interpretation of distributive justice that we come to understand what it is that the very proceduralist account of the least advantaged member teaches us, namely, that the least advantaged member is embodied in the historical development of the public institutions of society, and in this way has an *ethical* and not an individualist or purely moral signification. Ricoeur and Rawls's sociologization of the Kantian conception of moral autonomy configures a civic *phronēsis*, a citizenship narrative, from which we may respond to contemporary attempts to divorce persons' autonomy from their shared life in public institutions. Such a divorce represents a punitive and exclusionary regression from the historical development of the solicitous, and thus pubic, institutions of citizenship. Where contemporary attempts to divorce autonomy or liberty from the grounds of equality represent a punitive and *sacrificial* conception of membership, the model of civic *phronēsis* developed by Ricoeur and Rawls recovers the historical development of the *solicitous third party*, that is, of the public institutions of citizenship. The pursuit of moral authorship, and thus moral autonomy, is structured not only by the solicitous interpersonal affirmation of this authorship by the self-constitutive community, but by the solicitous configuration of the third party on the institutional plane of just institutions. Just as *moral autonomy* is configured by mutuality, it is the law of mutuality, of reciprocity that *preserves* the capability for moral authorship and liberty.

By interpreting the Kantian categorical imperative of the respect owed to persons as ends in themselves, and thus the respect owed to persons in their irreducible plurality, is itself an expression of the norm of reciprocity. We already saw the norm of reciprocity at work in Aristotle's ethical conception of friendship, governed by the practice of giving and receiving esteem, and again in the emphasis on equality in our distributive practices on the institutional plane. Ricoeur notes the biblical tradition of the Golden Rule that expresses the norm of reciprocity animating Aristotle's ethics:

> We can read it in Hillel, the Jewish master of Saint Paul (Babylonian Talmud, *Sabbath*, 31a): "Do not do unto your neighbour what you would hat him to do unto you. This is the entire law; the rest is commentary". We read the same thing in the Gospels: "Treat others as you would like them to treat you" (Luke 6: 31). (Ricoeur, 1992: 219)

The context against which the demand for reciprocity is made is the relation of inequality between the agent of an action, she who performs the action, and the patient of an action, who submits to the action. It is to this initial inequality that the norm, the "no" of morality addresses itself. While solicitude governs the relations of mutuality amongst friends on the ethical plane, it is the norm, the law, that replies to the lack of mutuality, to inequality. And this transition from the rule of reciprocity to the "no" of the moral norm can have the effect of breaking the tie between solicitude and the norm altogether. This break between the solicitous exchange between persons and the moral norm becomes wider as the inequality between the agent and the patient grows, culminating in the prohibition—the absolute law—against murder: "You shall not kill." Here, the tie between the solicitous concern with equality and the law becomes buried beneath the weight of the prohibition itself. But does it follow that the law of reciprocity, articulated by the prohibition, no longer expresses the public intention to live together in a cooperative society?

But if the norm's point of application is the inequality characterizing the agent–patient relation, it already finds itself on the plan of mutuality. Each of the moral prescriptions—you shall not kill, you shall not lie, and so on—in their opposition to the inequality between agent and patient, are pleas for equality and for solicitude in the face of inequality: "On the level of the ethical aim, however, solicitude, as the mutual exchange of self-esteems, is affirmative through and through. *This affirmation, which may well be termed original, is the hidden soul of prohibition* (my emphasis). It is what, ultimately, arms our indignation, that is, our rejection of the *indignities* (original emphasis) inflicted on others" (Ricoeur, 1992: 221). In its pursuit of equality, the norm of reciprocity seeks to preserve the moral status, the irreducible plurality, of both the agent and the patient of action, through its demand that I respect an-other as a one-self, and one-self as an-other.

A nice test case examining the relationship between the norm and solicitude emerges with the prohibition against lying, because this prohibition expresses a duty owed to others (Ricoeur, 1992: 264). Duties owed towards others, Ricoeur argues, fall within the second formulation of the categorical imperative, namely, the duty to consider persons as ends in themselves and never merely as means. The prohibition against lying is an essentially affirmative rule couched in the language of a prohibition. The prohibition is affirmative because it involves a commitment to another. It is this commitment to another that creates the obligation to keep a promise. Ricoeur refers to this obligation as the "principle of fidelity," which he argues has a dialogic structure (Ricoeur, 1992: 266). The dialogic structure of the principle is in turn grounded within a civic context of mutual trust:

> This dialogic structure, moreover, is to be analyzed into a dyadic, or dual, structure, involving two persons—the one who promises and the one to whom the former makes a commitment—and a plural structure, involving, possibly, a witness before whom a commitment is made and, then, behind this witness, the institution of language which one pledges to safeguard, *even the reference to some social pact in whose name a kind of mutual trust may reign among members of a community prior to any promise. Through this plural structure, the principle of fidelity is indistinguishable from the rule of justice* . . . (Ricoeur, 1992: 266, my emphasis)

Thus, the rule of reciprocity underlies the obligation to keep a promise, and this rule, as we have already noted, implies an external other. Thus, the very logic of the promise owes its coherency to its genuinely dialogic structure, backed by institutionalized codes and practices of trust. We already begin to see, then, that obligation, and specifically the duty to maintain an obligation over a period of time, requires an institutional context. Thus, Ricoeur argues, a given duty does not gain its adhering force from its internal coherence, i.e., in terms of a lack of contradiction "internal to the maxim itself" (Ricoeur, 1992: 263). In order to understand this, Ricoeur argues, we must follow the descending path from the universalization of the norm to its point of application in "concrete situations," in which the plurality of persons, in their otherness as such, are affected by the norm (Ricoeur, 1992: 265).

In the case of the prohibition against murder, the norm, in the strong sense of a prohibition, is necessarily monologic; it is a commandment against violence: "to all the figures of evil responds the *no* of morality" (Ricoeur, 1992: 221). The commandment against violence, however, gains its sense, its meaning, from solicitous affirmation of self-esteems. Thus, the prohibition that is voiced by the monologic structure of the norm of the norm is first articulated by the ethical aim of inclusion, of affirmation itself: "This affirmation, which can well be termed original, is the hidden soul of the prohibition. It is what, ultimately, arms our indignation, that is, our rejection of indignities inflicted on others" (Ricoeur, 1992: 221, my emphasis). Our cultural, legal, and political responses to the victimization of persons, then, are grounded in our civic institutions of inclusion and our wish to live well together. Our cultural modes of punishment, then, must themselves reflect this ethical aim of inclusion and equality. Here, then the evaluative moral norm and the Golden Rule are revealed to have the same (civic) configuration, namely: "to establish reciprocity wherever there is a lack of reciprocity" (Ricoeur, 1992: 225, my emphasis). In this way, the ethical aim of inclusion and of equality is prior to the moral prohibition. Prior to the rule of law is the giving and receiving of esteem. Benevolent affirmation is in this way productive; it implies that one ought to do something for one's neighbor.

It is the obligation, owed to another that lends self-constancy its structure. This very structure of obligation is dialogic; that is, it is a response to the situation of inequality. Following Gabriel Marcel, Ricoeur argues that self-constancy is tied up with availability and stands in contrast to non-availability, which is a denial of the dialogic dimension of selfhood. Kant places commitment to others, in the form of self-constancy, at the heart of the structure of the universal will. In so doing, he defines self-constancy entirely monologically, that is, in terms of non-contradiction within this universal will. However, constancy of self owes its very structure to the principle of reciprocity. In keeping one's word, one applies the rule of reciprocity which underwrites the *institution of language* through which mutual trust between interlocutors is preserved: "Not keeping one's promise is betraying both the other's expectation and the institution that mediates the mutual trust of speaking subjects" (Ricoeur, 1992: 268).

Availability is structured by the norm of reciprocity as a response to a situation of inequality. The structure of self-constancy is dialogic: it is the other's expectation that underwrites the normative structure of self-constancy as a response to an obligation owed to another.

The contradiction of the universal norm, then, arises when we do not take into account the ethical context to which the norm applies and from which it gains its sense. Given the principle of fidelity, the rule of self-constancy, of not breaking a commitment, has its point of application in the expectation of the other who is counting on me. The rule, then, gains its sense from its *other*; it is with reference to the other that I understand what my obligation consists in: "If fidelity consists in responding to the expectation of the other who is counting on me, I must take this expectation as the measure for applying the rule" (Ricoeur, 1992: 268). This is the same as saying, I must take the principle of reciprocity, structured by the dissymmetry of self and other, as the determining ground for rule. If reciprocity is to be understood as the principle of fidelity, then the concern with the problem of inequality, which forms the heart of reciprocity, is in turn understood as the structure of social solidarity. Understood in this way, *social* obligation is no longer external to norm but is rather constitutive of it. It is social obligation that is expressed in the norm, and in this way constitutes the ethical aim, that is, transforms our naïve wish to live together into a critical solicitude, which requires an awareness of inequality. The teleology of the ethical aim is here no longer opposed to the obligatory nature of the norm. In fact, the teleological conception of the good, by providing a cultural context of social solidarity articulate a "sense of justice" from which our principles of justice spring. This idea of mutual affirmation, central to solicitude, frames the question of justice in terms of the orientation that we take with respect to one another.

Justice as the Norm of Reciprocity: The Golden Rule

Ricoeur argues that justice as a system of distribution both reflects and reinforces this solicitous orientation. This *sense* of justice, expressed in the orientation that we bear to one another, central to solicitude, must then be examined in relation to the principles of justice. As we have seen, solicitude informed the norm of reciprocity embodied in the Golden Rule. It is in the Golden Rule, wherein solicitude joins with the norm of reciprocity, that the problem of distribution is articulated. The prohibition articulated by the norm: "Do not do unto your neighbor what you would hate him to do unto you . . ." rests upon the recognition of the plurality of persons, namely, the agents and the patients of action, and thus, of the original dissymmetry marking the agent–patient relationship:

> The most remarkable thing, however, in the formulation of this rule is that the reciprocity demanded stands out against the background of the presupposition of an initial dissymmetry between the protagonists of the action—a dissymmetry that places on in the position of agent and the other in that of patient. This absence of symmetry has its grammatical projection in the opposition between the active form of doing and the passive form of doing and the passive form of being done, hence of suffering or submission. (Ricoeur, 1992: 219)

The significance of the grounding of the norm of reciprocity in solicitude must not be undermined. This is so because the irreplaceable character of the other presupposes a structure of reciprocity, precisely so that the other is distinguished from oneself. The plurality of persons, central to solicitude, is assured by the norm of reciprocity, which prohibits the victimization of another by oneself. The role of solicitude, signifying the ethical intention, is crucial here: because solicitude signifies the mutual exchange of self-esteems, it grounds the norm in a distributive context. Herein lies the meaning of the norm of reciprocity. Outside of a redistributive context, the norm becomes hyper-moralized. That is, the separation of the norm from solicitude has the effect of replicating and even exacerbating the initial forms of dissymmetry or inequality recognized by the Golden Rule. The prohibition against murder represents the culmination of the weakening between the ethical aim of civic equality in just institutions and the moral norm in the complete separation of the prohibition "You shall not kill" from the civic practices constituting the ethical aim of the wish to live together: "*The tie between this prohibition and the Golden Rule seems even to have been obliterated here*" (Ricoeur, 1992: 119–120, my emphasis).

We shall examine the specific meaning and implications of the hypermoralization of the law in Chapter 4, where we will take up the moralization of the law in relation to the retributive practices of the state such as disenfranchisement and imprisonment, in contrast to the recognitive aspect of law, wherein issues of crime and poverty are treated not along retributive lines, but as issues for social policy, that is, in terms of social justice. For now, it is important to note the essential intersection between the ethical and moral traditions in the norm of reciprocity. By way of anticipation, we can say that the norm of reciprocity embodied by the Golden Rule has an *ethical aim*: "to establish reciprocity wherever there is lack of reciprocity," and thus is to be understood not solely along moralistic lines, but in terms of social justice (Ricoeur, 1992: 225). As we shall see, the ability of the norm to establish reciprocity, or equality, and thus to locate inequalities, requires that the norm be understood as the state, whose laws work to locate the social and economic facts of inequalities.

It is because solicitude is characterized by its concern for inequality that it is placed by Ricoeur between the first and second Kantian formulations of the categorical imperative. The general formulation of the categorical imperative, we will recall, reads as follows: "I ought never to act except in such a way that I could also will that my maxim should become a universal law" (Kant, 1997: §4: 402). The second formulation of the categorical imperative, which develops from the first formulation, reads as follows: "Act in such a way that you always treat humanity, whether in your own person or in the person of any other, never simply as a means, but always at the same time as an end" (Kant, 1997: §4: 429). Kant explicates a progression between the categories of the maxims in the following way: "A progression takes place here, as through the categories of the *unity* of the form of the will (its universality), the *plurality* of the matter (of objects i.e., of ends), and the *allness* or totality of the system of these" (Kant, 1997: §4: 437). Each of the three categories are to be understood in terms of the other, such that the *plurality* of ends is nothing other than the rational being acting in accordance with her very nature, that is, by acting in accordance with the law of freedom to which she may be subject; therein lies the meaning not only of her freedom, but simultaneously the freedom of all other rational law-givers and thus of the very constitution of the kingdom of ends:

> Now, from this it follows incontestably that every rational being, as an end in itself, must be able to regard himself as also giving universal laws with respect to any law whatsoever to which he may be subject; for, it is just this fitness of his maxims for giving universal law that marks him out as an end in itself; it also follows that this dignity (prerogative) he has over all merely natural beings bring with it that he must always take his maxims from the point of view of himself, *and likewise every other rational being, as lawgiving beings* (*who for this reason are also called persons*). Now in

> this way a world of rational beings (*mundus intelligibilis*) as a kingdom of ends is possible, through the giving of their own laws by all persons as members. *Consequently, every rational being must act as if he were by his maxims at all times a lawgiving member of the universal kingdom of ends.* (Kant, 1997: §4: 438, my emphasis)

In this way, the continuity between the rational being and the kingdom of ends (allness) is assured by the self-givenness of law (*unity*), rendering the category of the plurality of ends superfluous, insofar as in giving himself a universal law, the rational being is simultaneously recognizing all other rational beings as ends in themselves, that is, in their plurality.

Ricoeur focuses on the relationship between the first category of unity and the second category of plurality in order to draw out the relationship between the first and second formulations of the categorical imperative. Specifically, it is in the category of plurality that the mediation of the Golden Rule is made apparent (Ricoeur, 1992: 225). Let us turn now to his argument.

Ricoeur notes a tension within the second formulation of the categorical imperative, namely, between the notion of humanity and of persons as ends in themselves. It is with reference to the solicitude characterizing the Golden Rule that the tensions between these two terms is brought to light. The two terms of the imperative, humanity and persons as ends in themselves have roles that are at once complementary, but which operate at two distinct levels. While the term humanity functions as the criterion of universality constitutive of the principle of autonomy, persons as ends in themselves articulates the plurality of persons such that persons as ends in themselves pass the criterion of universality through the globalizing idea of humanity, and not in terms of otherness as such:

> Everything in Kant's natural's explicit argumentation aims at giving priority to the continuity, assured by the idea of humanity, with the principle of autonomy, at the expense of the idea of humanity, with the principle of autonomy, at the expense of the unavowed discontinuity that marks the sudden introduction of the idea of an end in itself and of persons as ends in themselves. (Ricoeur, 1992: 220)

The term humanity, then, functions as the condition of universality applied to persons as ends in themselves. What remains to be seen, however, is whether the condition of universality, satisfied by the term humanity, may be said to fully account for the operation of the second categorical imperative, and whether something new is not added with the pairing of humanity with persons as ends in themselves.

It is here between the terms *humanity and persons as ends in themselves*, that the full meaning of the Golden Rule emerges as the *norm of reciprocity*. As we noted above, the Golden Rule expresses the intersection of solicitous concern with the otherness of persons and the normative articulation of this concern through the principle of reciprocity. Ricoeur, by placing the Golden Rule in the intermediary position between solicitude and the second categorical imperative, allows for the possibility for the *demonstration* of the Golden Rule itself. That is, it allows for the possibility, and indeed of the necessity, for the second categorical imperative to be treated as the formalization of the Golden Rule.

The demonstration of the Golden Rule through the second categorical imperative takes places in two stages. In the first stage of the demonstration, Ricoeur notes that the Kantian category of "matter" or "plurality" constitutes the place of those interactions between agent and patient, characterized by the problem of dissymmetry or inequality. It is here that the norm of reciprocity responds to the dissymmetry characterizing the agent–patient interaction. The idea of humanity, then, applies a formalizing process on the norm of reciprocity articulated in the Golden Rule. Where the norm of reciprocity enacted by the Golden Rule responds to the *dissymmetry* of the agent and patient of action, and thus to their *plurality*, the idea of humanity in the second categorical imperative provides a universal gloss on the plurality assured by the norm of reciprocity. The principle of autonomy asserts itself through the idea of the idea of humanity. By universalizing the norm of reciprocity, the idea of humanity works to undermine the very plurality that is preserved by the norm (Ricoeur, 1992: 223). The norm of reciprocity assures the plurality, the otherness, of agent and patient through the anti-sacrificial principle, which states that each person is to be accorded the dignity inherent to self-respect; that is, persons are to be treated as ends in themselves and not as means. The Kantian precept of treating persons as ends in themselves, expressed in the second categorical imperative, however, requires the mediation of the solicitous concern for the otherness of persons be clarified and structured through the norm of reciprocity. The universalization of the norm of reciprocity leads to the separation of the norm from solicitude and the concern with the otherness of persons, highlighted by the problem of inequality:

> In this regard, the notion of humanity can be considered the plural expression of the requirement of universality that presided over the

> deduction of autonomy, hence taken as the plural unfolding of the very principle of autonomy. *Introduced as the mediating term between the diversity of persons, the notion of humanity has the effect of lessening, to the point of eliminating, the otherness that is at the root of this diversity, otherness which is dramatized in the dissymmetrical relation of the power one will holds over the other, opposed by the Golden Rule.* (Ricoeur, 1992: 223, my emphasis)

Because the idea of humanity assures the universalization of the norm of reciprocity, it assures once more the primacy of the principle of autonomy that figured the general formulation of the categorical imperative. In this way, the idea of humanity provides a plural articulation of the principle of autonomy itself. Humanity, then, occupies a similar structure with respect to autonomy as solicitude does with respect to the good life.

In this first stage of the demonstration, the process of formalization through which the principle of autonomy is affirmed in the deontological tradition, works to undermine the Golden Rule. In this respect, Ricoeur notes Kant's dismissal of the Golden Rule precisely because it fails the rigorous test of formalization that applied to the first formulation of the categorical imperative. The Golden Rule is only partially formal because while it includes the order of inclinations, such as liking and disliking, it does not provide these inclinations with content. According to the Kantian critique, the norm of reciprocity cannot constitute a standard of judgment amidst these affections. A standard of judgment would make possible the delineation the grounds of respect between oneself and another. This criterion of judgment would require the delineation of the universality of the grounds of respect owed to persons. This universality, as the condition of the respect owed to persons as ends in themselves in constituted by the idea of humanity. It is the idea of humanity in the second categorical imperative that constitutes the grounds of respect between oneself and another without thereby crediting the plurality of persons as such.

In this way, the idea of humanity constitutes in the second categorical imperative the equivalent of the principle of universalization in the general formulation of the categorical imperative. The idea of humanity expresses the *dialogic* structure of the principle of universality, and thus assures the passage from *unity* to *plurality*, both of which are moments of autonomy itself. *Because the idea of humanity constitutes the condition of universalization with respect to persons as ends in themselves, it occupies the same dialogic position as solicitude. Thus, the plurality of persons can be shown to be internal to the principle of universalization, of autonomy, itself.* This means that the imperative of respect owed persons as ends in themselves is internal to the formal categorical imperative, thus "robbing the respect owed to persons in their diversity of any original significance" (Ricoeur, 1992: 224).

The idea of humanity formalizes the requirement for equality between agent and patient articulated by the Golden Rule. However the Golden Rule, underwritten by the solicitous concern for the otherness of others comes to the fore precisely at this juncture between *humanity* and *persons as ends in themselves*: the second categorical imperative distinguishes between my "own person" and "the person of any other," thereby introducing the plurality of persons:

> It is here that the notion of *person* as an end in itself comes to balance that of *humanity*, to the extent that it introduces in the very formulation of the imperative the distinction between "your person" and "the person of anyone else" [original emphasis]. *With the person alone comes plurality* [my emphasis]. (Ricoeur, 1992: 224)

Respecting the humanity in oneself and in others, that is, never treating humanity as a means, has a two-fold meaning: On one hand, this prohibition works as the test of universalization assuring the autonomy of the imperative. On the other hand, however, the prohibition against treating humanity as a means demands respect for the plurality, or the otherness, of persons. The subtle discordance created by the idea of persons as ends in themselves remains hidden because of the Kantian emphasis on the universalism central to the principle of autonomy, which prohibits treating humanity as a means. This emphasis on universalism, then, conceals the very point of its application of humanity, namely, the plurality of persons. It is the Golden Rule that safeguards the humanity of persons from being treated as a means and in this way grounds Kant's rejection of the principle of utility in the introductory pages of the *Groundwork* as candidate for the unconditionally good. *Treating the humanity of another as a means entails a violation of the norm of reciprocity, which ensures the insubstitutibility of persons through the distributive commandment to treat one self as an-other.* Here, then, the second categorical imperative emerges as a clarification of the norm of reciprocity, or the Golden Rule:

> What is said here that is new is precisely what the Golden Rule states on the level of popular wisdom, before it is shifted through the critique. For it is indeed the deepest intention of this rule that now emerges clarified and purified. What indeed is it to treat humanity in my person and in the person of others as a *means* if not to exert *upon* the will of others that

> power which, full of restraint in the in the case of influence, is unleashed in all the forms that violence takes, culminating in torture [original emphasis]? *And what is the occasion for this progressive violence of power exerted by one will upon another if not the initial dissymmetry between what one does and what is done to others* [my emphasis]? (Ricoeur, 1992: 225)

Treating the humanity in oneself and in others as a *means* translates into the denial of the *plurality* of persons, which is a violation of the norm of reciprocity. What the Golden Rule reveals here is that the idea of humanity, as the condition of the universal, is not sufficient for the preservation of persons as ends in themselves, precisely because it cannot account for the problem of inequality. That is, the norm of reciprocity, by distinguishing between actor and patient through the problem of inequality, prohibits treating the humanity in oneself and in the other as a means. This plurality or otherness of persons as ends in themselves, Ricoeur argues, introduces something new into the very structure of the imperative. The prohibition in the second categorical imperative against treating humanity as a means places the plurality of persons within a structure of reciprocity:

> The Golden Rule and the imperative of the respect owed to persons do not simply have the same field of exercise, they also have the same aim: *to establish reciprocity wherever there is a lack of reciprocity*. And in the background of the Gold Rule there reappears the intuition, inherent in solicitude, of genuine otherness at the root of the plurality of persons. At this price, the unifying and unitary idea of humanity ceases to appear as a copy of the universality at work in the principle of autonomy, and the second formulation of the categorical imperative assumes once more its entirely original character. (Ricoeur, 1992: 225, my emphasis)

The idea of humanity, then, is fundamentally to be understood in terms of the norm of reciprocity. In this way, humanity is tied up with the solicitous concern with the otherness of persons, for it is the configuration of reciprocity through the norm that prohibits the victimization of the other by the self, thereby violating the otherness of the other. Thus, the imperative to treat the humanity in oneself and in others as an end in itself is grounded in the structure of reciprocity safeguarding the plurality of persons through the recognition of inequality. In this way, the imperative of the respect owed to persons joins with the aim of the Golden Rule, namely, "to establish reciprocity wherever there is a lack of reciprocity" (Ricoeur, 1992: 225).

I want to remark briefly on the significance of this intersection of the Golden Rule with the imperative of respect owed to persons as it applies to the search for equality amidst inequality, insofar as it informs the third plane of the ethical field explored by Ricoeur, namely, just institutions. We have argued above that it is the Golden Rule that grounds the recognition of self and other as distinctive persons within a distributive context. In this way, the Golden Rule provides, on the ethical plane what Ricoeur refers to as "the sense of justice" that informs the deontological formulation of dialogic or interpersonal relationships (Ricoeur, 1992: 225). Because the Golden Rule places the recognition of self and others within a distributive trajectory, it already points to an *institutional* context. On the institutional plane, we shall see that the *aim* of the norm of reciprocity articulated by the Golden Rule, namely, to reestablish reciprocity, becomes constitutive of *redistributive justice*. That is, it is through the term *distribution* that the ethical and deontological terms intersect once again on the institutional plane. The same nuances characterizing the norm of reciprocity on the dialogic plane will make themselves felt on the institutional plane. Thus, a just system of distributions will also be concerned with the plurality of persons, or the distinctiveness of the individuals taking part in the system of distributions, and at the same time, the system of distributions acts as a guarantor of this plurality by recognizing persons as *members* of the distributive system, of society.

Ricoeur's Distributive Interpretation of the Kantian Principle of Non-Violability

The principle the non-violability of persons governing the relationship between the agent and the patient of action is an expression of the norm of reciprocity, and thus of a shared or distributed conception of personhood. The principle of the non-violability of persons also governs the relations among members who take part in a cooperative society on the institutional plane. But the order of sharing on the institutional plane is necessarily distinct from the mutuality governing the plane of friendship. This difference is due to the fact that the political community is not—as we shall argue against dominant conceptions of communitarianism—a constitutive community, or a community of friendship, in which members identify with one another's ends and with one another's conception of the good.[9] A political community is a community of *moral strangers*. That is, what enables and preserves membership in a political community is the *separation* between members of a community and their constitutive ends. In anticipating Rawls's method for distinguishing between memberships in the public or shared institutions of society, and membership within particular associations and constitutive communities, we say that while we may calculate a person's worth—her capabilities and her disabilities—with respect to her contributions to the latter, they have no place in the former. We cannot intelligibly speak of the worth of a person with respect to her contribution of a society: the order of mutuality on the institutional plane is distinguished from that of the community of friendship, because while the latter is defined by its constitutive ends, on the basis of which may grant or deny membership, society has no such ends according to which it may accept or reject members in accordance with the capabilities and disabilities. In short, what distinguishes membership in society from membership in a constitutive community "is the fact that it is not optional (up to us) whether or not we belong to society" (Rawls, 1977: 165). With Hegel, we may say that society is not to be configured by the association of private individuals; its public character extends far beyond the limits of civil society. We shall argue that it is *separation* between persons and their ends that underwrites a mutual and thus inclusive—or to borrow Jean-Pierre Dupuy's language—*anti-sacrificial society*.[10]

It is here, on the institutional plane, that the deontological and the teleological conceptions are at once most distinct and at the same time intersect in remarkable ways. Their intersection is demonstrated by their two-fold determination of the norm of reciprocity. We have already begun to appreciate the intersection of the deontological and the teleological traditions in the very *distributive structure* of the norm of reciprocity. On one hand, the norm of reciprocity, in articulating the Golden Rule, configures the solicitude that underwrites the inviolability of persons. On the other hand, by virtue of its solicitous grounding, the inviolable status of moral personhood extends to *each* person. The distributive character of the norm of reciprocity, then, faces the good and of our indebtedness to others, and in the direction of the just in its extension of mutuality to the moral stranger, which implies a mutual disinterest in the interest of others. We may say, then, that the norm of reciprocity articulates the distributive conception of personhood which remains under the aegis of the ethical intention to always treat *one*self as an*other*. But this very distributive conception of personhood requires the aid of a deontological *procedure* so as to prevent the exclusion of any-*one* from the status of moral personhood, that is, from the capability to recognize herself as the author of her conception of the good life. It is in terms of the reciprocity that governs the relationship between redistributive justice and recognitive justice that we are to understand Ricoeur's civic interpretation of the lexical ordering of Rawls's principles of justice.[11] The reciprocal relationship between redistributive justice and recognitive justice goes to the heart of the figuration of the self's capacities, so dear to Ricoeur, for action, speech, narration, and imputation.[12] The figuration of selfhood in terms of the capabilities for childhood, parenthood, for life in neighborhoods, for health, for education, and for work, depends upon a distributive understanding of selfhood, wherein one-*self* is translated as an-*other*:

oneself as another

capable self distributive self

A distributive conception of selfhood configures what Ricoeur refers to as the "paradox of exchange at the very place of the irreplaceable", that is, the distribution, the sharing of the *inviolable* status of moral personhood (Ricoeur, 1992: 193).

We shall show later how this distributive conception of the Kantian principle of the inviolability of persons stands in contrast to its *possessive* interpretation. At this stage, we simply wish to suggest that the deontological conception of justice, traditionally aligned with the preservation of the autonomy of persons, is itself an articulation of the demand for equality that is conjoined by the demand that *all* persons are to be treated as ends in themselves. The proceduralist conception of distributive justice advanced by Rawls, which demands that we separate the status of moral personhood from its constitutive ends is itself a *demonstration of a society—a fellowship—of moral strangers*. But if a fellowship of moral strangers is not founded on an identification of constitutive ends, can we still speak of its foundation, of its history? It is here that the most profound connection between the ethical *tēlos* to live together and the deontological emphasis on the inviolability of persons as ends in themselves are conjoined in the most profound way: the ethical foundation of a society of moral strangers—of free and equal persons—is founded on the distributive conception of the capabilities and disabilities for moral selfhood. Just as equality amidst the search for inequality animated the preservation of the plurality of persons, or the inviolability of persons as ends in themselves articulated by the second categorical imperative on the interpersonal plane, so our convictions regarding the injustice of inequality grounds what I will call the proceduralist demonstration of the public *phronēsis* on the collective will t live together.

But just as the order of sharing on the institutional plane will be distinct from that of friendship, so the figure of inequality will be distinct from that of friendship, so the figure of inequality will no longer be the individualized patient of action, but rather the distributed figure of the least advantaged citizen in the institutions of health, education, transportation, social transfers, and old age and disability pensions. *What Rawls teaches us, or rather reminds us, is that it is the institutionalization of the least advantaged member that configures the basic structure of society.*

It will be the figure of the least advantaged member that animates Rawls's thick as opposed to think theory of the good. Thus, while Rawls will eschew the transcendental and metaphysical grounding of Kantian morality in favor of a minimal empiricism which will permit a thin rather than a constitutive or thick account of the good to structure the reasonable or the fair terms of cooperation between members of a society. *But the very thinness of Rawls's account of the good has a deeply ethical signification.* That is, it is the thin account of the good that furnishes what Rawls refers to as the *reasonable* conditions of cooperation will signify the profoundly social character of the capabilities for moral personhood. Rawls's deontological conception of a thin theory of the good configures the mutual and the reciprocal grounds of cooperation, of the ethical intention to live together.

We find the social-ethical grounding of the deontological conception of a thin theory of the good, Rawls argues, in the *anti-sacrificial* character of Rawls's serial ordering of the principles of justice (Ricoeur, 1992: 236; 2000: 53). Ricoeur here draws on Jean Pierre Dupuy's observation in his "Les paradox d Théorie de la justice: Introduction à l'ouvre de John Rawls" that the ordering of the two principles of justice, namely the priority of what Dupuy refers to as the principle of political justice, which emphasizes the liberties of citizenship—freedom of expression, of assembly, of the right to vote, of eligibility for public office—over what he calls the principles of economic justice, in which social and economic inequalities are to be arranged so as to maximize the minimum share, is aimed *against* the sacrificial vice of another teleological tradition, namely utilitarianism.[13] It is crucial to bear in mind that Rawls's deontological conception of justice directed against utilitarianism, to which the Golden Rule is also opposed. With Dupuy, Ricoeur argues that on the institutional plane the utilitarian logic of max-min works to rationalize a sacrificial principle. When confined to individual reasoning, max-min's sacrificial reasoning is circumscribed in terms of a short-term pleasure in exchange for long-term satisfaction. But when the utilitarian max-min principle is extrapolated from the individual to the societal plane, the scale of the sacrifice envelops an entire social stratum.

It is with the sacrificial principle that the problem of inequality emerges on the institutional plane. As we saw on the intersubjective plane, the problem of inequality was inextricably tied up with the problem of the plurality of personhood. In recognizing the initial dissymmetry between the agent and the patient of action, the norm of reciprocity distinguishes and preserves the plurality of agent and patient through their reciprocal affirmation. On the institutional plane, the dissymmetry between agent and patient is reflected in the sacrificial principle of utilitarianism. Ricoeur's argument is that the norm of reciprocity expressed in the Golden Rule interjects once more on the institutional plane as a response to the sacrificial principle.

The principles of justice in their lexical ordering prohibit the purchase of greater social or economic advantages at the price of the loss of liberty for any-one member. In other words, no-*one* may be sacrificed, even for the greater social or economic advantages that may accrue to society as a whole. The sacrifice of the least advantaged member will entail the sacrifice of society itself: on a distributive conception of society, we cannot legitimize the jettisoning of members without thereby endangering membership itself. This is so because a distributive conception of society rests upon the norm of reciprocity which prohibits the separation of the capabilities of oneself from the capabilities—or disabilities—of another. On the institutional plane of justice, Rawls will demonstrate, the norm of reciprocity is institutionalized by the publicity requirement.

It is the institutionalization of the requirement for publicity that is represented by the principles of justice in their lexical ordering. The publicity requirement on the institutional plane of the distributive or the solicitous society is directed against the individualization of disadvantage inherent in utilitarianism: it is the very *sharing* of the position of the least advantaged member that underwrites society itself. It is this profound connection between the institutionalization of the publicity requirement and the norm of reciprocity—the demand for equality—that prompts Ricoeur to argue that Rawls's proceduralist conception of justice is a demonstration of the ethical intention of justice is a demonstration of the ethical intention to "aim for the good life, with and for others, in just institutions," and thus as providing a *methodology* for public *phronēsis*, for critical public deliberation, on this aim.[14] If Ricoeur is correct, then Rawls's proceduralism itself serves as a profound defense of the inclusionary, and this historically informed, society.[15] But before we can advance our ethical interpretation of Rawls's moral constructivism any further, we must address the serious charges of anti-communitarianism advanced against Rawls. This will prompt us to take a closer look at the social implications of Rawls's argument for a Kantian constructivism.

Chapter 3

The Sacrificial Ethics of Constitutive Communitarianism

We began our study with an account of Ricoeur's philosophical anthropology of the capable subject. The subject's capabilities for speech, action, narration, and moral and ethical imputation, Ricoeur argues, unfold within the social, economic, and political narratives embodied in the public culture of a society. Capabilities are not the possession of any-*one*, but are both articulated and preserved by the law of mutuality and as such belong to everyone. Ricoeur's conception of a capabilities approach to social justice, then, rejects the divide between methodological individualism and holism: the capabilities constitutive of moral autonomy attest to the mutual or public configuration of liberty and equality. Where the "ultra-individualistic" tradition in liberal thought, in emphasizing the capabilities for selfhood as such, treats these capabilities as the accomplishments of the autonomous or self-grounding self, the civic tradition in liberal thought articulates the *distributive* character of the capabilities for selfhood, and in this way, refuses their separation from the public institutions of society.

I then introduced an idea that will preoccupy us for the remainder of our studies, namely, that while the deontological conception of justice, articulated by John Rawls, has traditionally been thought to be opposed to the teleological conception of justice articulated by Ricoeur, the very deontological character of Rawls's theory of distributive justice is intended to demonstrate in a profound way Ricoeur's Aristotelian ethics of *oneself as another*. Just as fairness, by configuring the grounds of mutuality, prohibits the sacrifice of an-other for greater social or economic advantages that may accrue to one-self: this kind of comparative deliberation, in which the very moral status of persons may be weighed against potential advantages or disadvantages, is itself rendered impossible by the "thick" demands of mutuality in the original position. That is, the "thin" theory of the good advanced by Rawls, often thought to serve as an attack on communitarian or ethical ideals, is itself a "thick" defense of the norm of reciprocity, of the ethical refusal to separate the capabilities of one-self from the disabilities of an-other. Rawls's *anti-sacrificial* conception of capability justice is articulated by the demand for full publicity.[1] I want to turn now to consider the way in which the full publicity condition is in turn demonstrated by the reasonable constraints on the rational deliberations in the original position. In this way, the proceduralist articulation of the publicity condition—or of the norm of reciprocity—figurates a conception of an inclusive society, which refuses to exclude members from its public culture by moralizing the disadvantages of illness, poverty, homelessness, disability, and unemployment. Nor does a fully public or inclusive society sanction the withdrawal of the elite from public life by moralizing wealth, health, the capabilities for literacy and economic and political responsibility. But before we are able to go any further with our argument that the very proceduralist character of Rawls's theory of justice constitutes an ethical defense of a public or inclusive society, we must first spend some time considering compelling communitarian critiques of Rawls, which argue that the proceduralist character of Rawls's theory of distributive justice, far from articulating a defense of community, advances a disembodied and asocial conception of personhood. One of the most powerful articulations of this position is the by now classical work of Michael Sandel, entitled *Liberalism and the Limits of Justice* (1982), and developed further in his *The Procedural Republic and the Unencumbered Self* (1984). Sandel's communitarian critique of Rawls's political philosophy has in turn informed other dominant critiques of modern liberal thought, such as Charles Taylor's argument that Anglo-American liberal thought is unable to accommodate the needs of multicultural societies.[2] We shall turn to consider powerful arguments such as Taylor's, which urge us to take seriously citizens' demands for political, economic, and cultural *recognition* in the next chapter. Let us first consider the communitarian tenants that underwrite these claims for *recognitive justice*.

The Communitarian Defense of the Constitutive Self

In his reading of Rawls, Sandel traces the Kantian foundations of Rawls's proceduralist account of justice to the priority Rawls grants to the right over the good. Where Kant emphasized the universal character of moral law, Sandel argues, Rawls designates justice– and not any particular conception of the good—as "the first virtue of social institutions" (Sandel, 1984: 83). Just as the universalist conception of moral law cannot be grounded in the contingencies of the empirical world, so justice cannot rely for its articulation on the particular conceptions of—and particular attachments to—conceptions of the good. If moral law is to delineate the grounds of freedom, it requires a categorical and not a merely contingent foundation. If justice is to regulate amongst competing conceptions of the good life, it too must have recourse to a categorical grounding that stands above merely particular notions of the good. Thus, theories of justice, and indeed of ethics, which aim to realize a human conception of the good, to borrow Aristotle's language, through their endorsement of a particular conception of the good, risk violating the capacities of individual subjects to choose their own conception of the good. In short, a theory of justice that rests upon a conception of the good risks violating the *freedom* of the individual subject. Recall that for Kant the subject is free when she gives herself the law of freedom, in short, when she is self-determining. It is this essential freedom of the subject, Sandel argues, that Rawls seeks to endorse with his proceduralist account of justice. But if it is the subject, and not the ends she pursues or to which she is attached, that is given priority in the proceduralist account of justice, then are we not merely advancing a theory of the subject as such? For if what matters is the autonomy of the self, are we not then advancing a view of what Sandel calls the "unencumbered self," a self that is *necessarily* separated from her commitment to a conception of the good, to her community and to the goods she exchanges with members of her community and which are thereby imbued with a social meaning (Sandel, 1984: 86)? And it is the subject as such, not the particular subject immersed in its attachments to the objects and persons of the empirical world, that serves as the foundation of freedom: "Nothing other than what Kant calls 'the subject of all possible ends himself' can give rise to the right, for only this subject is also the subject of an autonomous will" (Sandel, 1984: 84). We—that is, the empirical you and I—are not simply assured of our status as autonomous agents, and it is precisely at this empirical limit that our essential capacity for freedom reveals itself: despite our empirical trappings, we nonetheless feel that we are free, we experience a sense of freedom. This sense of freedom would be impossible unless the subject is at least *capable* of participating in the transcendental realm of freedom, in which our wills are the first cause, that is, in which we are genuinely self-determining agents. The subject, then, is defined by its capacity for freedom and thus the status of the subject is in a fundamental sense prior to the social goods and the social relations of the empirical world. In short, the status of autonomy, or right, is prior to the social character of the good.

Rawls, Sandel argues, is firmly committed to this view. He seeks with Kant to preserve the priority of the subject's capacity for freedom, and thus of the right over the good, but he configures moral personhood not in light of a transcendental idealism, but rather by clarifying a set of principles of justice, through the original position, which will design the social, political, and economic circumstances constitutive of moral personhood. But here the role autonomy plays in political institutions becomes even more urgent: what kind of community is possible from within a proceduralism that prioritizes autonomy? Rawl's proceduralism—centered in the original position—is an attempt to mediate the relationship between autonomous moral persons and the basic or the institutional structure of society. The question that Sandel raises concerns the nature of this relationship: what sort of membership are persons conceived independently of their religious and moral convictions, their material, social and cultural capital, and their attachment to others, capable of? For in the original position, the contracting parties—autonomous (or rational) persons—are to agree upon the principles of justice according to which the basic structure of society is to be designed, without knowledge of these prior social, economic, and political commitments. The principles of justice which arise from the procedure of deliberation set forth in the original position will themselves be autonomous of particular ends.

But while the procedure of deliberation represented by the original position—a procedure that we have yet to give a full account of—frees the contracting parties from their commitment to particular ends, it nonetheless articulates a very specific view of the persons for whom justice is the first virtue of social institutions. "This," Sandel argues, "is the picture of the unencumbered self, a self understood *a priori* to and independent of purposes and ends" (Sandel, 1984: 86). Sandel notes that a society in which justice is the first virtue structures a certain distance between the status of moral personhood and the possessions and attachments of any given person, or to borrow Sandel's language, "between the values that I *have* and the person I *am*: To identify any characteristics as *my* aims, ambitions, desires and so on, is always to imply some subject 'me' standing behind them, at a certain distance, and the shape of this 'me' must be given prior to any of the aims or attributes I bear" (Sandel, 1984: 86). On Sandel's account, the original position conceptualizes a view of self-identity in which the subject—"me"—is forcibly separated from what is "mine"—my ambitions, commitments, and possessions. What this separation between "me" and "mine" signifies, Sandel argues, is that the priority in the Kantian proceduralist account of moral personhood is not the ends to which a particular self is committed, but rather *anyone's capacity* to choose these ends. In order to be able to view myself as a free agent and as being capable of autonomous choice-making, my self-identity must not be connected with what is "mine"—my values, ambitions, possessions and so on. It is this view of the "unencumbered self" of moral personhood that represents the preoccupation of the proceduralist account with the autonomy or the freedom of the self. Kantian proceduralism does not permit a conception of identity such that the separation between me and what is mine might render my ability to recognize myself impossible. That is, Kantian proceduralism eschews the view that the self is *constituted* by its ends in favor of the unencumbered self, and the significance of this for Sandel is that this is done to preserve the freedom of the subject.

The price that we pay for our allegiance to the Kantian view of the unencumbered self—a conception of the self that is antecedent to its ends and commitments—is that this self is always antecedent to community itself. The privileging of the subject's capacity for choice-making, for freedom, means eschewing the possibility of the community membership of the self prior to its status as an autonomous choice-maker. In short, on the Kantian proceduralist view of the autonomous self, membership in a community cannot be a constitutive end. Certainly, the unencumbered self may choose to participate in a community, thereby joining a community in a voluntary sense. To borrow Sandel's language, the unencumbered self is capable, at best, of membership in a cooperative community; it is incapable of membership in a constitutive community, which "would engage the identity as well as the interests of the participants, and so implicate its members in a citizenship more thoroughgoing than the unencumbered self can know" (Sandel, 1984: 87).

The implication of the impossibility of a constitutive community in the Kantian proceduralism, from which Rawls will develop his conception of moral personhood, is vast: if the autonomy of the subject prevails over the constitutive ends of persons, then even Rawls's vision of community—a community in which benefits and burdens, rights, and responsibilities are to be distributed—is itself threatened. In particular, the difference principle, or the principle of equality, is threatened. For the difference principle underwrites the lexically prior principle of liberty by prohibiting the exclusion of persons from the principle of liberty—that is, from the capacity to recognize themselves as autonomous moral agents—by holding that only those inequalities which are to the benefit of the least advantaged member are fair or just. What this means is that arbitrary inequalities—evidenced by social and economic unequal starting positions in terms of such variables as poverty and poor health, and which as starting positions cannot be said to have been merited or earned in any way—may not be permitted in the design of the basic structure of society. The difference principle enacts this prohibition by designing the basic structure of society so as to *distribute* or *share* both arbitrary advantages and arbitrary disadvantages. The equality principle is of course key for Rawls's distributive account of justice, because it is through the inclusion of all persons in the principle of liberty—through the distributive work of the difference principle—that a cooperative community is created and maintained. But even in the distributive work of the difference principle, we can see the endorsement of the unencumbered self—that is, the difference principle, in characterizing the advantages that I might accrue from, say, my wealth or natural talent, reinforces a separation between who I am and what is mine:

> I cannot be said to deserve the benefits that flow from, say, my fine physique and good looks, because they are accidental, not essential facts about me. They describe attributes I *have*, not the person I *am*, and so cannot give rise to a claim of dessert. Being an unencumbered self, this is true about me. And so I cannot, as an individual, deserve anything at all. (Sandel, 1984: 89, original emphasis)

By characterizing what is mine as arbitrary, the difference principle renders my capability to recognize myself by virtue of what I have, and the very idea of merit, unintelligible.[3]

But if the ascription of my advantages that flow from what I have to the person I am is completely arbitrary, on what grounds does the difference principle demand that I be willing to *share* these advantages with others? What makes this sharing legitimate and not merely arbitrary? If the advantages accruing from what I have are considered to be arbitrary when used to serve my ends, it is not at all clear why, on the cooperative view of society endorsed by Rawls's proceduralism, that distribution of these advantages to others would be any less arbitrary: "And if their arbitrariness in *me* makes them ineligible to serve *my* ends, there seems no obvious reason why their arbitrariness within any particular society should not make them ineligible to serve that society's ends as well" (Sandel, 1984: 893, original emphasis). If we accept that the distribution or sharing of advantages (and of disadvantages) in the cooperative view of society advanced by Rawls is merely arbitrary, then the very relationship between distribution, of sharing, and of cooperation, is thrown into question.

But while sharing practices in a cooperative society are voluntary at best and arbitrary at worst, the constitutive society supports relations of mutuality amongst its members, thereby supporting distributive practices. In a constitutive view of society—because each person recognizes herself by virtue of her commitment to the society in which she lives, she views the demands for the sharing of advantages and disadvantages not as external, arbitrary demands, but rather as part and parcel of her very self-identity as a member of society. It is crucial to understand the force of Sandel's argument here: only a constitutive society may provide the norms of mutuality that underwrite redistributive practices. A cooperative society, governed by the difference principle, is unable to do so:

> What the difference principle requires, but cannot provide, is some way of identifying those *among* whom the assets I bear are properly regarded as common, some way of seeing ourselves as mutually indebted and morally engaged to begin with. But as we have seen, the constitutive aims and attachments that would save and situate the difference principle are precisely the ones denied to the liberal self; the moral encumbrances and antecedent obligations they imply would undercut the priority of right. (Sandel, 1984: 90, original emphasis)

In fact, it is the imposition of the difference principle upon the cooperative society governed by the autonomy of the subject that has worked to *undermine* any substantive notion of community. The autonomous subject, standing outside of society, regards its distributive demands with increasing indifference, and even with hostility. And yet, the distributive demands imposed by the state continually presuppose a conception of community, which it at the same time rejects. For it is the state that guarantees us our individual liberties and entitlements, and at the same time demands a high level of mutuality, as articulated by the difference principle. Here Sandel returns us, in a communitarian guise, to an old complaint, namely, that the principle of equality is incompatible with the principle of liberty: "The point so far is that we cannot be persons for whom justice is primary, and also be persons for whom the difference principle is a principle of justice" (Sandel, 1984: 90).

Does the "procedural republic" foster a mode of deliberation in which the norm of distribution, of sharing, stands over and against the autonomous individual? (Sandel, 1984: 91). Does not this opposition represent, to once again borrow Sandel's language, an "official rejection of community" that it nonetheless presupposes? If Sandel's diagnosis is correct, then it seriously undermines the role of the proceduralist conception of justice as a *public* model of deliberation on the basic structure of society. How are we to better understand the roots of this antinomy between the anti-communitarian interpretation on the one hand and the proceduralist republic as the embodiment of publicity and of community on the other? Is it possible that the antinomy is false? The classical opposition between redistribution (the equality principle) and autonomy (the liberty principle) runs like this: so long as persons are prohibited from identifying with their ends, that is, from being constituted by their ends, no community is possible (difference principle). Is Rawls's argument against the constitutive self necessarily an argument against community, or might the classical opposition between redistribution (the equality principle) and autonomy (the liberty principle) runs like this: so long as persons are prohibited from identifying with their ends, that is, from being constituted by their ends (articulated by the principle of liberty), no community is possible (presupposed by the difference principle, or the principle of redistribution). Is Rawls's argument against the constitutive self necessarily an argument against community, or is the Rawlsian prohibition against the constitutive self a prohibition against the sacrifice of the or the exclusion of our least advantaged member from the social, economic, and political institutions of society, and in this way an argument for a more inclusive conception of society than the constitutive model of society might allow? But before we begin to unpack the contradiction between the anti-communitarian and the communitarian renderings of the Kantian proceduralist conception of justice, let us examine Rawls's argument for the role that Kantian constructivism plays in configuring the relationship between the conception of the moral or the autonomous person and community, or the background structure of society. Our aim will be to clarify how autonomy and the basic structure of society are defined in Kantian constructivism. This will in turn presuppose a clarification of the original position and its attendant features, which as we have said embodies the Kantian conception of proceduralism.

Kantian Constructivism: Moral Objectivity as a Social Point of View

In two major essays published after *A Theory of Justice*, "Kantian Constructivism" (1999) and "The Basic Structure as Subject" (1977), Rawls is careful to stress that the Kantian form of constructivism is not an endorsement of Kantian moral thought as such, but rather borrows from the fundamental structure of Kant's moral thought and extends this structure to the development of a model for public political reasoning. But even at the level of structure, the Kantian view of community, or the Kantian "social point of view," differs radically from the constitutive sense of community advanced by communitarians, the paradigmatic model of which can be found in Sandel's work (Rawls, 1999: 305). We arrive upon a Kantian social point of view through a procedure that connects a conception of the person to the first principles of justice. This procedural relationship between persons and the principle of justice which are to design the basic structure of society is a *social* proceduralism because it requires that all persons who are regarded in a certain way publicly agree upon, and thereby render as mutually acceptable, the grounds of their social cooperation. Against this procedural clarification of the relationship between persons and society, from which the grounds of social cooperation are established, the communitarian view holds that persons are constituted by their social, material, and political ends and thus the relationship between the conception of the person and the basis of social cooperation do not permit of this kind of proceduralist clarification.

And yet, as difficult as this kind of philosophical and political clarification is, it is demanded by the *social role* of a conception of justice itself. On the Kantian view advanced by Rawls, a conception of justice may be justified only when the conditions of justification itself meet the publicity requirement. That is, a public or shared understanding of justice constitutive of human community presupposes a public procedure of justification that is inclusive of all members of society: "The social role of a conception of justice is to enable all members of society to make mutually acceptable to one another their shared institution and basic arrangements, by citing what are publicly recognized as sufficient reasons, as identified by that conception" (Rawls, 1999: 305).

Rawls is careful to stress that the justificatory task of political philosophy is a fundamentally practical, and not merely theoretical, task (Rawls, 1999: 306). Rawls's version of Kantian constructivism does not aim to reveal universal moral truths, nor even to reason from universally correct premises; it takes as its starting point the historical, and thus considered, convictions constitutive of the public culture of a democratic society. The social role of the proceduralist conception of justice is itself determined by the social character of the considered convictions it sets out to shape and to clarify. By grounding his version of Kantian proceduralism within the considered convictions of an historical society which has sought to balance the competing aims of equality and liberty, the considered convictions or agreements constitutive of the history of democratic society itself provide the content for the proceduralist exercise. For it is in the excavation and the clarification of these considered convictions constitutive of democratic society that historical and perhaps latent agreements on a public conception of justice are reinforced and strengthened. Moral objectivity in Kantian proceduralism has a fundamentally social role: It aims to reaffirm the grounds of reciprocity by ensuring the inclusion of all citizens in a public understanding of justice. The social role of the proceduralist conception of justice is itself determined by the social character of the considered convictions it sets out to shape and clarify:

> What justifies a conception of justice is not its being true to an order antecedent to and given to us, but its congruence with our deeper understanding of ourselves and our aspirations, and our realization that, given our history and the traditions embedded in our public life, it is the most reasonable doctrine for us. *We can find no better basic character for our social world.* Kantian constructivism holds that moral objectivity is to be understood in terms of a suitably constructed social point of view that all can accept. (Rawls, 1999: 306–7, my emphasis)

There is a sense of urgency characterizing the practical social clarification of our considered convictions regarding the relationship between liberty and equality as it is translated on the institutional plane in the pursuit of a mutual fitness between society and economy by the modern welfare state.

The social-proceduralist view applies in the first instance to the basic structure of society, that is, to the social, economic, and political institutions of society and viewed as one system. It is for this reason that Rawls will refer to the proceduralist conception of justice as fairness: fairness or justice prevails when the capacity for freedom is distributed to all persons. This distribution in turn crucially depends upon the just arrangement of the institutional relationships into which each person is born. Rawls's adherence to the Kantian view of the inviolability of persons—that moral persons are fundamentally free—has a *social signification*: it underwrites the kind of initial agreement on the design of the basic structure of society that persons who regard themselves as being free (and on this basis are fundamentally equal) would agree to. On the Kantian view of moral personhood adopted by Rawls, persons are free to choose and revise their ends and pursuits over a lifetime and regard others as being equally free to do the same. Taken together, this means that moral persons have a sense of morality: that is, persons are willing and able to tie their conduct and the conduct of others to publicly affirmed principles of justice. In short, moral persons are able to pursue their rational ends and aims within a context of reciprocity and mutuality, that is, in accordance with fair or reasonable terms of cooperation.

In what follows, we see that in the original position, it is the conditions of reciprocity—which will ultimately be embodied in the basic structure of society—that represent the moral status of free and equal persons who are capable to pursuing their conception of the good. The conditions of *full autonomy* are represented by the demonstration of reciprocity, or of publicity, in the original position. Outside of this procedural demonstration represented by the constraints on the deliberations of the rational parties in the original position, even the rational pursuit of individual conceptions of the good remains unintelligible. That is, the rational autonomy of the contracting parties is itself an artificial, though indispensible, part of the construction of the fuller or more inclusive conception of autonomy modeled by the conditions of reciprocity which frame the deliberations of the rational parties (Rawls 1999: 320). It is for this reason that Rawls can say that the principles of justice arising from the mutuality that frames self-preservation, when self-preservation is defined as persons' rational pursuit of the good, themselves express the basic institutional structure of society, and thus that the basic structure of society is the primary subject of justice. It is not the rational autonomy of the contracting parties, anxious to advance their interests, that is the subject of justice and prior to community, but rather the social conditions of freedom and equality that constitute the primary subject of justice. The proceduralist construction of the basic structure of society represents the social point of view that is "authoritative with respect to all individual and associational points of view" (Rawls, 1999: 340). That is, it represents how moral persons, who regard themselves as being free and equal, would ideally choose to arrange the basic social, political, and economic institutions of their society so as to adequately represent their self-understanding as free and equal persons. As soon as persons who regard themselves as being free and equal contract to design the principles of justice which are to structure the terms of their cooperation, certain constraints on the parties' deliberations become necessary so as to preserve the freedom and equality of the contracting parties in the deliberative procedure. For if the conditions or the situation of deliberation on the principles of justice preserve the freedom and equality of the contracting parties, that is, if they are fair, then the hope is that this fairness will transfer to the principles of justice themselves. This situation is the original position: we conjecture that the fairness of the circumstances under which agreement is reached transfers to the principles of justice agreed to; since the original position situates free and equal moral persons fairly with respect to one another, any conception of justice they adopt is likewise fair. Hence the name "justice as fairness." The very procedure of deliberation will engender the principles of justice constitutive of the basic structure of society: this is the very definition of Rawls's Kantian conception of procedural justice. It is not the autonomy of the contracting parties, but rather the conditions of their deliberations on the principles of justice as free and equal moral persons that configures the just society. In other words, it is the relations between persons that the procedure of deliberation, embodied by the original position and structures, thereby overcoming the false divide between individual and society, between liberty and equality.

Distributive personhood in the original position

Justice as fairness, we said, has as its practical aim the mediation of the relationship between freedom and equality, between the conception of the moral person and social cooperation. In so doing, it seeks to clarify a conception of the person that is implied in the considered convictions of democratic society. Justice as fairness enacts this mediation by formulating two ideal or model conceptions—the model conception of the person and the model conception of a well-ordered society, a society in which the relationship between freedom and equality is publicly articulated and agreed upon. A third model conception—that of the original position—mediates between the model conception of the person and the principles of justice, and is constitutive of the social cooperation among citizens in a well-ordered society (Rawls, 1999: 308). The original position configures moral personhood so as to adequately represent its constitutive features, namely the liberty and equality characterizing moral persons. If free and equal moral persons in the original position are able to agree upon principles of justice, then we can say that the principle of justice, and thus the basic structure of society, , themselves express the freedom and equality constitutive of moral personhood.

Let us turn now to examine how the original position performs its mediation between the model conception of the person and the model conception of social cooperation. From the outset, we notice that the contracting parties are not fully autonomous in themselves. That is, they reflect only a part of the ideal conception of moral personhood. Rawls refers to this partial aspect of moral personhood embodied by the contracting parties as rational autonomy. The rational autonomy of the contracting parties is expressed first by the requirement that the conditions of their deliberation in the original position, and not any preunderstanding of the just or the good, is to guide their agreement on the principles of justice. This is, as we have said, the very meaning of the purely proceduralist conception of justice. Moral persons are also rationally autonomous because they are moved solely by what Rawls refers to as their highest order interests. It is interesting to note here that Rawls also refers to these highest order interests or moral powers, as *capacities,* namely, the capacity to freely choose and thus to act from within the principles of justice and the capacity to formulate, to revise, and to pursue a conception of the good (Rawls, 1999: 313). But these moral persons also have a determinate character, that is, to borrow Sandel's language, they have a conception of their constitutive good. While moral persons have a higher-order interest in advancing their constitutive good, they do not know what the content of this constitutive good is from within the original position. It is essential to note that while the capacity to act from within the fair terms of social cooperation (the capacity for a sense of justice) and the capacity to formulate and revise a conception of the good are the highest order interests, the determinate or constitutive conception of the good is a higher and not a highest order interest, just as importantly, does not qualify as a *capacity* constitutive of moral personhood as such (Rawls, 1999: 313). This is so because in articulating the ideal conception of the moral person, we are concerned with specifying the moral capacities constitutive of moral personhood and how these capacities constitutive of free and equal moral persons are to be engendered by fair terms of social cooperation. That is, in specifying the moral conception of the person, in relation to fair terms of cooperation, we are necessarily concerned first with how these moral capacities are to distributed amongst all free and equal persons, and questions regarding the pursuit of specific ends must be subordinated to the conditions of fair distribution.

It might be argued that by excluding constitutive ends, we are artificially narrowing our conception of the moral person. But the conception of the free and equal moral person itself demands this constraint, so that the agreements on the terms of cooperation reached in the original position are based solely on the consideration of the equality and freedom of *all* moral persons, and not on the constitutive ends or goods of some one person. By ensuring the inclusion of all representatives in the original position in the status of moral personhood, we expand, and not restrict, our conception of the moral person. This is the inclusionary role that is played by the veil of ignorance in the original position. The veil of ignorance sets up the "background conditions" of the deliberations in the original position by ensuring that all members in the original position are similarly situated, that is, so that no-one is arbitrarily advantaged or disadvantaged in the deliberations that are to result in the design of the basic structure of society. Thus the veil of ignorance excludes from the original position the contracting parties' "place in society, their class position, or social status, nor do they know their fortune in the distribution of natural talents and abilities. It is also assumed that they do not know their conception of the good, that is, their particular final ends; nor finally, their own distinctive psychological dispositions and propensities, and the like" (Rawls, 1999: 310). Another way of saying this is that in the original position, no-one is regarded as possessing, or being constituted by, the arbitrary advantages and disadvantages that accrue from wealth, education, culture, on the one hand, and poverty, poor health, and disability on the other. It is when persons are regarded as being constituted by their fortune or misfortune that we exclude persons from the status of moral personhood, because a possessive account of fortune and misfortune excludes persons from the moral capacity to regard themselves—and to be regarded by others—as free and equal moral persons.

When the parties deliberate on the design of the basic structure of society from within the original position, then, they do so by regarding others as they regard themselves—that is, by virtue of their shared moral capacities to act from a sense of justice and to formulate and revise a conceptions of the good, as well as advancing their determinate, though unknown, conception of the good. The shared character of persons' moral capacities is reflected by the shared character of the primary goods that are necessary for any-one to realize their moral capabilities: once we have an adequate conception of the capacities constitutive of moral personhood, we may specify "the social background conditions and general all-purpose means normally necessary for developing and exercising the two moral powers and for effectively pursuing a conception of the good" (Rawls, 1999: 313). The contracting parties in the original position are charged with the task of justifying a conception of justice that fairly distributes these primary goods—income, wealth, responsibility, etc.—so as to extend the capacities for moral personhood to everyone. Since the parties in the original position do not know their particular social and economic status, but regard themselves as free and equal moral persons by virtue of their shared moral capacities and by their rational desire to advance their constitutive ends—whatever they may be—as far as possible, they work to justify a conception of justice that will distribute the primary goods necessarily for their self-recognition to all persons irrespective of their particular socio-economic position. In other words, in choosing and ordering the primary goods, in the form of the principle of justice, the contracting parties configure the basic institutional structures of society. *The very deliberative process between the contracting parties, who regard themselves as being free and equal, reveals the shared or distributive character of moral capacities and thus of moral personhood.* And it is this distributive character of the moral capacities for personhood, modeled by the original position and the constraints of the veil of ignorance, that serves to connect the conception of the moral person with the conception of social cooperation, or the basic structure of society. The distributive character of goods also applies to the distributive figuration of advantages and disadvantages: once advantage and disadvantage are interpreted distributively, they are rendered *public,* thereby prohibiting the exclusion of the least advantaged member from the status of moral personhood.

While it is rational for contracting parties, as individuals, to pursue the primary goods that will allow them to develop their moral capacities and to advance their conception of the good, this rational advancement of an individualized conception of the good is itself grounded by the reciprocal or fair terms of cooperation, represented in the original position by the constraints on individual or rational deliberation in the original position by the veil of ignorance. Through the application of the veil of ignorance, the possessive or constitutive conception of advantage and disadvantage is given a redistributive reading, and the capacities for moral personhood are extended to everyone through the public agreement of the contracting parties on the principle of justice. It is the distributive or reciprocal conception of moral personhood represented by the mediating conception of the original position that allows us to connect the conception of the moral person with the conception of social cooperation in a well-ordered society. And it is as citizens in a society in which principles of justice are mutually or publicly known that moral persons achieve *full autonomy*:

> So not only do citizens have a highest-order desire , their sense of justice, to act from the principle of justice, but they understand these principles as ensuing from a construction in which their conception of themselves as free and equal moral persons who are both reasonable and rational is adequately represented. By acting from these principles, and affirming them in public life, as so derived, they express their full autonomy. (Rawls, 1999: 320)

It is in a society governed by mutuality, embodied in the principle of justice, that the conception of the free and equal moral person is realized.

It is not, then, the rational autonomy of the contracting parties, standing at a distance from society, that governs the design of society. On this reading, all the veil of ignorance represents is reinforcement of the absolute, even senseless, autonomy of the contracting parties from their relation to society and even to themselves. But far from reinforcing the divide between individual and society, the veil of ignorance undermines the possessive conception of moral capabilities, of advantages and disadvantages, by giving a distributive account of advantage and of disadvantage. And it is through this distributive account of the capabilities for moral personhood that the full autonomy of citizenship in a well-ordered society emerges:

> *The intent of justice as fairness is badly misunderstood if the deliberations of the parties and their rational autonomy are confused with full autonomy.* Rational autonomy is not, as such, an ideal at all, but a device of representation used to connect the conception of the person with the definite principles of justice. (Rawls, 1999: 321)

The figure of the self-constituting self, to borrow Ricoeur's language, is a myth, for the very autonomy of the self develops from the relations of mutuality governing the background structure of society. It is the conditions of mutuality, of reciprocity, demonstrated by the original position, that is constitutive of moral autonomy: in other words, the conditions of the mutual or cooperative society, to return to Sandel's language, configures the capacities for moral autonomy for *all persons*. On Rawls's distributive interpretation of selfhood, it is the *constitutive self*—that is, the self that cannot be separated from its particular community, its goals, its ambitions, its religious and ethical convictions—that undermines the just society, because the constitutive self reflects a *possessive* conception of the moral capacities of selfhood. It is this possessive conception of selfhood that legitimates a *separation* of the constitutive self from the bonds of mutuality, from society. For the constitutive self does not concern itself with whether others have similar capabilities to author and to revise their conception of the good, to enjoy a sense of membership in their communities. In fact, as Sandel himself has emphasized, the practice of distributing, of sharing, these capabilities, is an *arbitrary encumbrance*. In short, it is the constitutive self, and not the distributive self, that expresses Sandel's conception of the unencumbered self. If the constitutive self regards its moral capacities as simply given, then it is not surprising that it would find the demands of the norm of reciprocity as somehow external to itself and thus as arbitrary.[4] The self-constituting self views its moral capacities as given, and thus opposes its freedom to the demands of sharing, of equality. Here is the surprising conclusion of the communitarian complaint against the procedural configuration of distributive personhood.

The distributive conception of selfhood advanced by justice as fairness, my capability to recognize myself as the author and agent of my conception of the good, as a member of my community, depends upon similar capabilities for an-other. It is the norm of reciprocity, of fairness, governing *oneself-as-another* that extends the capacities of Sandel's notion of constitutive selfhood to all persons, thereby configuring an inclusive conception of society.

The norm of reciprocity as the background condition of justice

Sandel is correct, then, in his argument that justice as fairness is directed against the idea of the constitutive self. But Sandel confuses both the nature of the constitutive self and why the proceduralism of justice as fairness sublimates the constitutive self in favor of a distributive self. Sandel equates the proceduralist undermining of the constitutive subject—namely, the idea that the self is constituted by its communal associations, its aims and ambitions, and by the goods to which its community assigns social meaning—with the rejection of community itself. But the proceduralist sublimation of the constitutive self for the distributive self represents the *social view* that the moral capabilities constitutive of autonomy are engendered by the bonds of mutuality articulated by the principles of justice and institutionalized by the basic structure of society. It is the basic structure of society—the overall organization of the social institutions of society that distributes rights and opportunities and benefits and burdens amongst its members—that frames the development of citizens who recognize themselves as the authors of their conception of the good and as members of their society, just as the original position and its constraints represented subordination of rational autonomy by reasonable autonomy. That is, for the proceduralist conception of justice, it is the basic structure of society that forms the subject of justice, for it is the background conditions of justice that preserve the freedom and equality of moral personhood and extends the status of moral personhood to everyone. It is this capacity of the basic structure of society to distribute the status of moral personhood to everyone, and the nature and character of the original agreement that underwrites the basic structure of society in the form of the principle of justice, that distinguishes this social pact from all other individual agreements and associations:

> [. . .] in view of the distinctive features of this structure, the initial agreement, and the conditions under which it is made, must be understood in a special way that distinguishes this agreement from all others, and

> doing this allows a Kantian view to take account of the fully *social nature* of human relationships. (Rawls, 1977: 159)

Abstracting from the constitutive commitments and ends of particular persons, associations, and communities, and asking ourselves which principles of justice persons who regard themselves solely in terms of their equal status as free persons would choose, distributes societal membership to all persons. In order for all, as opposed to some, persons to enjoy the moral capacities of full citizenship, the background institutions (or conditions) of individual transactions must themselves be fair; that is, they must embody the norm of reciprocity, of publicity, against which individual interactions take place. *What this means is that constitutive selfhood is not sufficient* for a distributive conception of selfhood, or of an inclusive society. It is the original agreement that represents the social point of view, and it is the social point of view that is institutionalized in the basic structure of society.

The Anti-Social Viewpoint of the Constitutive Self

There are several reasons, Rawls argues, that lead us to identify the basic structure of society, and not the moral person as such, as the subject of justice. First, even if we begin with the idea that the historical development of society ought to reflect fair agreements reached by free persons, we still need a way of determining when the social circumstances in which the agreements between individuals are reached are indeed fair. For it is entirely possible that while specific agreements between individuals appear to be fair and freely taken up, the background or the social conditions of the agreements may, due to certain historical and social contingencies, no longer be, in fact, fair. And while it is difficult—and, in the context of a democratic society, undesirable—to impose rules on individual agents so as to ensure a fair outcome of their transactions with other individuals agents, "the role of the basic structure is to secure just background conditions against which the actions of individuals and associations take place" (Rawls, 1977: 160). Thus, for example, we say that market transactions freely entered into cannot be characterized as being fair unless the background conditions of these market transactions, such as the distribution of income and wealth, the distribution of opportunities to acquire the skill and the income to participate in the market system, as well as the market system itself, are themselves fair. Just as we cannot take the fairness of the background conditions of individual transactions for granted, justice as fairness does not take as given the capabilities of the individual persons engaged in these transactions. Members' realistic hopes and ambitions for their futures are greatly determined by the kind of society into which they are born and in which they live out their lives:

> Nor, similarly, can we view the abilities and talents of individuals as fixed natural gifts, even if there is an important genetic component. These abilities and talents cannot come to fruition apart from social conditions and as realized they always take but one of many possible forms. An ability is not, for example, a computer in the head with a definite measurable capacity unaffected by social circumstances. (Rawls, 1977: 160)

Capabilities are not, at a fundamental level, the possessions of the individualized self. In other words, the capabilities for education, for example, and for wealth are not the possessions of the self. Capabilities configure not the constitutive self, but the distributive self, for they are developed, or diminished, by the social attitudes and institutions into which persons are born. In other words, the capabilities for moral personhood are part of the public culture, of the background conditions of society: "So not only our final ends and hopes for ourselves but our realized abilities and talents reflect, to a large degree, our personal histories, opportunities, and social position. *What we might have been had these things been different, we cannot know*" (Rawls, 1977: 160, my emphasis). The very identity of the constitutive self is unknowable outside its configuration by the institutional make-up of society, and how the capabilities for selfhood are distributed therein. And because this distribution of the capabilities for selfhood is uneven—the basic structure of any society inevitably contains social and economic inequalities—the case for treating the basic structure of society as the subject of justice becomes all the more urgent.

If we step back now from the basic structure of society to the ideal expression, it receives in the original agreement, we can appreciate not only the impossibility of the capacity of the self-constitutive self to found its own identity, to recognize itself in its possessive conception of its capacities and for personhood, but also why the viewpoint of the constitutive self is exclusionary rather than one that is inclusionary of all moral persons, why the conditions of deliberation in the original position are necessary to configure the inclusive society. The conditions of the initial agreement, we will recall, are represented by the constraints of reasonable autonomy, represented by the veil of ignorance, on the rational-individualistic deliberations of the contracting parties. We will recall as well that the veil of ignorance served to separate the moral status of personhood from the constitutive social, economic, political, and religious and ethical ends of the contracting parties. In doing so, the veil of ignorance assures the status of free and equal moral persons, irrespective of socio-economic contingencies. The contracting parties' rational pursuit of the primary goods necessary for the preservation of the moral capacities of free and equal persons may not be influenced by their contingent positioning in the basic structure of society. It is by excluding arbitrary inequalities that result from socio-economic contingencies that the contracting parties arrive at an initial agreement on the principles of justice that is based not their contingent advantageous or disadvantageous position in the basic structure of society, but rather solely on their status as participants in a community of moral personhood. For this reason, we require a thick, rather than a thin, veil of ignorance. That is, because the contracting parties' abilities and interests are excluded in the initial agreement, the agreement has a hypothetical character—it represents the agreement that *would be* reached among persons who consider themselves free and equal. But the hypothetical character of the initial agreement itself has a historical significance: the initial agreement represents not only the terms of cooperation that all persons would freely enter into, but also the terms of cooperation that they would will for future generations. In this way, the initial agreement represents an intergenerational pact.

The most distinctive way that the initial agreement differs from constitutive or particular agreements is the role that advantages and disadvantages play in the latter. In constitutive agreements, that is, where contracting parties, be they individual or associations, identify with the ends and advantages they seek to secure, will naturally weigh the advantages and disadvantages of entering into the contract, since of course, the parties' abilities, opportunities, and interests, as they have been developed in the basic structure, are already known: "Under certain conditions someone's contribution to a joint venture, or to an on-going association, can be estimated: one simply notes how the venture or association would fare without the person's joining, and the difference measures their worth to the venture or association" (Rawls, 1977: 161). The person joining the on-going association similarly weighs the advantages and disadvantages of membership, in contrast to other opportunities. The constitutive character of the contract permits parties to weigh the advantages and disadvantages of membership, because the abilities, assets, opportunities, and interests of each of the parties are already known, already determined. What this information permits, to be precise, is the exclusion of potential membership if her abilities and assets are judged to not be advantageous. Similarly, the constitutive person may also determine whether membership in an association is more advantageous than non-membership, and as such, the constitutive person may reject membership. In short, constitutive or particular contracts can exclude the possibility of membership on the basis of rational calculations of advantage and disadvantage.

Conversely, membership in society is given, that is, the weighing of advantages and disadvantages is not permitted, and even rendered senseless, in the initial agreement. This is represented by the distribution or the sharing of advantages and disadvantages, of ability and disability, through the veil of ignorance: since no one knows their socio-economic position, each must agree to share the primary goods necessary for the preservation of moral capacities for everyone, irrespective of socio-economic position:

> [. . .] the veil of ignorance not only establishes fairness between equal moral persons, but by excluding information about the parties' actual interests and abilities, it represents the fact that *apart from our place and history in a society, even our potential abilities cannot be known and our interests and character are still to be formed.* (Rawls, 1977: 162 my emphasis)

The initial agreement, then, confirms the *shared character* of the abilities and opportunities constitutive of selfhood, and in this way configures an *inclusive* reply to the exclusionary and even *sacrificial* character of constitutive agreements and associations.

Our reply thus far to the communitarian conception of the constitutive self has been that the figure of the constitutive self is itself anti-communitarian. That is, the figure of the constitutive self may be seen to stand in opposition to the shared or the distributive conception of the self advanced by justice as fairness. And yet, there is a very real objection that can be raised here, and that is: does not the distributive conception of selfhood, what we have been referring to as the ethics of *oneself as another*, governed by the norm of reciprocity, represent a rather *simple* conception of equality? Does not redistributive justice, by emphasizing a shared conception of primary goods by virtue of which we extend the moral capacities for everyone, end up undermining the very *complex* character of these primary goods? Are not social goods, as Michael Walzer (and David Miller) have argued, historically and socially configured, and if so, does not the method of this distribution depend upon their socially and historically specific context (Walzer, 1983)? How—and why—does Rawls give what Walzer calls a "universalistic" account of distributive justice? Surely, the mere distribution of a primary set of goods according to universalistic criteria cannot achieve equality for all. The claim here is that Rawls's distributive account of justice as fairness advances a "resourcist" or "economistic" solution to complex social ills. The danger of such an economistic approach is that it is not equipped to address the plural character of injustice in the modern global order. Paradigmatic of this critique is the work of Wolff and De-Shalit, who credit their pluralist approach to political philosophy to Walzer and Miller's theory of complex equality. The pluralist critique of "economistic" approach of justice as fairness is also grounded in contemporary articulations of the capability approach to social justice, most significantly in the work of Martha Nussbaum.[5]

The conception of complex equality as developed by Walzer rests on his theory of goods. If the aim of distributive justice is equality, Walzer argues, then we must first develop an adequate conception of the goods we seek to distribute. The reason we ought to start with a theory of goods, rather than with a theory of distribution as Rawls does, arises from the very diversity of the goods we seek to share, from basic material goods such as money, food, housing, health care, and transportation to social goods such as esteem, honor, community membership, family life, etc. (Walzer, 1983: 1). The multiplicity of these goods that we share points to a multiplicity in our practices of distributing these goods. Even the dominant medium of distribution—the market—cannot encompass all the multifarious forms of exchange; it continues to be the case that certain goods cannot and ought not be exchanged for money. What is more, there is no centralized basis, not even the state, from which all distributive decisions may be controlled and regulated—informal, criminal, and religious systems of exchange, for example, routinely escape the regulative purview of government. Finally, and perhaps most importantly, Walzer argues that there has never existed a universal criterion or standard according to which distributive decisions are made: "Desert, qualification, birth and blood, friendship, need, free exchange, political loyalty, democratic decisions—each has had its place, along with many others, uneasily coexisting, invoked by competing groups, confused with one another" (Walzer, 1983: 2).

A philosophical attempt, such as Rawls, to identify a universal distributive criterion seems counterintuitive, Walzer argues, especially when we take stock of the diverse historical configurations of distributive justice. Rawls is able to arrive at a universal set of distributive principles by—and here we are reminded of Sandel's argument for the constitutive community—constructing a hypothetical original agreement that excludes the way in which persons are constituted by the historical and social specificities of their society. According to Walzer, the contracting parties in the original position are required to *choose a set of goods* that they would want, in abstraction from their historically and socially specific constitutive commitments. This demand is simply too abstract: *the contracting parties agree to a system of distribution based solely on an abstract set of goods.* Given this excessively abstract situation in which the parties are merely rationally and not constitutively linked together, it is not surprising if "those same men and women, if they were transformed into ordinary people, with a firm sense of their own identity, with their own goods in their hands, caught up in everyday troubles, would reiterate their hypothetical choice or even recognize it as their own" (Walzer, 1983: 3). In short, Rawls's proceduralist conception of justice fails at its task to clarify our considered convictions on our sharing practices because it does not in fact account for our considered convictions at all:

> [But] the first impulse of the philosopher is to resist the displays of history, the world of appearances, and to search for some underlying unity: a short list of goods, quickly abstracted into a single good; a single distributive criterion or an interconnected set; and the philosopher himself standing symbolically at least, at a single decision point. (Walzer, 1983: 2)

In order to better understand our considered convictions, we need simply to examine the decisions we have already made about how, when, why, and according to what criteria, we share. Without the aid of these constitutive commitments, the proceduralist conception of justice simply distributes a set of abstract goods among rational agents, far removed from the challenges and the meanings constitutive of social and historical societies. The social and historical lineage of these goods, and the relation this lineage might bear to their distribution, is overlooked by the proceduralist account of justice, in which distribution precedes a theory of social goods. All the work is done by the hands of rational agents who, by agreeing to share a set of abstract goods, also agree to the distributive system according to which they will carry out this sharing.

The result is simple equality: so long as goods, abstractly conceived, are equally apportioned among all persons, equality has been achieved. This view has been widely referred to as the "resourcist" approach to economic equality and social justice, because it concerns itself not with the multiplicity of meanings different goods hold for different persons and community, but rather with the simple distribution of some dominant good, such as the primary goods of income and distribution of wealth, among all persons. But while simple distribution is critical of the monopoly over dominant goods by certain groups, Walzer argues, it does not question the dominance of goods—such as money and income –itself. It is the dominance of these goods that leads to inequality, because dominant goods such as money and income enjoy a wide range of *convertibility* into other goods. Persons who enjoy a monopoly over a dominant good, such as money, are able to *convert* this good into other goods, thereby expanding their monopoly into different spheres of society (Walzer, 1983: 15). Thus, wealth may be converted into such diverse goods as political power, good health, education, literacy, and social esteem. We need a way to challenge not only certain citizens' monopoly over dominant goods, but the dominance of goods themselves. The way to do this, Walzer suggests, is by ensuring the *autonomy* of different spheres of goods themselves. But this requires that we develop a better understanding of the principles of distribution internal to each of the separate social goods. In so doing, what we discover is that the multiplicity of goods corresponds to a multiplicity of distributive practices. Equality, then, requires an understanding of the social meanings conveyed by the conception and the exchange of each type of good, and not merely an "identity of possessions" endorsed by the conception of simple equality (Walzer, 1983: 18).

Walzer is here proposing a *complex* conception of equality, which prevents the large-scale conversion of a dominant good into other goods in different spheres of society. By recognizing the autonomy of each of the distributive spheres corresponding to each social good, dominance is challenged. Now each distributive sphere is monopolistically held, but the control of a person or persons in a particular sphere is the result of what Walzer refers to as a "natural conversion" between the person's personal attributes and the social good over which she enjoys a monopoly. Thus, someone who possesses such traits as persuasiveness, public mindedness and enthusiasm will naturally and thus justly enjoy a monopoly over the social good of political power. There will be a relation of inequality, then, between the person X who possess these characteristics and as a result has a monopoly over the social good of political power, and person Y who neither possesses these qualities nor as a result enjoys control over political power. At the same time, however, her monopoly over the social good of political power cannot be converted into another, unrelated sphere of social goods, such as health care. Thus, the inequality between person X and person Y will be limited to the sphere of political power, because the sphere of political power is autonomous from the sphere of health care. *Complex equality, then, is constituted by a series of small inequalities*: "Though there will be many small inequalities, inequality will not be multiplied through the conversion process.

Nor will it be summed across different goods, because the autonomy of distribution will tend to produce a *variety of local monopolies*, held by different groups of men and women" (Walzer, 1983: 14, my emphasis). A society comprised of such small inequalities, Walzer argues, is able to combat the tyranny of dominance.

Walzer's emphasis on the multiplicity of goods and the complex character of equality, and its critique of the "resourcist" or "economistic" character of justice as fairness, which Walzer argues is content with simply equating an "identity of possessions" amongst citizens with equality, has influenced contemporary thinking on the plural character of *inequality*, of disadvantage (Walzer, 1983: 18). In their recent work, *Disadvantage* (2007), Wolff and De-Shalit credit Walzer's pluralist conception of social goods with their pluralist approach to understanding the character of disadvantage, and in particular, their pluralist account of the Rawlsian conception of the least advantaged member.[6] In order to understand what equality would look like, and how to go about achieving it, Wolff and De-Shalit argue, we must first be able to appreciate the plural character of disadvantage itself. Wolff and De-Shalit share Walzer's conviction that the simple distribution of one dominant good is an inadequate approach to the complex character of both equality and inequality. Wolff and De-Shalit's work seeks to refute such "monist" or resourcist accounts of equality in favor of a more complex picture of each of the social goods that constitute both advantage and disadvantage. In want to turn now to consider how Walzer's conception of complex equality informs a pluralist understanding of the "worst off" or the least advantaged member of society. As we go along, I also want to consider in particular the role that Walzer's figuration of equality through a series of "small inequalities" plays in Wolff and De-Shalit's analysis of the relationship between advantage and disadvantage. Once we understand this comparative approach, in which equality is achieved through the balancing of advantage *against* disadvantage, and grounded in the pluralist conception of justice, we will return to consider whether Rawls's distributive conception of the least advantaged member is able to address the pluralist conception of disadvantage.

The Conversion of Advantage and the Clustering of Disadvantage: The Pluralist Approach to Social Justice

It is our least advantaged citizen, Wolff and De-Shalit argue, who ought to be the focus of government policy reform so that we may achieve a more equal society. But identifying who the least advantaged is—what Wolff and De-Shalit refer to as the indexing problem—is complex, because disadvantage is itself complex and plural. We recognize disadvantage in such diverse figures as the "chronically unemployed, the rough sleepers, the illiterate who dropped out of school very early, those fourteen-year-old girls who become teenage mothers, and so on" (Wolff and De-Shalit, 2007: 17). But because of the plural character of disadvantage articulated by each of these groups or persons, it is a very difficult task to identify whether it is the loss or the absence of the capability for literacy, or for health, or for parenthood, or for community membership, or some combination of these disadvantages defines our least advantaged member. The plural character of these capabilities and disabilities, these advantages and disadvantages, prevent us from attempting to ameliorate disadvantage through what Wolff and De-Shalit refer to as "monist" solution, that is, through the distribution material resources (Wolff and De-Shalit, 2007: 24). Following Walzer, Wolff and De-Shalit argue that equality cannot be achieved through distributive justice alone; that is, not all forms of disadvantage and advantage may be understood in terms of wealth. The distributive or resourcist approach to equality needs to be coupled with a better understanding of the *social* or *relational* interpretation of goods. Our distributive or resourcist practices must go hand in hand with a better understanding of how social exclusion—citizens' sense of belong to a community—impacts disadvantage: "Thus distribution—and redistribution—on this rather communitarian view, concerns not only the possession and transfer of material wealth, but the diverse ways in which people's lives can be affected government policy, by the nature of the society they live in, and by how they regard and treat each other" (Wolff and De-Shalit, 2007: 6). Thus, public policy ought to extend a sense of membership and belonging, of social equality, along the distribution of material goods, and this pursuit of social and material equality ought to be organized around our duty to help our least advantaged members. Wolff and De-Shalit, then, share Walzer's view that redistributive justice is insufficient for a fully social or relational view of equality.

And yet, disadvantage is a relation concept. We recognize the figures of disadvantage by comparing them to other more advantaged members of society, who have in some sense abandoned their less advantaged neighbors. Rather than abandoning our least advantaged members, Wolff and De-Shalit argue that public expenditures ought to be directed towards improving their life circumstances. The problem of course lies in determining how and where public monies ought to be spent so as to improve the diverse circumstances of, for example, the homeless, young single mothers, poor children, the chronically ill, etc. in the most efficient and effective way. We need a way to recognize both the plural character of disadvantage, what Wolff and De-Shalit refer to as the realism constraint. And at the same time, the indexing problem requires that we be able to "identify the least advantaged, and, ideally, *to place each member of society on a scale of relative advantage and disadvantage*, as well as being able to identify absolute disadvantage. This is the indexing constraint which gives rise to what we call the indexing problem" (Wolff and De-Shalit, 2007: 21, my emphasis). The indexing constraint represents a *comparative framework* that would help us in our aim to identifying who is better off and who is worse off. But how do we identify which loss—the loss of the capability for health, or for housing, or for literacy—is determinant of the least advantaged, and conversely, which capability determines the most advantaged? To complicate matters further, "for some reason, several disadvantages cluster together" (Wolff & De-Shalit, 2007: 10). We recall here Walzer's caution regarding the conversion of a dominant good into other goods across the spheres of society: the conversion of a dominant good, or to use Wolff and De-Shalit's language, the clustering of advantages corresponds to a clustering of disadvantages; and it is this clustering of advantages on the one hand and disadvantages on the other that creates an unequal or stratified society. The task of public policy is to combat the growing inequalities in society by breaking up the conversions of advantage and the clustering of disadvantage.

In order to achieve this declustering, Wolff and De-Shalit argue, government needs to pay closer attention to the conversion of advantages and to the clustering of disadvantages. Wolff and De-Shalit propose to start by asking disadvantaged persons themselves which capabilities they value most, or are most significant to their well-being, and then to determine how persons are fairing in each of the capability categories. Six "core" capability categories that emerge from this interview process are: life, bodily health, bodily integrity, affiliation, control over the environment, and sense, imagination, and thought (Wolff and De-Shalit, 2007: 122). Given the wide agreement on the importance of their capabilities, we may assume that persons who are fairing badly on all or even some of these capabilities are at risk of losing some of these capabilities will be among the least advantaged. One way to understand disadvantage across these capability categories, and to thereby identify the least advantaged persons, is to determine whether and how disadvantage clusters across categories by examining correlations between disadvantages. Where the clustering of disadvantage may become *corrosive*, when disadvantage in one category is shown to cause disadvantage in another, the successful realization of a capability category, referred to as functioning, may either directly or indirectly be related to other functioning. Wolff and De-Shalit refer to this clustering of functions as "fertile functioning" (Wolff and De-Shalit, 2007: 122). By better understanding the patterns of corrosive disadvantages and "fertile functionings," we will be better able to identify who our least advantaged members are, thereby satisfying the indexing constraint, and at the same time to appreciate the multidimensional character of both advantage and disadvantage, thereby satisfying the realism constraint.

It is by breaking up these clusters of advantage and disadvantage that government can improve the circumstances of our least advantaged members. The comparative character of Wolff and De-Shalit's approach to equality becomes apparent here: when governments are able to de-cluster both advantage and disadvantage, such that "we *can no longer say who in society is worst off*, then they have every reason to claim that they have moved society in the direction of equality" (Wolff & De-Shalit, 2007: 10, my emphasis). There appears, then, to be a correlation between the pluralist or complex conception of equality and a comparative conception of society in which goods, advantages and disadvantages, abilities and disabilities are assumed to be separated from, and even opposed to, one another. It is by virtue of this opposition that we can compare advantages to disadvantages, and even go so far as to rank them on a scale. We may go so far as to say that the comparative conception of society advanced by the pluralist conception of disadvantage introduces a *competitive* logic into our deliberations on inequality. Thus, the problem Wolff and De-Shalit face of trying to make sense of seemingly disparate advantages and disadvantages—satisfaction here, single motherhood there, education here, homelessness there. Wolff and De-Shalit know that they must try and make sense of these seemingly disparate advantages and disadvantages, and they attempt to do so, following the complex or plural approach to equality, by referring to this problem as the problem of "clustering," where "for some reason, disadvantages cluster together" (Wolff and De-Shalit, 2007: 10) The clustering of both disadvantage and advantage is then organized into a comparative scale. The very problem of creating a scale of relative disadvantages and advantages reveals that Wolff and De-Shalit's conceptualization of the least advantaged member individualizes disadvantage by separating and even opposing disadvantage to advantage. On their pluralist approach, disadvantage is tied to particular individuals or groups. *The very plural character of disadvantage emphasized by Wolff and De-Shalit is itself the result of the individualization of disadvantage.*[7] In both Walzer's and Wolff and De-Shalit's pluralist conceptions of equality, it is simply taken for granted that some individuals suffer from employment, that they possess the "personal skills" requisite for the command of certain social goods such as political power or education or good health; still others happen to suffer from homelessness, social alienation and loneliness, and poor health. But even when referencing the social context of health, Wolff and De-Shalit still treat social determinants such as homelessness, unemployment, and a sense of alienation as a set of separate factors that happen in some way to be related to one another.[8]

And yet, it can be questioned whether the significance of studies such as Wilkinson and Marmot's (2002) *The Social Determinants of Health: The Solid Facts* is merely to identify the—contingent—clustering of disadvantages. That is, the pluralist conception of disadvantage, by individualizing both advantage and advantage, tends to overlook, or remains silent on, the *institutional* figuration of advantage and disadvantage. The pluralist does not ask *how* persons become capable of literacy, health, political participation, or *how* persons become disabled in their capacity to recognize themselves as literate, healthy, housed, familied members of their community. The pluralist does not consider the possibility that persons' capabilities and disabilities, their advantages and disadvantages, are not merely possessed by them, but are engendered by the social, political, and economic institutions constitutive of the society into which they are born. Does not social epidemiological research into the social determinants of health point to the institutional relationships—the background or social conditions, to borrow Rawls's language—of population health and well-being? In other words, when social epidemiologists talk about the social determinants, or the social conditions, of the disadvantage of poor health, are they not referring to the way in which societal practices of cooperation, of reciprocity, and in particular, the relative strength or weakness of these norms of reciprocity, configure the health of citizens? And if it can be shown that the strength or the weakness of a society's norms of reciprocity determine population health, then it turns out that the character of disadvantage, such as poor health, is shared or distributed. On this interpretation, the least advantaged member is not an individual, but rather a distributive figure constitutive of the background social, economic, and political institutions of reciprocity, of sharing, of society: It is the redistributed figure of disadvantage that is articulated by the social institutions of society. *As such, there can be no distinction between individual and society*: this is what justice as fairness articulates through its distributive conception of personhood. The distributive figuration of both advantage and disadvantage is accomplished by the conditions imposed upon the deliberations of the contracting parties: the significance of the prohibition on the contracting parties from identifying with their advantages or disadvantages, or from identifying others with their advantages or disadvantages, is that it prohibits the *individualization* of advantage and disadvantage. This is what permits Rawls to say that the reasonable conditions, represented by the veil of ignorance, that frame rational self-pursuit, are constitutive of the basic structure of society. The distributive account of the least advantaged member, demonstrated by the conditions of deliberation in the original agreement, represents an account of the development of the *public institutions* of society. It is this institutionalization of the distributive or public account of personhood that is expressed by the principles of justice: "[I]t is no accident that once the parties are described in terms that require some social expression, the first principles of justice are themselves institutional and apply to the basic structure of society" (Rawls, 1977: 163).

Chapter 4

Civic *Phronēsis*: Rawls's Anti-Sacrificial Ethics for Capability Justice

We have thus far argued that Rawls constructs a social proceduralism that demonstrates the thoroughly social character of the inviolability of moral personhood. The principles of justice, when read in their serial ordering, articulate the institutionalization of distribution or the sharing of the capabilities for moral personhood, and thus of the ethical intention to live together. Citizens' capabilities for health, literacy, parenthood, childhood, and social, political, and economic participation in their communities are not the possessions of the wealthy, nor do the disabilities of chronic illness, homelessness, and unemployment, illiteracy, and poverty the possessions of the poor. Both capabilities and disabilities are configured by the historical development of institutions that represent the *capabilities of the third party*, that is, of *every-one*, embodied in public health care, public child care, public education, social transfers, and old age and disability pensions. The liberal commitment to *neutrality* articulated by Rawls' social proceduralism, then, fare from advancing an a-social or anti-communitarian conception of autonomy, works to remind us of the institutional, and thus deeply historical and communitarian character of the capabilities for moral personhood—that is, for meriting or recognizing ourselves as the authors of our conceptions of the good. I want to now try and develop this argument a little further by linking up the distributive and thus institutional interpretation of capability advanced by Ricoeur and Rawls to the problematic with which we opened this book, namely, the growing stratification between rich and poor, between capability and disability, between advantage and disadvantage, that characterize modern neo-liberal societies.[1] The argument we want to put forward here is that when we divorce the liberal requirement for neutrality from its solicitous context which fosters the recognitive capabilities for every-one, we contribute to growing compassion gap between capability and disability.

But first we need to examine another important source of criticism against Rawls' conception of neutrality. This criticism will also significantly be a critique of our argument that the figuration of neutrality by the reasonable constraints on the rational constraints on the rational deliberations of the contracting parties in the original position represents a figuration of the third party. We recall here Ricoeur's argument that the institutional figuration of the third party represents the "fiduciary base" of all interpersonal interactions, or to recall Michael Walzer's language, of all constitutive relationships. The charge we must consider now tackles head-on our argument that the ethical figuration of neutrality distributes capabilities for self-recognition to everyone. This charge comes from the capabilities approach to social justice itself, which has traditionally been associated with the thought of another Aristotelian philosopher, Martha Nussbaum, and with Indian economist Amartya Sen. It is especially important that we take up Nussbaum and Sen's conception of capability justice, because both take as their starting point the argument that Rawls' conception of distributive justice does not include a conception of capability: that is, Rawls' conception of distributive justice, and in particular, its proceduralist character, cannot account for what persons are able to do and to be (Nussbaum, 2000; Sen, 1985). Behind this claim is the "resourcist" or the "economist" characterization of redistribution: merely distributing material resources, the argument goes, does not tell us anything about whether these material resources translate into the capabilities constitutive of autonomous personhood. We already have at least some footing from which to reject this resourcist reduction of Rawls' conception of redistributive personhood, and we shall return to developing a better understanding of its sources, but I want to pause for a moment to underscore a significant distinction between Sen's and Nussbaum's critique of Rawls' conception of distributive justice: while Sen does not reject the lexical ordering of Rawls' principles of justice, Nussbaum, in developing her theory of capability justice in distinction from Sen's, forcefully rejects the lexical figuration of the principles of justice. I shall argue that Nussbaum's rejection of the lexical ordering of the principles of justice that leads her to her resourcist reduction of Rawls' distributive conception of personhood. Sen differs from Nussbaum significantly in this respect by framing his capability critique of Rawls as an extension of Rawls' distributive and thus institutional figuration of capabilities.

We shall, therefore, focus on Nussbaum's critique of Rawls, because while she attempts to retain certain features of Rawls' theory of distributive justice, most notably his emphasis on the neutral or universal character of the principles of justice that are to furnish the basic structure of society, she also distances herself from Rawls' conception of distributive personhood. A certain contradiction will plague Nussbaum's twofold enterprise, and it will culminate in the wholesale rejection of society, as will be evidenced by contemporary neoliberal readings of capability justice, which themselves take root in Nussbaum's rejection of the lexical ordering of the principles of justice.[2]

Nussbaum's Defense of Capability Justice: A Normative Pluralism

What distinguishes Nussbaum's approach to social justice is her attempt to mediate between relativist and pluralist conceptions of justice on one hand, and universalist or essentialist approaches on the other (Nussbaum, 1992). Her view accords with Walzer's emphasis on the fundamentally plural character of the goods we divide and share, and on their social significance. Nussbaum would also agree with Sandel's emphasis on the way in which the particular community in which a person's life unfolds constitutes, in a significant way, his or her self-understanding or identity. What Nussbaum also encourages us to do, however, is to think across the boundaries of these spheres and the boundaries of constitutive communities, and to recognize certain normative principles that hold across social and cultural boundaries. Here she notes that even the principles of "pluralism and respect for difference are themselves universal values and are not everywhere observed; they require a normative articulation and defense . . ." (Nussbaum, 2000: 32). Such a reflection on the normative grounds that express our shared convictions across particular spheres and communities is especially pressing, given the present era of globalization, in which the free market threatens to make all of our ethical decisions for us. This normative grounding is to be found in the moral conception of the inviolability of persons, which she argues has both an Aristotelian and a Kantian grounding. Nussbaum translates the Kantian principle of persons as ends in themselves as the capability of each person to live a truly human life, and not merely an animal life. Nussbaum connects the Arsitotelian conception of a truly human life with the Kantian conception of persons as ends in themselves by translating the Aristotelian emphasis on the capability to act and deliberate well as the function of man in terms of self-determination. That is, the capability for practical reason depends upon the principle of the non-violability of persons.

Nussbaum uses the example of women living in poverty in India to illustrate the connection she draws between and Aristotelian and a Kantian conception of self-determination. Both their poverty and their status of caregivers mean that these women do not enjoy the status of persons as ends in themselves; they are treated merely as a means. In Aristotlelian terms, the combined effect of poverty and its gender-specific implications, such as unequal access to education, physical and sexual violence against women, and the role of women's child care labor, mean that the capability for practical reasoning, for flourishing in a truly human way, are severely circumscribed for poor women. When we consider the issue of justice for women in international development, Nussbaum argues, it becomes apparent that we need to examine—and to come to some kind of agreement on—the central capabilities for truly human functioning. Although Nussbaum argues that it is possible, and indeed necessary, to agree to a set of central capabilities and in this way aligns herself with the liberal emphasis on universalism, she is at the same time careful to emphasize the irreducible plurality of the capabilities constitutive of a truly human life, as well as the disabilities that circumvent human flourishing. We have already seen the impact of Nussbaum's emphasis on the plural character of capabilities constitutive of human flourishing on the work contemporary capability theorists, Wolff and De-Shalit (2007).[3] We saw that, following Nussbaum, Wolff and De-Shalit interpret the Kantian principle of persons as ends in themselves as the principle of each person's capability: we need to check to see how each *individual* is affected by her disadvantage as well as by her advantage. Wolff and De-Shalit develop this conception of *each person's advantage and disadvantage* from Nussbaum's recasting of the principle of the non-violability of persons as "the principle of each person's capability"—to, we might add—live a truly human life. Living a truly human life, we recall, implies being capable of practical reason, which in turn implies being regarded as, and recognizing oneself as, an autonomous, self-determining agent. Nussbaum's recasting of the principle of persons as ends in themselves in terms of the principle of each person's capability will form the basis of both her critique and her extension of Rawls. But as we have already noted in our discussion of each *person's* capability and disability in Wolff and De-Shalit's effort, we will need to pay close attention to whether Nussbaum's principle of each person's capability does not lose sight of the distributive character of each persons' capability (of the capabilities of *one*-self *as* an-*other*). Let us turn now and take a closer look at how Nussbaum appeals to Rawls to develop a theory of capability justice that is at once universalist and pluralist.

From Primary Goods to Central Capabilities

Nussbaum, like Rawls, grounds her inquiry into a capability approach to social justice in the Kantian-Aristotelian principle of the non-violability of persons, and in this way shares with Rawls a deep liberal commitment to universalism. But while her conception of social justice has a universalist grounding in the idea of the non-violability of persons, her interpretation of this principle will differ radically from Rawls'. We find our first clue in Nussbaum's commitment to specifying a list of central capabilities, something that Sen has shied away from. It is Nussbaum's anxiety to develop and to defend a list of universal or cross-cultural capabilities that leads her to identify her approach with Rawls' conception of primary goods, i.e., goods that are rational to want whatever else you may want. The appeal of Rawls' list of primary goods—liberties, responsibilities, income, wealth—Nussbaum argues, is their cross-cultural appeal: irrespective of your identification with some constitutive community, you will require access to these goods in the pursuit of any kind of good life: "The basic idea is that, whatever else citizens pursue, they should be able to arrive at a working *political consensus* about the central importance of these basic resources and about some rough criteria for their fair distribution" (Nussbaum, 2000: 66).

It is very important to note how in Nussbaum's introduction to Rawls' primary goods, they are made to appear as though they stand independently of their lexical ordering, as articulated by the principles of justice. The significance of the divorce Nussbaum affects between Rawls' primary goods and the principles of justice is that the primary goods, to borrow Nussbaum's language, take on a "thing-like" quality (Nussbaum, 2000: 66). This is especially true of the income and wealth which Nussbaum claims (and here we recall Walzer's complaint against Rawls) "have a particularly central role on the list, since they are used to define the class of the least well-off" (Nussbaum, 2000: 66). Despite these concerns, to which we shall return momentarily, Nussbaum declares that Rawls' universalist approach to social justice provides a good starting point for the development of her theory of capability justice, because of its articulation of a set of liberties and opportunities for all citizens, thereby furnishing a context for practical reasoning and choice-making for all citizens, including the material basis of the capability for autonomous choice-making.

Contra Rawls: Resourcist Comparisons

Nussbaum, then, endorses the "liberal-political" spirit of Rawls' theory of distributive justice, by endorsing the universalist character of the primary goods, which all can agree to for political purposes, irrespective of their more comprehensive commitments. However, on Nussbaum's reading, the resourcist character of Rawls' primary goods actually works to undermine the very normative grounding upon which it rests, namely, the principle of the non-violability of persons. On Nussbaum's reading, Rawls engages in a *comparative* analysis of who is better or worse off on the basis of the mere possession of resources: "By measuring who is better off and who is worse off in terms of resources, the Rawlsian model neglects a salient fact of life: that individuals vary greatly in their needs for resources and in their abilities to convert resources into valuable functions" (Nussbaum, 2000: 68). This comparative analysis of advantage and disadvantage, based upon the possession of resources, ignores important distinctions between persons varying needs for resources as well as their abilities to convert these resources into valuable functionings. Thus, for example, newborns require a higher intake of fat that do adults; persons with cognitive disabilities require much more in the way of social supports than do persons with normal-range cognitive abilities in order to live as fully participating members of society.

The differences between persons in terms of their respective "struggles for flourishing" are erased by Rawls' resourcist approach to social justice, which, according to Nussbaum, is satisfied by ascertaining how much of a given resource a given person commands, and then determining who, on the basis of this comparison of the capability to command resources, is worse-off. We must find a way of recognizing each person's struggle for flourishing, for developing the capability for choice-making and for self-determination:

> Thus even the Rawlsian approach, in the end, doesn't sufficiently respect the struggle of each and every individual for flourishing. To treat A & B as equally well-off because they command the same amount of resources is, in a crucial way, to pretend that A's circumstances are interchangeable with B's, which may not be the case. (Nussbaum, 2000: 69)

We can now appreciate where Wolff and De-Shalit, who, in following Nussbaum's resourcist reading of Rawls, view the task of social justice as the identification of who the least advantaged member is: just as resources are commanded or possessed by persons, so too are the advantages of health, literacy, employment, and an adequate standard of leaving, and the disadvantages of illness, illiteracy, and poverty. [4]

On Nussbaum's resourcist reading of Rawls, primary goods are things that persons possess either more or less of, and this is what, she argues, enables Rawls to conduct a comparative analysis between the haves and have-nots, between advantage and disadvantage, ultimately enabling us to identify the *list advantaged member.* Notice that on this reading, a *comparative logic*, that is, a comparison between who has more of some*thing*/resource and who has less, underwrites the identification of the least advantaged member. This competitive logic is attributed to Rawls through Nussbaum's resourcist interpretation of his theory of distributive justice. Nussbaum takes her resourcist argument against Rawls even further: because she thinks income and wealth play an especially central role in Rawls' comparative identification of the least advantaged member, she characterizes his approach in economistic terms. It is crucial that we understand the significance of Nussbaum's economist interpretation of Rawls' conception of distributive justice: primary goods, especially income and wealth, are commanded or possessed by individuals. And it is this possession that underwrites the competitive comparison between have and have-nots: "[His] Rawls' emphasis on wealth and income as primary goods central to the task of indexing . . . sells short his own respect for the individual (Nussbaum, 2000: 69). But in our reading thus far, we have argued that the articulation of primary goods by the principles of justice configures not a comparative analysis of what persons can be said to *possess*, but rather a defense of a distributive or shared conception of personhood, embodied in the public institutions constitutive of the basic structure of society. That is, the principles of justice in their lexical ordering, figurate the public culture of a democratic society. It is significant that Nussbaum's resourcist interpretation of Rawls' primary goods extracts the primary goods from their articulation by the lexical ordering of the principles of justice. What this amounts to is *the separation of the primary goods a public or shared culture.* Once the primary goods have been separated from their role in the articulation of a shared or distributive conception of the capabilities for personhood, then they become the possession of the person as such.

But, as Nussbaum is quick to remind us, it is the person as such, the person as an end in herself, that matters. Distinctions between individual person's "struggles for flourishing" are significant. We need to be able to say, for each person, whether she is function in a truly human way, in the Aristotelian-Marxist sense, that is, whether she is capable of exercising practice reason, and whether this capability is nourished and fostered by the community in which she lives. Here, Nussbaum appeals to the kind of comparisons that social epidemiologists, physicians, and health practitioners use to make quality of life comparisons between populations.[5] Two things become clear, she notes, when we look at how such comparisons are made: taken together, this comparative data on population capabilities relies on a list of centralized capabilities, and what this reveals is our shared conviction that a society's public political arrangement is justice where it extends these central capabilities to each citizen.

If persons in a society are routinely falling below the threshold of developing any of these capabilities that are constitutive of living a truly human life, then we say that the society in which they live unjust and recognize their plight as being tragic. A twofold set of intuitions underwrite these observations: first, that certain capabilities signify the presence of human life, and thus, that there is a distinctively social-human way of exercising these capabilities that distinguishes them from their exercise on the instinctive-animal plane. In distinguishing between the instinctive-animal plane and the social-human plane, Nussbaum notes the intersection of Aristotle and Marx in their shared conception of truly human function as persons' capability for self-determination with the social and material support of the society in which they live:

> The core idea is that the human being as a dignified free being who shapes his or her own life in cooperation and reciprocity with others, rather than being shaped as pushed around by the world in the manner of a 'flock' or 'herd' animal. A life that is really human is one that is shaped throughout by these human powers of practical reason and sociability. (Nussbaum, 2000: 72)

It is the loss of the capability for self-recognition as the author of one's life that is the stuff of tragedy: the tragic character is over-determined by her fortune, by the arbitrariness of her luck, to borrow Rawls' language. As Kant has taught us, the worth of the person as an end in herself transcends her noumenal trappings. Marx and Aristotle, on the other hand, stress that the capabilities for moral authorship require social and material support.

And at the same time, Nussbaum argues, Marx's Aristotelian conception of truly human flourishing is itself Kantian in character in its emphasis on the *inviolability of persons*. Nussbaum locates source of Marx's Kantianism by arguing that Marx conceptualizes exploitation: persons who are exploited are treated as means rather than as ends in themselves. On this Kantian interpretation of Marx, we need to know whether each person possesses the capabilities for human flourishing, that is, possesses the capabilities to be treated as ends in themselves: "we may thus rephrase our *principle of each person as an end*, articulating it as a *principle of each person's capability*: capabilities are sought for *each and every person*, not, in the first instance, for groups or families or states or corporate bodies" (Nussbaum, 2000: 24, original emphasis). Capabilities are sought for each person, as an end in herself. It is for this reason that Nussbaum focuses specifically on the struggles for flourishing of Indian women living in poverty: we cannot ascertain whether these women are capable of truly human functioning simply by ascertaining the material well-being of their societies, nor even the resources that are available to them. Rather, what we need to do is to be able to identify and to enumerate a list of central capabilities constitutive of a truly human life:

> Taking a stand for political purposes on a working list of functions that would appear to be of central importance in human life, we ask: Is the person capable of this, or not? We ask not only about the person's satisfaction with what she does, but about what she is in a position to do (what her opportunities and liberties are). And we ask not just about the resources that are sitting around, but about how those do or do not go to work, enabling her [Vasanti] to function in a fully human way. (Nussbaum, 2000: 71)

It is Nussbaum's defense of the capabilities of persons as ends in themselves (and thus her defense of the moral status of persons as ends in themselves) that leads her to identify a list of "irreducibly plural" list of capabilities (Nussbaum, 2000: 81). Where Rawls' lexical figuration of the primary goods, on Nussbaum's resourcist reading, works to eliminate the distinct character of each person's struggle for flourishing, each of the capabilities on Nussbaum's list is equally fundamental, and demands that we consider whether each person has the opportunity to develop each of the identified capabilities. Only when she has the opportunity to develop each of the capabilities which Nussbaum argues, following Rawls, everyone would want, whatever else they may want, can a person be said to be living a truly human life. In other words, the central capabilities identified by Nussbaum enables her interpretation of Rawls' conception of a *political liberalism*, in which citizens can come to a mutual agreement on the basic structure of society. This mutuality, we have argued, governs the *public* character of the institutional make-up of the basic structure of society. In turn, it is the public character of the basic structure that enables the inclusion of every-*one* in the public culture of society: it is the very public or inclusive character of the basic structure of society that renders it a political, as opposed to a metaphysical or a comprehensive society. For, as we have seen, a comprehensive membership by definition excludes persons who are not already constituted by the moral, political, social, and cultural commitments of that society. A constitutive conception of society violates the ethical translation of oneself *as* another, from which public institutions and public culture are born and maintained. But while it is the ethics of mutuality that underwrites Rawls' conception of an *overlapping consensus*, or of the public conception of the basic structure of society, Nussbaum interprets the Rawlsian conception of an overlapping consensus in terms of the pursuit of the capabilities of each person as an end in herself. In this way, Nussbaum's list of the central capabilities represents a very significant break from Rawls' articulation and defense of the public character of political membership.

In what follows, I want to consider some of the important social and implications of this methodological break, unforeseen by Nussbaum: Nussbaum's rejection of the lexical ordering of the principles of justice ends up justifying the erosion of the very public institutions which underwrite the very capabilities she holds so dear. We will end by considering social epidemiological research on the relationship between the public institutions of the welfare state, such as health care, education, and the redistribution of income and the provision unemployment insurance, and the development and preservation of population capabilities for health. This research helps us to clarify the inextricable tie between the basic structure of society and citizens' capabilities for freedom and self-determination.

Regressive Genealogies Versus Civic Narratives

In his "From Primary Goods to Capabilities: Distributive Justice and the Problem of Neutrality," Eric Nelson traces the "genealogy of an error" in contemporary moral reasoning to John Rawls' interpretation of the Kantian maxim to respect persons as ends in themselves which grants priority to our least advantaged citizens (Nelson, 2008: 114).[6] Rawls's distributive figuration of the principle of inviolability of persons is a violation of the norm itself seen from the capabilities approach to distributive justice developed in the Aristotelian tradition by Amartya Sen and Martha Nussbaum. *Any* attempt to distribute either social primary goods, emphasized by Rawls, or central human capabilities, emphasized by Sen and Nussbaum, leads to the violation of the Rawlsian liberal commitment to persons as autonomous choosers of their own good and as exercisers of their capabilities for moral choice-making. The sectarian character of Rawls's civic imperative to distribute primary social goods to everyone in society is revealed by Nussbaum's interpretation of the Rawlsian overlapping consensus in terms of a list of capabilities that everyone would want, whatever else she or he may want. Each of the capabilities may be shown to violate someone's conception of the good and Nussbaum's list of capabilities may be shown to be exclusionary of many conceptions of the good. The sectarian and exclusionary nature of Nussbaum's list of capabilities serves to expose the sectarian and exclusionary character of Rawls' civic interpretation of persons as ends in themselves. Thus the distributive model of deliberation on the moral status of persons developed by Rawls violates the deliberative capabilities of persons as autonomous choosers of their own good.

Where Nelson begins to trace his attack on the Rawlsian civic interpretation of the principle of the inviolability of persons as ends in themselves with his critique of the sectarian character of Nussbaum's list of capabilities, I trace Nelson's elitist interpretation of the norm of persons as ends in themselves to Nussbaum's rejection of the lexical ordering of the Rawlsian principles of justice which configures a distributive interpretation of our least advantaged citizens. That is, whereas the Rawlsian dialectic between moral autonomy and redistribution configures the moral capabilities of oneself *as* another, Nussbaum's list of capabilities, divorced from distributive understanding of vulnerability, becomes vulnerable to the neo-liberal picking and choosing of capacities.[7] Nussbaum like Nelson confines herself to the moral capabilities of *oneself* in abstraction from, and ultimately in opposition to, the moral capabilities of *another*. Nelson's elitist interpretation of moral autonomy represents a neo-liberal consequence of Nussbuam's recognitivist interpretation of Rawls's theory of justice.

The distributive interpretation of vulnerability developed by Rawls represents a distributive understanding of capability by configuring the *non-seperability* of vulnerability from capability: herein lies Rawls's civic interpretation of the principle of nonviolability of persons as ends in themselves. I argue that we owe this insight into Rawls's ethics of *oneself as another* to Paul Ricoeur's Aristotelian interpretation of the Rawlsian principle of civic inclusion. Drawing on Ricoeur's argument that the *telos* of good society is the non-exclusion of its most vulnerable members from capabilities for health, education, work, parenthood, care giving, and an adequate standard of living, I argue that we may develop an historically informed methodology for public deliberation with which to respond to Nelson's elitist withdrawal from the civic commons.

I end by considering how this Rawlsian model of public deliberation on vulnerability—of an Aristotelian *phronēsis*—is used by social epidemiological research to investigate how population capabilities for health are fostered through the long, slow development of redistributive practices of societies such as the civic provision of education, social transfers, and public health care. In this way, we will have demonstrated how Nelson's individualist configuration of capability itself represents a regressive genealogy of the historical, social, and political narratives which underwrite the institutionalization of the recognitive capabilities of each person. The Rawlsian methodology of public deliberation on vulnerability—of an Aristotelian *phronēsis*—reveals how Nelson's individualist configuration of capability itself represents a regressive or sacrificial genealogy of the historical, social and political anti-sacrificial narratives which configure the ethical *telos* of the modern welfare state that underwrite the institutionalization of the recognitive capabilities of each person.

Possessive Individualism and the Principle of the Nonviolability of Persons

Nelson begins his defense of the absolute liberty of persons' ability to choose their own conception of the good life by demonstrating how the primary goal of the Rawlsian theory of distributive justice is to promote each individual's capability to choose his or her good through a political configuration of justice that remains neutral towards citizens' comprehensive views of the good life. Rawls' political conception articulates those primary goods—"rights, liberties and opportunities, income and wealth, and the social basis of respect"—that underwrite every-one's capability to pursue his or her conception of the good life (Rawls, 2003: 54–55). The Rawlsian primary goods configure those solicitous narratives that engender anyone's life-story as it unfolds from childhood, youth, adulthood to old age within families, schools, work, and in communities. But Nelson interprets the Rawlsian civic narrative in terms of the *neutrality* of the state vis-à-vis the pursuit of the recognitive capabilities of *one*self as the sole author of his or her good. Rawls's primary goods support the basic structure of civic society, of an "overlapping consensus," through which a distributive interpretation of capability is fostered that overcomes the false dichotomy between methodological individualism and holism. Nelson, however, offers an ahistorical interpretation of the Rawlsian overlapping consensus in terms of the rational choice-making practices of *oneself* (Rawls, 2003: 340). Herein lies the significance of Nelson's emphasis on Rawls's argument that primary goods are those goods that it is "rational to want whatever else one wants" (Rawls, 2003: 92): if we are to respect persons as ends in themselves, that is, as the autonomous choosers of their own good, we must be able to convince them that their inclusion in the distributive narratives of rights, liberties and opportunities, income and wealth, and the social bases of respect does not violate their moral capacity to recognize themselves as the authors of their own good.

The Rawlsian reply to this classical opposition between methodological individualism and holism is to demonstrate that the moral capabilities of oneself to author one's good depends upon similar capabilities for self-recognition of another. The Rawlsian understanding of primary goods as those goods "which it is rational to want whatever else one wants" expresses the distributive character of our recognitive capabilities, of our capacities to recognize our dignity of persons capable of authoring our own conception of the good. Nelson, however, interprets the Rawlsian overlapping conception purely recognitively, namely, in terms of the capabilities of *oneself*. The Rawlsian *distributive* ethics of *oneself as another* are replaced with a competitive strategizing wherein one seeks to advance his or her good *against* an-other: equality of moral autonomy between persons here means that my capabilities for self-recognition as the author of my conception of the good will *always* be in competition with your capabilities to recognize yourself as the author of your conception of the good.[8] The members of the original position, anxious to advance their own conception of the good, then, will only get as far as the first Rawlsian principle of moral equality: it will be impossible for them to proceed beyond the recognitive right to recognize themselves as the authors of their own good, to move beyond the state at which each member vies to protect and to advance his or her recognitive capabilities. Rawls's own commitment to the moral dignity of persons as ends in themselves itself guarantees the disjuncture between recognitive justice and redistributive justice:

> The claim that I am making is that, after Rawls's parties in the original position have agreed to provide equal liberty and have arrived at the question of what further primary goods to place on the list (income, wealth, the social basis of respect, etc.), they will not be able to agree on *any* additional items. There is no possible overlapping consensus they could reach which would not exclude certain non-rights violating conceptions of the good. (Nelson, 2008: 11, original emphasis)

Rawls cannot appeal to the principle of equality of moral autonomy in order to come to some kind of agreement upon which primary goods ought to be shared because, although the parties in the original position agree to distribute equal liberty of moral autonomy through the contractual exercise, the principle of equality of moral autonomy is constitutive of the original position itself and not derived from it: "Parties in the original position would then *by definition* agree to maximize and equally distribute primary goods in Rawls's "category 1" (equal liberty, rights); or rather what it *means* to be a party in the original position is that one would be committed to the provision of goods in this category" (Nelson, 2008: 11, original emphasis).

A question arises here for the parties in the original position that does not arise for Nelson: *How* do the contracting parties configure the equal distribution of liberties for each person to recognize himself or herself as the author of his or her good? In other words, *how* do the parties come to recognize the *inviolability of an-other as one-self*? Is this not precisely the question that the members of the original position pose to themselves? Is it sufficient, as Nelson claims, for each party to recognize himself/herself as the "inviolable chooser of [his/her] own idea of the good"? (Nelson, 2008: 11). What are the social, political, and economic conditions that will underwrite the recognitive capabilities of each person once the veil of ignorance is lifted? *It is because the parties in the original position must ask themselves this question that the first principle of moral equality forms a dialectic with the second distributive principle*: taken in their dialectical relationship, the principle of moral equality and the principle of distributive justice configure the moral status of our least advantaged citizens by arguing for the priority of the moral equality of all persons through an *anti-sacrificial regard* towards our least advantaged citizens (Dupuy, 1988).[9]

Rawls refers to this dialectic between the principle of moral equality and the principle of distribution in terms of the lexical priority of the principle of moral equality (or political justice) over the principle of distribution (or economic justice): the principle of the equal moral status of all persons may not be violated through the sacrifice of our least advantaged citizens for the sake of greater social or economic gain. The second principle, by prioritizing our least advantaged citizens in the distribution of wealth, opportunity, and social status, then, ensures the extension of moral status to all persons. Thus, the lexical priority of the principle of moral equality does not signify, as Nelson would have it, its separation from the principle of redistribution. Even less does it signify the opposition between the principle of moral equality and principle of redistribution: the principle of political justice (equality of moral liberty), which underwrites the equality of all moral persons, itself configures the ethical significance of the principle of economic justice. A society's capabilities or norms for reciprocity configure each person's capacities to recognize herself/himself as a worker, parent, student, caregiver, neighbor, teacher—in short, as the author of his or her good along with or *as* an-other worker, parent, student, caregiver, neighbor, teacher.

In order to understand how Nelson comes to interpret the lexical relationship between the Rawlsian principles of moral equality and redistributive justice as the *separation* between the moral capability for the authorship of one's good and the similar capability of an-other to recognize himself/herself as a good will, we must begin where Nelson begins: with Martha Nussbaum's interpretation of the Rawlsian capabilities approach to social justice. Nelson's neo-liberal complaint against Rawls's distributive interpretation of the non-violability of persons as ends in themselves is itself grounded in Nussbaum's interpretation of this principle. Nussbaum's argument is that Rawls's distributive interpretation of persons as ends in themselves undermines what she refers to as the Aristotelian "principle of each person's capability" (Nussbaum, 2000: 5).[10] The question that we will ask ourselves is whether the Aristotelian principle of each person's capability is not configured by civic narratives of reciprocity. If capability is separated from its distributive configuration, are we not lead to an elitist conception of capability, such as Nelson's, which divorces capability from disability, thereby moralizing advantage and disadvantage and thus undermining the dignity of our least advantaged citizens as moral persons?[11]

Nussbaum's Recognitive Interpretation of Distributive Justice

In order to be able to reply to elitist interpretations of the capability approach to social justice, we will need to critically evaluate the underdevelopment of certain methodological issues that arise from Nussbaum's rejection of Rawls's distributive interpretation of capability. Developing a socio-historical methodology that responds to the neo-liberal attacks on the civic state will return us to Rawls's principles of justice in their lexical ordering by way of another Aristotelian approach to capability—that of Paul Ricoeur's.

One of Nussbaum's major objectives is to develop a universalist or non-metaphysical political conception of capabilities justice. As Nelson notes, Nussbaum ties this aim up with the Rawlsian concern with an *overlapping consensus*, which permits the formulation of the principles of justice without favoring or prioritizing any particular conception of the good:

> The capabilities approach must now be shown to take seriously each person's prerogative to identify and pursue his or her own conception of the good life; it may not "be dictatorial about the good" and must leave

individuals "a wide space for important types of choice and meaningful affiliation." (Nelson, 2008: 99)

Nussbaum refers to her interpretation of the Rawlsian overlapping consensus—wherein each individuals' capabilities to pursue his or her conception of the good are preserved—as the "principle of each person as an end" and this principle forms a central aspect of her capabilities approach to justice (Nussbaum, 2005: 5). She is of course correct to underscore Rawls's Aristotelian concern with the capabilities of persons to achieve the status of being ends in themselves, of being good in themselves because they have the capabilities necessary to recognize themselves as the authors of their choices and of their life plans and that these capabilities furnish the political conception of justice. To this end, Nussbaum develops a list of central human capabilities, which articulate the constitutional principles that underwrite the flourishing of everyone in a political community. Because she insists upon the essential character of each of the capabilities, Nussbaum's list suffers from a certain endlessness:

1. Life. The capability to achieve a normal, high-quality life span.
2. Bodily health. The capability to achieve good health, to become adequately nourished and sheltered.
3. Bodily integrity. The capability to achieve and maintain bodily integrity through the enjoyment of freedom of movement, sexual satisfaction and through the freedom of reproductive choice free of sexual and domestic violence.
4. Senses, imagination, and thought. The capability to make use of one's senses, imagination and thought to produce cultural, artistic and social artifacts and to have these capabilities protected by constitutional laws.
5. Emotions. The capability to develop and express emotional attachments to people and things outside of oneself.
6. Practical reason. The capability to exercise one's practical reasoning by articulating and setting out to achieve a life plan in accordance with one's conception of the good life.
7. Affiliation
    - 7.A. The capability to develop and express empathy for other human beings and to engage in social interaction.
    - 7.B. The capability to enjoy the social bases of self-respect and to be recognized as having moral dignity, protected by constitutional guarantees against discrimination on the basis of race, sex, sexual orientation, ethnicity, caste, religion, and national origin.

8. Other species. The capability to develop and express empathy towards animals, plants and towards nature.
9. Play. The capability to engage in play, laughter, and recreational activities.
10. Control over one's environment.

A. *Political.* The capability to exercise freedom of political choice-making, freedom of association and freedom of speech.

B. *Material.* The capability to own property and to attain work and the capability to form relationships and exercise practice reasoning in the workplace. The capability to be free of unwarranted search and seizure practices.[12]

Each of the items on the list of capabilities, Nussbaum argues, is equally significant for human functioning and the capabilities are "of central importance in any human life, whatever else the person pursues or chooses" (Nussbaum, 2000: 74). We may thus reformulate the principle of the non-violability of persons, or the good of each person as an end as a "*principle of each persons' capability*" (Nussbaum 2000: 74, original emphasis).[13] While each of these capabilities are essential for the preservation of each person's capabilities as autonomous choosers of their own good, their very essential character prohibits their configuration by a law of distribution or of reciprocity, as argued by the Rawlsian lexical priority of the least advantaged member(s). Nussbaum's list of capabilities develops a *purely recognitive interpretation* of the Rawlsian overlapping conception—it insists on the capabilities of each person to recognize herself as the author of her good but these recognize capabilities are not configured by a principle of redistribution. Nussbaum's claim is that in identifying a list of central capabilities which she argues all political constitutions, which take seriously the status of persons as ends in themselves, ought to articulate, she is endorsing Rawls' own conception of an overlapping consensus:

> By "overlapping consensus" I mean what John Rawls means: that people may sign on to this conception as the free standing moral core of a political conception, without accepting any particular metaphysical view of the world, any particular comprehensive ethical or religious view, any particular view of the person, or of human nature (Nussbaum, 2000: 76).

The major advantage of Nussbaum's interpretation of Rawls' overlapping consensus is that she is able to preserve a recognition of the unique or singular circumstances of each person's struggle for flourishing. It is the moral significance of each person's singular struggle to flourish, to live a truly human life, that is erased by Rawls' lexical ordering of the primary goods. As we have noted, Rawls's solution to the problem of inequality, according to Nussbaum, is to redistribute primary goods. So long as people may be said to possess these primary goods, they may be said to enjoy the status of moral personhood, and are in this way considered to be equal. The problem with Rawls's "resource-based" approach is that it does not ask why or how persons fail to avail themselves of the rights, liberties, opportunities, and resources they are said to possess, and in order to understand this, we need a deeper understanding each person's struggle for flourishing. I want to suggest here that Nussbaum's resourcists characterization of Rawls's conception of distributive justice is rooted in her rejection of his lexical figuration of the principles of justice: "My own view holds that *all capabilities are equally fundamental, and does not announce a lexical ordering among them*" (Nussbaum, 200: 12, my emphasis). Nussbaum's resourcist critique of Rawls itself depends upon her rejection of the lexical ordering of the principles of justice in favor of the irreducible plurality of her list of central capabilities. But as we have seen, what the lexical ordering of the principles of justice demonstrate is not merely the priority of individual liberty (for this would only capture the rational aspect of human deliberation), nor even an argument for the possession of primary goods by all, but rather through the public or the reciprocal constitution of personhood. For Rawls, it is the public institutions of a society, which represent the norm of reciprocity governing the ethical configuration of oneself as another, that articulates an overlapping consensus. Put differently, an overlapping consensus is not chosen by rationally self-interested persons, but rather is realized in our collective reasoning on the shared or distributive status of the least advantaged member, recorded in the development of the public institutions of our society. By rejecting the lexical ordering of the principles of justice, Nussbaum enacts a separation between primary goods or primary capabilities, if you will, from the basic structure of society. On this reading, persons are ends in themselves and possess the status of moral personhood independently of the configuration of their life-story within the basic structure of society: primary capabilities are no longer embodied in the public or shared institutions of health, education, housing, and old-age and disability pensions, but *rather in persons as ends in themselves*. Herein lies the irony of Nussbaum's principle of each person's capability: by detaching the principle of each person's capability from the basic institutional structure of society, she ends up treating *primary capabilities* as the possessions of persons as ends in themselves.

In the absence of the Rawlsian lexical dialectic between each person's freedom for self-recognition as the author of his or her own conception of the good and the ethics of reciprocity that extend this capability for recognition to *each* one, or between recognitive justice and redistributive justice, Nussbaum's list of capabilities loses its coherence as a program for social justice and becomes vulnerable to the neo-liberal complaint launched by Eric Nelson that *any* argument for the sharing of a given capability violates the individual's inviolable autonomy of his or her conception of the good life. That is, because Nussbaum's capability approach to social justice lacks a *distributive methodology* for ensuring that *no-one's* status as a good in him/herself is violated, she is left without an historically informed defense against the neo-liberal denial of the *distributive character* of the *capability for self-recognition.* Once recognitive capabilities become divorced from their redistributive grounding, the principle of *moral equality*, which underwrites the dignity of persons as ends in themselves, becomes a justification of the *moralization* of inequality and the justification of the withdrawal of the elite from the civic commons.[14]

Nelson's Moral Blindness: Justice Without History, Politics, Society

Nelson advances his attack on redistributive justice—on the very possibility that we may achieve consensus on goods or capabilities that ought to be shared so as to furnish the basic public institutions of society—using Nussbaum's recognitive refiguration of Rawls's distributive conception of capability. Nussbaum's list of capabilities, through its rejection of the dialectic between recognitive and redistributive justice, which configures the moral status of our least advantaged citizens, and thus binds the moral capabilities of one-self with the moral capabilities of an-other, is left open to the neoliberal practice of picking and choosing of capabilities, wherein the capabilities of selfhood may be reduced to each person's right to defend her recognitive capabilities *against* the recognitive capabilities of another. The Rawlsian redistributive or reciprocal configuration of recognitive capabilities, where my capability to recognize myself as the author of my good—that is, to recognize myself as an artist, writer, entrepreneur, neighbor, parent—is opposed to your capabilities for self-recognition. The inviolability of persons comes to be interpreted not through the solicitude of one-self *as* an-other but through the competitive withdrawal of one-self from an-other.

Nelson begins by demonstrating how Nussbaum's list of capabilities is bound to violate the dignity of persons as autonomous choosers of their own good, thereby rendering impossible the construction of an overlapping consensus on the basic structure of society. Many interpretations of the good, such as that of the celibate, the Christian scientist opposed to the practices of Western medicine, and of anti-social persons, are violated by Nussbaum's list and thus excluded from the construction of the basic institutions of society. Nussbaum's list, divorced from the Rawlsian figuration of oneself as another, leaves us without a methodological justification for the redistribution of capabilities (Nelson, 2008: 74). Why, Nelson asks, do you get to decide what I want?: "In this connection, we should recall that, on the Rawlsian view which Nussbaum shares, it is not enough for the state to avoid institutionalizing *any one specific* conception of the good; a state which excludes all but three accounts of the good has still failed the neutrality test" (Nelson, 2008: 99). The conclusion that Nelson draws from Nussbaum's recognitive approach to redistributive justice is that the exclusion or the violation of any-*one's* good violates the liberal commitment to the preservation of the good persons as ends of themselves, what Nelson refers to as the liberal commitment to neutrality.

Nelson here begins to radicalize Nussbaum's recognitive interpretation of the Rawlsian overlapping consensus by *completing Nussbaum's rejection of the Rawlsian dialectic between the principle of moral equality and the principle of redistribution which figurates the priority of our least advantaged citizens*: he argues that there can be *no* relationship between the principle of moral equality (or the principle of political justice) and the principle of redistribution (or the principle of economic justice), without the coercive undermining of persons' capabilities to choose their own good.[15] Nelson here invokes the Foucauldian bio-political fantasy in which the autonomy of persons is stripped by their coerced participation in the disciplinary practices of state institutions of health, education, housing, and so on. The claim that underwrites the bio-political fantasy, of course, is that distributive state practices fail to respect the differences between persons. And on Nussbaum's and Nelson's account of capability, it is precisely the failure of the redistributive practices of society to recognize the differences between individuals that makes it necessary for us to pay closer attention to each person's capability to recognize his or her conception of the good. The question that arises here is whether the recognitive capabilities of the person, of *one*-self, is not inextricably tied to the recognitive capabilities of an-*other*, that is, whether there the moral dignity of persons as ends in themselves does not necessarily have a *distributive* structure.

It is the distributive structure of the recognitive capabilities of selfhood that the lexical ordering of the Rawlsian principles of justice articulates. But Nussbaum's and Nelson's interpretation of capabilities is founded on the *separation* between the principle of the equality of persons based upon their moral autonomy and the principle of distribution, and is thus divorced from the Rawlsian distributive configuration of vulnerability or of disadvantage. The separation that Nussbaum and Nelson presuppose between the principle of moral autonomy and the principle of distribution amounts to a rejection of the lexical priority of our least advantaged citizens in all moral deliberations on the distribution of resources and capabilities that underwrite moral dignity. That the priority of the principle of moral equality over the principle of distribution is *lexically* structured does not mean that the principle of equality and the principle of distribution are separate principles, wherein the priority of the principle of moral autonomy may be understood separately from its dialectic relationship with the principle of distribution. That is, Nussbaum and Nelson interpret for their purposes the lexical ordering of the principle of equality of moral autonomy over the principle of distribution in terms of a *separation* between moral autonomy and distribution, and thus privilege the equality of moral autonomy over the principle of distribution outside of their lexical ordering, which articulates their *non-separability*. In their lexical ordering, the principle of equality of moral autonomy and the principle of distribution express the *non-violability of the dignity of our least advantaged citizens.*

The lexicographical ordering of the Rawlsian principles of justice addresses the issue of civic exclusion and those requisite social, political, and economic rights that *enable* citizenship:

> The first statement of the two principles reads as follows:
>
> First: each person is to have an equal right to the most extensive scheme of equal basic liberties compatible with a similar scheme of liberties for others.
>
> Second: social and economic inequalities are to be arranged so that they are both (a) reasonably expected to be to everyone's advantage and (b) attached to positions and offices open to all. (Rawls, 2003: 53)

The first principle guarantees equal access to those social, political, and economic rights constitutive of citizenship, such as the right to vote and to hold public office, freedom of expression, freedom of thought, and freedom of the person. The second principle holds certain inequalities as being preferable over strict egalitarianism, provided these inequalities do not legitimate the exclusion of citizens from those basic institutions of citizenship outlined in the first principle:

> The second principle applies, in the first approximation, to the distribution of income and wealth and to the design of organizations that make use of differences in authority and responsibility. While the distribution of wealth and income need not be equal, it must be to everyone's advantage, and at the same time, positions of authority and responsibility must be accessible to all. (Rawls, 2003: 53)

Inequalities which may be permitted but are not to undermine the institution of citizenship are bound through the "*lexical ordering*" connecting the two principles:

> These principles are to be arranged in a serial order with the first principle prior to the second. This ordering means that infringements of the basic equal liberties protected by the first principle cannot be justified, or compensated for, by greater social and economic advantages. (Rawls, 2003: 53–54)

The lexical ordering of the two principles of justice prohibits the exclusion of certain members from the basic civic institutions of societies for greater economic or social advantages. Thus, the second principle, known as the "difference principle," is only intelligible in its positioning vis-à-vis the principles of political justice (Rawls, 2003: 57). The difference principle credits those inequalities essential to a productive economy, whilst prohibiting the sacrifice of the least advantaged for the greater whole. That the least advantaged ought not to be sacrificed for the good of the greater whole is represented in the "lexical ordering" of the principles of justice: the priority of the principles of equality, which taken together constitute the principle of civic inclusion tells us that only those inequalities that would benefit everyone are permissible: "Taking equality as the basis of comparison, those who have more must do so on terms that are justifiable to those who have gained the least" (Rawls, 2003: 131). In this way, the difference principle is to be understood as a principle of *economic justice.*

We may summarize the ethical significance of the Rawlsian principles of justice in the following way:

1. The political institutions that configure the respect owed to persons as ends in themselves must be equally accessible to all. That is, the

dignity of one-self depends up on the capacity for dignity of an-other. The moral characterization of persons as ends in themselves—or moral autonomy—is necessarily a *distributive* category.

2. Differences in socio-economic status, necessary for a healthy economy, may not lead to the violation of the *distributive principle of political institutions*—that is, socio-economic inequalities may not lead to the exclusion of our least advantaged citizens from membership in political institutions and thus the capabilities constitutive of moral dignity.
3. *Thus, the Rawlsian concept of the least advantaged is a distributive figure representative of the historical logic of the political institutions of civic states that seeks to maximize the capabilities for moral autonomy for our least advantaged citizens, or to "maximize the minimum share"* (Rawls, 2003: 132–136). Rawls, then, is an historian of the development of institutions that configure civic capabilities.

Yet the principle of persons as ends in themselves is given a possessive interpretation by Nelson. The idea that persons can be autonomous choosers of their own good outside of solicitous narratives of reciprocity is the unintended effect of Nussbaum's rejection of the lexical ordering of the Rawlsian principles of justice. The question that arises here is whether the Rawlsian original position configures such possessive individualism as Nelson argues or whether it configures a model of public moral deliberation—*phronēsis*, to borrow Aristotle's language—wherein the capabilities constitutive of selfhood, such as literacy, health, housing, employment, culture and political participation are interpreted *distributively*, that is, where both capabilities and vulnerabilities are shared. This is what is at stake in Rawls's *civic* interpretation of the principle of persons as ends in themselves. Treating an-other as an end in him/herself means treating *an-other as one-self*: the capabilities of *one*-self may not be achieved without similar capabilities for an-*other*.[16]

Nelson has it backwards, then, when he argues that the redistribution of capabilities violates the liberal principle of neutrality:

> In asking whether the "bread and butter" capabilities are genuinely things we all want no matter what else we want, we must recall a central fact: we are not being asked whether we all want to be well-nourished, but whether we all want to be well-nourished *by the state*. It is simply not the case that we all want an *entitlement* to nourishment whatever else we want. (Nelson, 2008: 103, original emphasis)

But in a modern state, we *demoralize* or destigmatize illiteracy, poverty, illness, homelessness, single parenthood, and unemployment through our *norms of reciprocity, through our practices of sharing.* Nelson reduces the historical, political, and social development of our norms of reciprocity and our civic practices of deliberation that underwrite the solicitous regard for oneself as another to an exercise of individualist choice-making.[17] Nelson's possessive interpretation of the good leads him into the kind of moral blindness characterizing the extreme stratification between rich and poor in modern neo-liberal societies. He reduces the historical-institutional practices of deliberation on the civic well-being of both rich and poor to the moral autonomy of the individual to *choose* whether his/her participation in the development and preservation of the civic commons accords with his/her idea of the good. Think, for example, of what happens when party Z emerges from behind the veil of ignorance and discovers that he is Robert Nozick, whose conception of the good requires that his capability to engage in moral reasoning and decision making, "in all its contingent particularity" be preserved. Ipso facto, Nozick's good cannot be subsumed into the "privileged vantage point" of the original position (Nelso, 2008: 115). In order to not violate Nozick's conception of the good—that is, that redistributive justice be carried out by the individual who decides how much of what he/she possesses he/she will share, and one might further suppose, if individuals do decide to share some part of their possessions, they will also need to decide *who* the benefactor of this sharing will be. But to preserve his status as a moral agent, we must then commit ourselves to the logic of a divided or stratified society. Such a society divides those who have goods they may or may not choose to share and thus possess the recognitive capabilities accorded by these goods, such as education, health, housing, and an adequate social minimum or standard for living, from those who do not possess these recognitive capabilities and whose vulnerabilities—illiteracy, homelessness, poverty—are then *moralized* by those persons who possess the capabilities which grant them the moral status that they deny to vulnerable others!

Not only is the moral autonomy of the elite violated when we make a claim for their participation in the civic commons, but the civic interpretation of moral autonomy is irrelevant for their status as autonomous choosers of their own good: "But here Nozick would again complain that he had been tricked: in the original position the question "Do you desire bread and water?" is deceptive. It turns out to be shorthand for the question "do you desire an *entitlement* to bread and water?" (Nelson, 2008: 113, original emphasis). On Nelson's account, persons as ends in themselves may be said to possess the genuine autonomy for moral choice-making only when they are capable of rendering the history, politics, and sociology of narratives of reciprocity irrelevant to their practices of moral choice-making. But Rawls's account of the original position introduces a "coercive" idea of state distribution of certain social goods—that is, liberty and opportunity, income and wealth, and the social bases of self-respect—once each contracting party concedes that he or she would want these goods, no matter what else he or she may want. The affirmation of each contracting party to wanting certain goods does not justify Rawls's second argument that the provision of these social primary goods ought to furnish the basic structure of society: acceding to wanting a certain good, Nelson argues, is not the same as wanting an entitlement to that good from the state.[18] The Rawlsian original position permits the first move, that is, the establishment of the moral equality of each person to assert what he or she would want, but it cannot go further than that, that is, it cannot, without violating the very principle of moral equality that it has established, make the second move of configuring what every person would want to maintain his or her moral dignity, *distributively*, that is, by interpreting the goods desired by *oneself* as goods that would be desired by *oneself as another*. A distributive interpretation of the good of oneself violates the principle of moral equality that says the good of each person is to be respected equally. The original position itself represents the violation done to oneself when interpreted as an-other. The deliberative model articulated by the Rawlsian original position *violates* the deliberative capabilities of oneself and thus the recognitive capabilities enjoyed by oneself by virtue of possessing these deliberative capabilities. The question "Do you desire bread and water?" respects the deliberative autonomy of persons as ends in themselves. But when an autonomous person is asked this question from within the original position, her very autonomy is endangered because she is no longer assumed to be the sole author of her good and the deliberative capabilities constitutive of her good. The good of *oneself* is irreducible to the good of *oneself as another*. Such a claim is not elitist, it merely respects the right of each person to posses his or her good(s) and to possess the deliberative capacities to determine whether and how these goods will be shared with others, as well as who these others will be.

Nelson bases his objection to Nussbaum's recognitive interpretation of distributive justice, that is, to her list of essential capabilities the she argues all members of a political community would want, no matter what else they may want, and which is not governed by the Rawlsian concern with the lexical priority of our least advantaged citizens. In this way, Nussbaum conceals Rawls's civic interpretation of the norm of persons as ends in themselves, where our least advantaged citizens are figured *distributively* or *solicitously*. This opens the door for Nelsons' argument that Rawls tricks us into abandoning our commitment to the principle of moral equality, or to the principle of neutrality, by coercing us into accepting state entitlements to social primary goods:

> This [Rawlsian] line of reasoning leads us back to an old observation, namely, that Rawls's two principles of justice rely on two incommensurable theories of the human person. The Kantian idea of the person as an inviolable, autonomous chooser, which underwrites the first principle, is incompatible with the "embedded" view of human beings that justifies the difference principle (i.e., the notion that none of our attributes is, strictly speaking, "ours"). *The former requires a respect for individual choices and for the distribution of assets that results from those choices; the latter allows for redistribution, but leaves us with no good reason to respect individual choices at all.* Rawls, as it turns out, cannot have both autonomy and redistribution, and the same applies to his disciples who have developed the capabilities approach. (Nelson, 2008: 115, original emphasis)

But Nelson's argument for a possessive or individualistic interpretation of the principle of persons as ends in themselves itself rests upon Nussbaum's rejection of the Rawlsian priority of our least advantaged citizens or the *civic* interpretation of the *principle of nonviolability* of persons as ends in themselves, which preserves the dignity of *an-other as one-self*. The original position exercise, then, figurates a *distributive conception of the good*: the *ethical aim* of a moral society, or a society that does not exclude its homeless, disabled persons, its unemployed, its illiterate, its children, its youth, its elderly, its parents, its caregivers and its workers from capabilities for health, education, work, culture, and community participation, constitutes the *civic inclusion of every-one* in public institutions of care such as education, health care, and social transfers. Rawls's civic interpretation of the principle of persons as ends in themselves underwrites a *distributive understanding of capability*: when our least advantaged citizens are excluded from the capabilities for health, education, and a minimum social standard of living, we are *all* worse off.

Nussbaum's list of capabilities lacked a methodological structure so as to realize the principle of capabilities for each person and thus rendered the distributive understanding of capability vulnerable to Nelson's neo-liberal charge of a kind of totalizing coercion, Rawls's distributive interpretation of our least advantaged citizen structures an historically informed methodology for civic deliberation on the preservation of persons as ends in themselves. It is a society's *norms of reciprocity*—its capabilities to continually engage in a distributive interpretation of vulnerabilities such as poverty, poor health, lack of education, and a decent standard of living—that underwrites its citizens' capabilities for dignity and for moral autonomy. The Rawlsian dialectic between the principle of moral equality and the principle of redistribution, which together figurate the distributive conceptualization of disadvantage and thus of advantage, of vulnerability and thus of capability; that is, the principles of justice figurate our *norms of reciprocity between advantage and disadvantage, between disability and capability*. These norms of reciprocity enable *every-one's* capabilities for moral self-worth, for self-recognition as the authors of their good. Our norms of reciprocity ensure that every-one develops capabilities for self-recognition, for moral reasoning and for moral authorship of their good by prohibiting the divide between the monied, educated, cultured self from an-other disabled, homeless, lone care-giver, unemployed self.

Nelson interprets our norms of reciprocity as coercively robbing persons of their capabilities for moral reasoning, but it is Nelson's own possessive conception of capability that creates the divide between capability and vulnerability. It is precisely such a stratified society that Nelson endorses when he argues that capabilities for moral dignity ought to be treated possessively and are thus undermined through societal practices of sharing:

> Any scheme of redistribution requires the existence of a "bird's eye view" from which a person or a group of persons is empowered to decide how much of what others have they may keep and what should go to whom—that is, to engage in moral reasoning on behalf of others. Any such scheme must depend on a theory of the human being which explains why this person or group of persons ought to be the locus of moral reasoning instead of the individuals themselves. (Nelson, 2008: 115)

Nussbaum's recognitive interpretation of Rawls's overlapping consensus, inspired by her Aristotelian concern with the preservation of each person's capability, underwrites Nelson's possessive interpretation of the good, which in turn articulates a vision for a highly stratified society in which some citizens enjoy capabilities for moral dignity and others are excluded from the capability to recognize themselves as the authors of their good. The result is a very impoverished conception of the capability for moral liberty, a capability that Nelson himself is anxious to defend.

Rawls's methodology for moral deliberation on distributive justice is not, as both Nussbaum and Nelson claim, limited to the consideration of the redistribution of wealth and income as primary goods, but rather with the way in which differences between citizens' socio-economic status (SES in social epidemiological speak), and more generally, the stratification or the *divide* between societies as a result of differences in socio economic status, *impact persons' capabilities for moral dignity* and for the autonomy to meaningfully realize their conception of the good: Thus, Rawls's argument is that extreme disparities in socioeconomic status lead to the civic and moral exclusion of citizens from those capabilities constitutive of genuine selfhood. *Distributive justice*, then, refers not simply to the fair allocation of income and wealth, but rather to the way in which societies organize their practices of reciprocity, of sharing, so as to preserve the dignity of our least advantaged citizens by prohibiting the *hyper-moralization* of vulnerability. Where societal practices of sharing are weak, as in the society that Nelson envisages for us, the disabilities of our most vulnerable citizens compound: poverty compounds poor health, poor education, and a lowered standard of living. A society that becomes divided along these capabilities for health, education, and a decent standard of living ends violates the principle of dignity of persons as ends in themselves by treating these recognitive capabilities as the possessive entitlements of the elite rather than as civic capabilities which in turn foster the capabilities for selfhood.

Civic *Phronēsis*: Ricoeur's Aristotelian Phenomenology of the Norms of Reciprocity

There is another Aristotelian interpretation of the Rawlsian overlapping consensus, advanced by Paul Ricoeur, which develops a distributive understanding of the recognitive capabilities emphasized by Nussbaum. A distributive understanding of the good of persons as ends in themselves, and thus of the principle of each person's capability, is historically developed within the *telos* or the *ethical aim* of the good society in which we pursue "the good life, with and for others, in just institutions" (Ricoeur, 1992: 172). On Ricoeur's Aristotelian reading, the Rawlsian overlapping consensus, configured by the lexical priority of our least advantaged citizens, structures ongoing public deliberation (*phronēsis*) on the slow-moving historical, sociological, economic, and political practices and institutions of reciprocity which underwrite—or undermine—the development of the dignity of each of its citizens. In developing Ricoeur's civic interpretation of *phronēsis* or deliberation, I argue that the Rawlsian figuration of *phronēsis*, guided by the Aristotelian ethical aim for the civic inclusion of our most vulnerable citizens figures a civic methodology for responding to the individualist model of deliberation which serves to attack our shared or distributive narratives on human vulnerability and capability.

The ethical aim of the good life "belongs to an Aristotelian heritage, where ethics is characterized by its teleological perspective" (Ricoeur, 1992: 170). While sharing Nussbaum's Aristotelian emphasis on human capabilities, Ricoeur interprets our capabilities for moral dignity from within Aristotle's ethical *telos* of the good society. The Aristotelian ethical aim is constituted by our *practices of sharing* which configure a *solicitous* response to relations of inequality, with and for others, in just institutions:

> It is the search for equality in the midst of inequality, whether the latter results from particular cultural and political conditions, as in friendship between unequals, or whether it is constitutive of initial positions of the self and the other in the dynamics of solicitude, as this defines the place of solitude in the trajectory of ethics. (Ricoeur, 1992: 192)

While it is the *mutuality* of solicitous giving and receiving which characterizes the Aristotelian conception of friendship, Ricoeur's phenomenology of mutuality has a triadic structure—reversibility, non-substitutability, similitude—that carries us from the benevolent spontaneity of friendship to the civic-historical pursuit of inequality on the plane of institutions. In our interlocutory practices, the reversibility of roles between listener and speaker is demonstrated by the use of personal pronouns: When one refers to another as "you," the other understands him/herself as "I," and when I am referred to in the second person, I receive this reference in the first person. Both listener and speaker are presumed to be equally capable of self-recognition or self-designation in interlocution. But while the *roles* of listener and speaker must be reversible, the *persons* occupying those roles are not:

> Solicitude adds the dimension of value, whereby each person is *irreplaceable* in our affection and our esteem. In this respect, it is in experiencing the irreplaceable loss of the loved one that we learn, *through the transfer of the other to oneself, the irreplaceable character of our own life. It is for the other that I am irreplaceable.* (Ricoeur, 1992: 193, my emphasis)

Friends engaged in the exchange of listening and speaking are *irreplaceable to one another* in a way that preserves the distinction between oneself and another. And yet, the *irreplaceability* of each is preserved by virtue of the solicitous regard in which each friend holds the other.

In turn, the reversibility of roles and irreplaceability of persons are realized through the *distributive* figuration of selfhood. Ricoeur places the *similitude* between one-self and an-other above the ideas of reversibility and irreplaceability. Similitude figurates the Aristotelian conception of "each-other" (*allēlous*) of mutuality. Similitude refers to my capacity to recognize myself as the author of my actions, as a neighbor, as a worker, as a caregiver, as a citizen by virtue of my recognition that you, too, are similarly capable of recognizing yourself in these roles and as the author of your own aspirations, actions, and speech. My capacities for well-being, work, health, education, culture, and community are dependent upon similar capabilities for you. It is by virtue of this similitude, this distributive interpretation of capability that we respond to the problem of inequality:

> The equivalence between the "you too" and the "as myself" rests on a trust that can be held to be an extension of the attestation by reason of which I believe that I can (do something) and that I have worth. All the ethical feelings mentioned above belong to this phenomenology of "you too" and of "as myself". For they well express the paradox contained in this equivalence, the paradox of exchange at the very place of the irreplaceable. Becoming in this way fundamentally equivalent are the esteem of the *other as a oneself* and the esteem of *oneself as another*. (Ricoeur, 1992: 193–194, original emphasis)

The figure of the other in the Aristotelian "each-other", then, already extends solicitude beyond the "I–you" dyad of friendship to the other who is also other than you—to the *moral stranger* [19]: "A plea for the anonymous in the literal sense of the term is therefore included in the fullest aim of the true life" (Ricoeur, 1992: 195). The "other," the moral stranger, is at the same time an "each"—a person as an end in himself or herself. My capability for self-recognition as the author of my actions and as a member of a political community, then, depends up on a *distributive* understanding of self-recognition, of self*hood*. This distributive understanding of selfhood carries us from the interpersonal plane to the institutional plane. The task of justice, posed by Aristotle and taken up by Rawls, is to structure the relationship between the recognitive and redistributive dimensions of selfhood in the ethical aim of the good life.[20]

The distributive interpretation of our solicitous regard for persons as ends in themselves is configured by the pursuit of equality on the institutional plane:

> By "institution" we are to understand here the structure of *living together* as this belongs to the *historical community*—people, nation, region, so forth—a structure irreducible to interpersonal relationships and yet bound up with these in a remarkable sense which the notion of distribution will permit us to clarify. (Ricoeur, 1992: 194)

The *historical* character of institutions constitutive of a political community expresses the considered convictions, the "*ethos*," of the community. The *ethos* guiding the political community is summarized in the *distributive commandment* or the Golden Rule, in both its negative and positive formulations:

> As was the case for the esteem in which we hold the good will, the Golden Rule appears to be part of the *endoxa* acclaimed by Aristotle's ethics, one of the received notions that the philosopher does not need to invent, but to clarify and justify. Now what does the Golden Rule say? We can read it in Hillel, the Jewish master of Saint Paul (Babylonian Talmud, *Sabbath,* 31a): "Do not do unto your neighbour what you would hate him to do to you. This is the entire law; the rest is commentary". We read the same thing in the Gospels: "Treat others as you would like them to treat you" (Luke 6:31). (Ricoeur, 1992: 218)

The Golden Rule, or the norm of reciprocity, grounds our practices of distribution in the historical-political community and its institutionalization of our wish to live together in *social time*.[21] That the law of distribution is necessarily housed in the institutions of the political community is testified to by the triadic structure of the Aristotelian phenomenology of mutuality: the reversibility of roles and the irreplaceability of the persons occupying those roles are configured by the *distributive recognition of oneself as an-other.* It is because the distributive commandment is embodied in the historical and political make-up of societies that the two-fold relationship between recognitive and redistributive justice may be preserved. Membership in a political community entails sharing in the community, and the distinction that is accorded by virtue of receiving one's share. The institutional structure constitutive of a political community mediates the conflicting distribution of valuable and precarious goods, the division and sharing of property, positions of responsibility, as well as advantages and disadvantages. Because of the complex nature of this sharing, this apportionment, Aristotle defined justice as having a particularly distributive character:

> And this sharing cannot help but pass through the institution. In fact, the first kind of particular justice is very exactly defined by a distributive operation that implies the political community, whether it is a matter of distributing "honour or money or the other things that fall to be divided amongst those who have a share in the [political community] (Aristotle, E.N. 5.2.11301, 30–33)". (Ricoeur, 1992: 199)

A distributive understanding of the political community, in turn, allows us to transcend the methodological, if not ideological, opposition between *holism* and *individualism*:

> The institution as the regulation of the distribution of roles, hence as a system, is indeed something more and something other than the individuals who play these roles. In other words, the relation is not reduced to the terms of the relation. But at the same time, a relation does not constitute a supplementary entity. An institution considered as a rule of distribution exists only to the extent that individuals take part in it. (Ricoeur, 1992: 200)

The ethical practices of a political community, understood as "a rule of distribution," are governed by the pursuit of intermediate and proportional equality over strict egalitarianism. Equality is characterized by Aristotle as having the virtue of intermediateness, of "*mesotēs*" between two extremes, as a corrective between sharing too much and sharing too little. Thus, equality seeks the proportional apportionment of shares to citizens' differential needs, merits, and responsibilities, of "equalizing two relations between, in each case, a person and a merit" (Ricoeur, 1992: 201). The intermediate and proportional character of equality pursued by distributive institutions of justice works to preserve the relationship between justice and equality, by preserving the recognitive capabilities of *each* for health, education, work, housing, for membership in a political community: "Justice in turn adds to solicitude, to the extent that the field of application of equality is all of humanity" (Ricoeur, 1992: 202). *The political community, configured by the rule of distribution, or the norm of reciprocity, is the solicitous or civic state.*

Historical Narratives of Civic *Phronēsis*: Norms of Reciprocity and Capabilities for Health

The distributive practices of the civic state, guided by the principle of equality, are concerned less with the individualist exercise of choice-making, exemplified by Nelson's monistic conception of moral deliberation than with the solicitous figuration of oneself as another.

INDIVIDUALIST MODEL OF DELIBERATION	CIVIC *PHRONĒSIS*
capabilities for *one*self *contra* capabilities for an*other*	oneself *as* another
recognitivist interpretation of "least advantaged"	distributive interpretation of "least advantaged
↓	↓
SACRIFICIAL	ANTI -SACRIFICIAL
possessive conception of the good	distributive conception of the good

If the rule of distribution or the *justice norm* refers to the historical development of the civic state, then *our practices of deliberation on equality and inequality*—what Aristotle referred to as *phronēsis*—*must also be structured by the historical configurations of the justice norm*, of our institutional practices of sharing, which configure our solicitous response to relations of inequality. Deliberation when guided by the justice norm concerns the *institutional interrelationships* that foster equality and entails investigating those institutional interrelationships that violate the justice norm because they exclude our must vulnerable citizens from public-civic practices of care. *Phronēsis*, or our civic practices of sharing, guided by the justice norm, is concerned with *maxi*mizing the *mini*mum share. This is the Aristotelian deliberative model that the Rawlsian principles of justice structure. Different welfare-state regimes represent different Rawlsian consensual histories of the long development of any given state's self-knowledge practices.[22] The *telos* or the *aim* of a political community is not the totalitarian imposition of a particular conception of the good, irrespective of the good of persons who make up the polity—whatever the philosophical fable of consequentialism teaches us. As Hegel has argued, the self-reflexivity of the civic state depends upon the teleological investigation of the interrelationship between the institutions of the state—the family, education, property, civil society, workers' guilds, social transfers—which continually configure and refigure the state.[23] The arrangement of the social institutions constitutive of the civic state expresses the *historical narrative*[24] of how that particular society organizes citizens' access to social transfers, employment insurance, health care, and education and how it organizes an efficient economy. The historical narratives embodied in institutions and policies constitutive of the polity–economy relationship, then, are not static or a-temporal, neither monadic nor holistic. Our practices of deliberation on the sociological and economic facts of inequality must be able to take into account changes in the structural relationships between polity and economy. For example, whereas the monopoly phase of capitalism was nationally bounded and required the mutual cooperation of capital and labor, the current global neo-liberal phase of capitalism succeeds by pitting market interests over and against labor and citizenship rights, which most Anglo-American welfare regimes, including liberal or market-based regimes, have historically employed. Such a division between social classes leads to a lowering of what Esping-Andersen refers to as the cross-class coalition gradient, or the level of social cohesion between socio-economic classes in a given society.[25] Deeply stratified societies, in turn, exhibit higher rates of income and social inequalities, crime, and poverty.[26] Here the search for *proportional equality*—wherein differences between citizens in terms of merit, responsibility and need are recognized from *within* the redistributive institutions of society and not by the *exclusion* of vulnerable citizens from the social institutions of the polity—is an *investigative category* that presupposes ongoing public deliberation. Proportional equality, then, is the *telos* of the civic state and represents an historical or civic interpretation of utilitarianism that is *anti-sacrificial* as articulated in the Rawlsian theory of justice.

Investigations into the way in which socio-economic status impacts citizens' capabilities for moral dignity requires an investigation into the historical-institutional figurations of the distributive practices of society. The Rawlsian principles of justice enable this kind of public *phronēsis* and knowledge-building. In what follows, we look at how the Rawlsian model of civic knowledge underwrites current social epidemiological research that employs long-term comparative research on liberal welfare state regimes to analyze how the impact of socioeconomic inequalities on citizen's capabilities for health is mediated by the differential distributive arrangements of welfare regimes. Recent studies have shown that in order to understand the role of income inequality on population capabilities for health, we must be able to contextualize the relationship between income inequality and health inequality in terms of the historical building-up, or tearing-down, of different welfare states' broader social infrastructure constituted by public education, public health care provision, unemployment, and social transfers through progressive taxation.[27] I argue that it is this kind of contextualized investigation of the historical-institutional development of the social infrastructure that works to mediate inequality that Rawls seeks to structure through the lexicographical ordering of the principles of justice. The *institutional configuration of the least advantaged engenders ongoing* public *phronēsis* on how our practices of distribution mediate the inequalities in population capabilities for health, education, and minimal standards of living that arise from the extreme stratification of rich and poor.[28]

The Priority of Institutional Modes of Sharing Over Socioeconomic Inequality: Background Institutions and Population Health in Modern Welfare State Regime

> Most important social processes take a long time—sometimes an extremely long time—to unfold. This is a problematic fact for contemporary social science, particularly in areas of inquiry where individual strategic action has become the central vantage point for framing questions and answers about social life. Especially in economic and political science, the time horizons of most analysts have become increasingly restricted. In choosing what we seek to explain and in searching for explanations, we focus on the immediate; we look for causes and outcomes that are both temporally contiguous and rapidly unfolding. In the process, we miss a lot. There are important things that we do not see at all, and what we do see we often misunderstand (Pierson, 2003).[29]

Recent social scientific research on the interrelationship between socioeconomic inequality and other inequalities, such as inequalities in health, have begun to look at a host of variables associated with the welfare state, such as the redistribution of income, public provision of health care and education, and unemployment insurance, as well as cross-class coalition building in the production of income inequality and to develop a more contextualized understanding of health inequalities in terms of the historical development of these institutionalized arrangements that both engender and undermine population health and well-being. In so doing, my aim is to demonstrate how the Rawlsian conception of the least advantaged is an *historical* category that figurates social scientific investigation of forms of civic exclusion, such as poor health and mortality.

That stratification between rich and poor has a significant impact on health outcomes has been widely acknowledged among social epidemiologists (Adler et al., 1994).[30] What social epidemiologists are increasingly interested in studying, however, is the idea that if socioeconomic status (SES) is significant for health inequalities, so are the differential institutional arrangements of both societies that produce these inequalities, and societies that manage to mediate these inequalities:

> The observation that SES gradients in health are ubiquitous suggests that institutional and policy determinants are also fundamental for population health . . . The extent of socio-economic stratification that exists in society is not innate. *Rather, it is strongly influenced by actions and inactions taken by societies that, cumulated over time, become embedded in institutions.* (Siddiqi and Hertzman, 2004: 590, my emphasis)

When we begin to ask questions about our institutionalized practices of redistribution and their impact on socioeconomic stratification, we are asking a necessarily historical question, one that requires that we take a long-term view on the causes of stratification and its relationship to other inequalities, such as inequalities in health. That is, stratification between rich and poor, and thus the configuration of our least advantaged citizens in terms of health, wealth, and civic well-being occur *over time* through the institutional practices of redistribution. SES alone cannot explain disparities in population health because the degree or the gradient of SES varies considerably across countries such that there is no predictable correlation between SES and health outcomes. Instead, the relationship between health status and SES is highly dependent on the extent to which different welfare states structure citizen's access to "health promoting resources" and to mediate citizens' exposure to those elements that are harmful to health:

> Institutional arrangements, then, play a role in distributing health promoting resources and buffering individuals from "exposures" adverse for health more successfully than others. In other words, in some societies, factors fundamental to health are provided as rights of citizenship, rather than according to socioeconomic status. (Siddiqi and Hertzman, 2004: 591)

What this means is that the gradient or the severity of socio-economic stratification is itself very significantly influenced by the differential redistributive orientation of different welfare state regimes and the extent to which societies manage to decommodify citizens' access to health, education, and social transfers. Income inequality is structured by different welfare configurations and is not a determinant of these welfare state typologies[31]: "In epidemiological speak, the function of societal policies can be thought of as *necessarily causally prior* to the effects of SES on health outcomes" (Siddiqi and Hertzman, 2004: 591).

Understanding the institutional figurations of population health and health inequalities necessarily entails that we take a long-term view of the causes of stratification and its consequent relationship to these other inequalities. In their case study comparing population health in Canada and the USA, Siddiqi and Hertzman utilize a longitudinal analysis in combination with a comparative approach in order to capture "big, slow-moving" institutional changes that shape the quality of population health:

> In particular, we focus on the manner in which structural changes in society are tantamount to the building up (or tearing down) of health-enhancing infrastructure, and that these changes occur in a gradual manner. So slow-moving are these effects on more meso-level and micro-level determinants of health shifts are discernible only from an historical, longitudinal perspective. (Siddiqi and Hertzman, 2004: 593)

In Rawlsian language, the civic well-being our least advantaged citizens is configured over time, and furthermore, institutional interrelationships are prior to socio-economic inequalities—that is, socio-economic inequalities are structured by the basic institutional arrangements of a given society. Distributive justice applies to the basic structure of society, to the design of a "social system" constituted by "background institutions" such as a fair constitution, equal opportunity for education for all through subsidized or public education, the provision of a social minimum through family allowances and sickness benefits as well as a taxation scheme. These background institutions are established and maintained by four branches of government, each of which is charged with "preserving certain social and economic conditions": The allocation branch preserves a competitive price system and the stabilization branch strives to maintain employment levels. Taken together, these two branches maintain an efficient economy. The branches that work to preserve the efficiency of the economy, however, is ill equipped to respond to considerations based upon need:

> It is clear that the justice of distributive shares depends on the background institutions and how they allocate total income, wages and other income plus transfers. There is with reason strong object to the competitive determination of total income, since this ignores the claims of need and an appropriate standard of life. (Rawls, 1999: 244–245)

The task of rendering distributive shares adequate to "common sense precepts of justice," or to our considered convictions, falls to the transfer branch. The final branch is the distribution branch, which structures the justice of distributive shares through the taxation of private property.

The social determinants of health, then, are configured by the historically embedded institutional arrangements of redistributive justice that may not be explained by a static conception of SES. Social epidemiological research into the institutional configuration of the relationship between SES and health inequalities, then, illustrates Rawls's observation that our practices of civic exclusion and civic inclusion structure the long-term expectations of our least advantaged citizens.[32] This research also lends support to the Rawlsian precept of max-min, or the maximizing of the minimal share of the least advantaged, is itself an historical process subject to social-scientific and policy investigations and that the social, economic, political, and cultural circumstances of our least advantaged citizen may be altered and thus are worthy of investigation. So, for example, Siddiqi and Hertzman's longitudinal study of the impact of welfare measures on the relationship between SES and health outcomes is an extension of Hertzman's earlier two-fold finding. From a comparative perspective, a pattern emerges such that, across societies, differences in health outcome at high levels of SES are far less pronounced than at low levels of SES. Thus, gains in terms of health outcomes from an increase in SES are more significant in some societies than in others. What this means is that societies that achieve "shallow" SES-health gradients—that is, where SES is not highly significant for population health—do so not by lowering the health status of higher SES groups, *but by raising the level of health of lower groups.* This is to say, societies that have achieved a shallow or insignificant SES-health outcome gradient have done so by raising the level of health for the most disadvantaged groups, and thus have better health on average than do steeply stratified societies:

> This pattern is sometimes referred to as the "flattening up" of the SES gradient and can only be uncovered through comparing whole distributions in *each* society to one another. The resultant conclusions are powerful. The link between SES and population health is modifiable, and thus worthy of investigation. (Siddiqi and Hertzman, 2004: 592, original emphasis)

The redistributive practices by which some societies are able to mediate the ways in which SES leads to forms of civic exclusion such as poor health cannot be understood by examining the effects of SES isolated from its broader institutional context, such as how different societies configure public provision and the gradual development of social institutions that support long-term population health: "Welfare measures in turn reflect basic social, political and economic institutions tied to the degree to which societies take care of their citizens or leave their citizens up to the market i.e., neo-liberalism" (Coburn, 2004: 43). Between 1971 and 1996, during which each income quintile in Canada gained equally in terms of life expectancy or where the socioeconomic gradients in health did not become steeper, Canada surpassed the USA in public social expenditures and in its redistributive efforts to reduce income inequality as well as in the provision of public education. During the same time period, socioeconomic gradients in health in the USA grew, with the richest income quintile gaining life expectancy more quickly than the poorest, despite the fact that the USA enjoyed a higher GDP per capita and lower unemployment rates than Canada and spent more money than Canada on health care. Thus, economic growth and direct spending on health care does not bear a significant relationship to population health (Ross et al., 2000: 899). Rather, the institutional configuration of welfare—redistribution of income, the provision of public health care and education, the provision of social transfers and unemployment insurance—is very significant for population health outcomes. Siddiqi and Hertzman argue that if it is the "redistributive work" of social transfers and the public provision of social services and not economic growth and direct spending on health care that underwrite population health and well-being, then we must also take into account the historical development of these institutions in post-recession Canada and the relative regression of the American post-war social infrastructure (Siddiqi and Hertzman, 2004: 599).

Chapter 5

Hegel's Philosophical-Historical Account of the Modern Interventionist State: The Social Figuration of Right

Thus far, we have been considering the tie between Ricoeur's teleological figuration of our ethical intention to pursue the good, with and for others, in just institutions, and Rawls' deontological figuration of the antisacrificial figuration of moral agency by the social institutions of society. What ties the ethical intention and the deontological figuration of moral personhood through the basic structures of society, what Ricoeur refers to as the "return path to the self" (Ricoeur, 1988): the identity of the self is not automatically generated but is actualized by the narrative of recognition embodied in interrelationships between the civic-social institutions of society. The capability to recognize oneself as the author of one's actions, speech, and life-story develops through the public institutions of the social state. The distinction David MacGregor draws in his *Hegel, Marx, and the English State* between the external state, such as the pre-regulatory English state at the dawn of industrialization and modern neo-liberal societies, in which the demands of the economy and civil society prevail, and the social state, in which the representative institutions of the state serve to connect government with each of the groups comprising civil society, is instructive here (MacGregor, 1996). In the social state, individual autonomy characterizing civil society is actualized in its passage through the social institutions of the state. In turn, the state is nothing other than the social figuration of the autonomy and the rights of its citizens. Another way of saying this is that the universal or the objective figuration of the moral subject—the inviolable status of persons as ends in themselves—is *ethically necessitated* through the development of the social state's knowledge of itself. The state develops reflexively through its continual investigation of the social and economic contingencies that shape the social and moral circumstances of its citizens. Historically, this mediation of the contingencies which shape the well-being and the legitimate expectations of citizens may be traced to the birth of the regulatory state, which instituted laws and social and political policies to intervene on the workings of free-range capitalism characterizing industrialization in order to foster the social context necessary for the preservation of the moral dignity of all persons.

This ethical preservation of moral personhood through the development of the social institutions of the state received its first philosophical articulation in Hegel's oft-misunderstood meditation on the state in his *The Philosophy of Right* (1967). We turn to Hegel's theory of the social state in order to illustrate the deontological-teleological figuration of moral personhood that we have been developing through Ricoeur and Rawls.[1] Our argument has been that the teleological or the ethical figuration of selfhood, at least as it is developed in the Aristotelian tradition, need not be opposed to the Kantian deontological or proceduralist figuration of personhood.

Illustrating the relationship between Rawls and Ricoeur through Hegel's philosophy of the social state is important for three reasons: it will demonstrate that Rawls's proceduralist figuration of moral personhood is not, as most major commentators would have it, anti-communitarian, that the teleological or ethical conception of personhood is not won at the price of totalitarianism.[2] Rather, through their distributive figuration of selfhood, grounded in the solicitous institutionalization of *oneself as another*, Ricoeur and Rawls overcome at the same time the false opposition between individual and society, and the false reduction of society to a possessive conception of individualism. Finally, the social figuration of moral personhood enables a civic *phronēsis* on the capabilities constitutive of moral autonomy—such as the capability for health, education, and work—are extended to every-*one*. Because the civic institutions of health, education, social transfers, and old age and disability pensions, are *public* institutions, no-*one* may be excluded from them, without undermining the very public status of civic institutions. And it is the solicitous public culture of society that underwrites the capabilities for moral authorship emphasized in the deontological tradition: my capabilities for health, well-being, literacy, parenthood, childhood, housing, and political membership depend upon similar capabilities for you. As such, the deep tie between the distributive figuration of personhood the public character of the basic structure of society enables a continual investigation by the social institutions of the state into the conditions that enable—and disable—citizens' capabilities for moral authorship and self-recognition. As the public culture of a society develops, so too does the social investigation into the capabilities of citizens for moral personhood: *the capability for moral authorship and choice-making develops in tandem with the development of the public institutions of society.*[3] We shall examine how both historical and modern civic *phronēsis* seeks to preserve individual autonomies, such as the right to an adequate standard of living the right to vote, appeal to *historical narratives of the inclusion of every-one* in the institutions of citizenship to legitimate individual rights and autonomy.[4] Equality between persons, contra Hobbes, is not self-founding, but develops through the unrelenting investigation by the social state—what Francois Ewald describes as societies based in solidarity—into the social and economic facts of inequality. The norm of reciprocity, which commands that we treat an*other* as *one*self, and which receives its moral tenor from the Kantian principle of the inviolability of persons, is not a moral fact, but is itself an *investigative norm into the social and economic facts of inequality and of reciprocity between oneself and another.* That is to say, the norm of reciprocity articulates a civic *phronēsis* on the capabilities of oneself as another. The historical narrative of the development of the public institutions of society is a story about the *reflexive* rather than the *linear* development of the modern welfare state. The civic narrative of the social state continually traverses, in a back and forth movement, the individual, interpersonal, and institutional planes, expanding the course of recognition governing each of the planes of the ethical intention to pursue the good, with and for others, in just institutions. It is in the course of its traversal of each of the planes of society that the state continually develops knowledge of itself, and thereby continually renders itself objective to itself.

This last point we shall demonstrate by arguing with David MacGregor that the *Philosophy of Right* is Hegel's philosophical conceptualization of the social or the rational state, which articulates a system of ethical interrelationships between the personal or familial realm, the realm of education, the realm of civil society or the market, the realm of social transfers and pensions, the realm of unions and workers' guilds, the legal realm, the political realm, and the realm of the monarch. Because the social state is an articulation of the ethical interrelationships between each of these civic realms, it does not reside above or outside of these ethical—or to recall Rawls's language—public interrelationships. The system of ethical necessity which draws together each of the realms of an ethical or a public society enables the continual development of a civic *phronēsis*, of social knowledge, on the social and moral circumstances of citizens. This kind of investigative knowledge building is only possible in a state that is not completely identified with civil society, or the market, but rather seeks to balance the social development of its citizenry with the demands of a productive economy. With MacGregor, we shall argue that in the *Philosophy of Right*, Hegel outlines a theory of the social or the interventionist state, which had not yet emerged in his time, that tasks the public institutions of the state to engage in the investigative work necessary to protect the well-being of worker-citizens. Hegel's philosophical defense of the role of the social state in preserving the moral status of personhood underwrites Marx's celebration of the role of the Factory Inspectorate in documenting the social and economic exploitation of the working class in industrial England, and his defense of the English state as one of the first interventionist states, or what is now known as the modern welfare state.

Ethical Life: The Figuration of Right through the *Rechtsstaat*

I propose to read Hegel's *Philosophy of Right* (1967) "backwards." In other words, rather than explicating Hegel's development of the rational Idea linearly, which culminates in the absolute objective freedom of the particular will (namely, the monarch), I propose to bring Ricoeur's conception of narrative to bear on the dialectic Hegel traces between subjective freedom and the objective or substantive grounds for this freedom (Hegel, 1967: §264). Hegel argues that the reflexive or substantial freedom is only possible within the ethical realm, once we have transcended the one-sided freedom of Abstract Right and Morality. I will begin, then, by explicating Hegel's three-fold argument on Ethical Life—namely, the ethical institutions of the family, civil society, and the state—and treating both his development and his critique of abstract right and morality therein. The *Philosophy of Right* (1967) is, after all, Hegel's meditation on human freedom. What I shall show is that for Hegel, human freedom requires an institutional context (Williams, 1997). Reading the text backwards allows us to re-frame the question of subjective individuality and universal necessity not in terms of the absolute identity of the monarch but rather in *teleological* terms. We find support for our teleological reading of the principle of determination employed by Hegel in the *Philosophy of Right* in Steven B. Smith's (1989) and Tony Burns's (1996) account of Hegel's structuration of right or individual freedom in its institutional contexts. Both Smith and Burns are careful to stress that the Hegelian conception of right cannot be fully appreciated without an understanding of his emphasis on the institutional structuration of right. Despite certain differences in the way that these authors conceive of the relationship between Aristotle and Hegel, both show convincingly that Hegel was heavily indebted to the Aristotelian conception of ethical community, *phronēsis* or practical deliberation, and the relationship between natural law and positive law.

In this reading, we will delineate the way in which objective and subjective freedom mediate one another through a two-fold determination (Hegel, 1967: §141). By emphasizing the structure of this reflexive determination, we will be less concerned with its (absolute) point of culmination, rather, our interest lies in the structure of this determination itself. This is so because Hegel argues that it is this reflexive determination that actualizes freedom. Freedom realized, then, presupposes a principle of structuration. For Hegel, substantive freedom is understood in terms of ethical necessity. Thus, he describes his explication of Ethical Life and the State as a "systematic development of the circle of ethical necessity" (Hegel, 1967: remark to §148). Freedom is structured, or to use Hegel's language, is necessitated through the state and the institutions of family and civil society. Hegel's concern with both the grounding and actualization of freedom coincides with our overarching concern with the acting and speaking subject. Another way of saying this is that subjective freedom, or the right of the subject is only realized when understood in terms of the citizen's relationship to the state. We thus return to Ricoeur's conceptualization of the good life as a reflexive precept that is developed on the ethical-cultural plane of distributive justice.

Only a teleological reading of Hegel's *Philosophy of Right* allows us to grasp conceptually the reflexive development of the good, in which the actualization of the good in the subject is not to be distinguished from its necessary grounding in the universal Idea of the good:

> The unity and truth of both these abstract moments—the Idea of the good not only apprehended in thought but so realized both in the will reflected into itself and in the external world that freedom exists as substance, as actuality and necessity, no less than as subjective will; this is the Idea in its absolutely universal existence—*Ethical Life*. (Hegel, 1967: §33)

It is through a reflexive configuration of the good that freedom and necessity are reconciled (Hegel, 1967: §264). Hegel emphasizes the *conceptual* nature of this mediation precisely in order to develop the two-fold figuration of the universal and the particular. The family or civil society as such does not make possible the existence of society. Rather, these institutions are only intelligible from within a broader conception of the state.

In *Hegel's Critique of Liberalism: Rights in Context* (1989), Steven Smith has argued that for Hegel, right (or freedom) is to be understood historically and culturally; this is Hegel's critical response to the natural law philosophies of the French Revolution. In the philosophies of Hobbes, Locke, and Rousseau, individuals are the possessors of certain natural or God-given rights. Today, we understand natural rights as universal human rights. According to natural law philosophies, these rights are not derivative of individuals' membership in the state, in families, or in estates. Because rights belong to individuals as such, the state or the political community cannot be said to endow individuals with these rights or to develop rights in any way. On the contrary, "government has its origins in the rational desires of individuals to protect and defend their preexisting rights as human beings" (Smith, 1989: 61). In contrast, Hegel's argument is that the development and the meaning of both will and right cannot be understood apart from an historical understanding of its institutional grounding; the will's freedom is historically and contextually developed. In other words, it is the state's laws that, at any given period in history, structure the will and make possible the freedom necessary for will's self-recognition as an autonomous agent:

> The Hegelian state is above all an organization of laws, a *Rechtsstaat.* Law is what purges the state of caprice and makes possible such modern freedoms as contract and property, career choice, religion, and speech. The result . . . is by no means some irrational state worship, *but the deepening of a recognition or respect for the wishes and ways of life of others, a manner of behavior that could be called civility.* The core of the modern state is, then, respect for the person, or "free personality". (Smith, 1989: 112, my emphasis)

It is through its laws and its political institutions that the state structures and thereby recognizes individual freedoms. It is through the laws of the state as they pertain to the maintenance of the family, to property, to education, to corporations, and the protection of workers that the universal will or right of the individual is actualized, that is to say, that the individual will recognizes itself in its universal willing. These civic laws relate the individual will to the universal through a process of juridification whereby each of the spheres of Ethical Life such as family, work, and education are brought into a system of laws that together constitute the state. Because it is through this process of juridification that the state is constituted, the state is nothing other than this process of juridification, whereby the particular social and ethical facts determining citizens' lives are recognized in terms of law. Furthermore, because individual will recognizes itself in this juridification of the ethical spheres of its life, i.e., the incorporation of Ethical Life into the laws of the state, the individual will is itself universalized through this juridification or ethical determination constitutive of the state. In this way, both the subjective and objective aspects of willing are brought together.

As we have seen, for Kant, the freedom of the will rests in its autonomy. That is to say, the good will is an end in itself. In chapter two, we explicated Ricoeur's argument that the second formulation of the categorical imperative, namely, the injunction to always treat others as ends in themselves and never simply as a means, represents a formalization of the Golden Rule. In his formalization of the Golden Rule, Kant sought to ground the ends of moral action in the principle of autonomy itself, which Ricoeur has argued undermines the ethics of respecting the plurality of the otherness of persons articulated by the Golden Rule. The first or universal formulation of the categorical imperative—always act such that your maxim may also become universal law—eclipses in a fundamental way the second categorical imperative which demands that the genuine plurality of persons be respected. That is to say, the second categorical imperative is absorbed into the monologic autonomy of the first categorical imperative.

As Smith notes, the difference between Kant and Hegel is to be found in their theories of objective ends. Where Kant locates the ends of moral action in the rational-autonomous constitution of the will, Hegel locates the will and the ends of its actions in terms of its practical and institutional modes of development:

> While Kant regarded the moral will as part of our "rational nature", as a "self-subsistent end" or a "fact of reason", Hegel regarded it very much as a specific historical accomplishment, something with a more pronounced developmental component in it. The will is not something prior to its actions. Put another way, a person cannot be totally detached from the kinds of commitments he has made. The will is always embedded in real life in an objective world of political and legal institutions which reach their fruition in the idea of the state. (Smith, 1989: 111)

Put simply, Hegel is concerned with the ways in which the self actualizes itself and thus becomes objective to itself, and is thereby able to recognize itself as the author of its actions. This process of self-actualization or the development of self-consciousness is a necessarily political and cultural endeavor; it is not a fact of reason. In other words, the development of self-consciousness requires a civic-ethical narrative, which it must continually traverse in its quest for self-recognition.

I shall argue that Hegel's Aristotelian argument is that self-actualization requires a civic configuration such that the self is able to recognize itself as the author of its actions. Self-actualization develops on the pre-dialogic, dialogic, and institutional planes. The acting and speaking self only recognizes itself within a community of actors and speakers who are in turn situated on the institutional plane. Hegel's practical philosophy draws out the autonomy of each of the aspects of the ethical spheres—the family, the corporations, or workers guilds in civil society, education, and private property—precisely by showing how each of these moments is related in the development of the state. Unless we are able to grasp each of these moments in terms of their development within the whole, we are not able to ascertain how the will actualizes itself within each of these ethical planes. The very ethical status of each of these institutional spheres in which subjectivity actualizes itself depends upon their interrelationships with the state. Thus, for example, the immediate right to property is developed within the family, supported by social provisions in the workers' guilds or the corporations, each of which are institutional moments of the continual development of the state's determinate knowledge of itself. Thus, the truth of the moral subject is in the familied, educated, and classed citizen of the state.[5] It is for this reason that I have chosen to explicate Hegel's critical development of the sections of abstract right and morality from within an explication of his development of Ethical Life constituted by the family, the institutions of civil society and the state.

Hegel's Aristotelian Conception of Ethical Community: *Phronēsis* and the Explication of Right in the Rational State

It is through an examination of the *practices* of the cultures and the social institutions of the state through which subjectivity gains actualization or self-recognition that the rationality or essentiality of each of the ethical-social institutions is revealed. Steven Smith has argued that in Hegel, the appropriate mode of examination for these cultural-institutional practices is through practical knowledge or *phronēsis*:

> [Philosophy] is rather a form of practice intended to bring out the structure of rationality from within the concrete embodiments and institutions of political life. As odd as it may sound, the *Philosophy of Right*, perhaps the most formidable and austerely written text in the history of political philosophy, was intended as a contribution to practical philosophy. (Smith, 1989: 136)[6]

Smith argues that Hegel's conception of Ethical Life or *Sittlichkeit* constituted by the practices of the institutions of family, education, property through which the state is itself constituted, reflects Hegel's Aristotelian grounding in practical philosophy. Aristotle's practical philosophy is concerned with the evaluative and practical dimensions of practice: "As originally conceived, practical philosophy dealt with all those domains relevant to the evaluation and direction of action (*praxis*). Custom (*ethos*), and household (*oikos*) were all deemed part of the philosophy of the practical" (Smith, 1989: 136). Ricoeur's Aristotelian figuration of the ethical aim helps us to clarify the teleological structure of Hegel's conception of the state in terms of the actualization of the moral self within the ethical institutions of the family, civil society, and the state.

Classical natural law theory as, articulated by Aristotle, offers a critique of modern natural law theory à la Hobbes and Locke in which the individual is presumed to be endowed with certain unalienable rights prior to her membership in society. Aristotle's practical philosophy as it is developed in the *Poetics* (1999) and the *Ethics* (1999) emphasizes the role of civic and cultural practices in the figuration of selfhood. What this means on the institutional plane emphasized by Hegel is that the particularities characterizing the lives of citizens such as employment, property, the raising of children, education, and so on, require a *normative* dimension for their very identification and articulation. I think it is in terms of his commitment to a normative-transcendental basis of society that Hegel is to be understood as a natural law theorist (Burns, 1996). At the same time, this transcendental basis is for Hegel meaningless unless it is codified and practiced in positive law and in the state's capacity for continual self-critique by virtue of the figuration of the state norm through the ethical institutions of family, property, workers' guilds, and so on. In order to understand Hegel's complex relationship to natural rights, we must understand Hegel's configuration of right vis-à-vis the civic laws and institutions of the political community. It is this configuration that we have been developing in our dialectic of emplotment and *phronesis* in our study of (civic) praxis.

In his analysis of Hegel's essay *On the Scientific Ways of Treating Natural Law* (Burns, 1996), Tony Burns has argued that Hegel puts forward a "formal conception of natural law" that is derived from the Aristotelian tradition (Burns, 1996: 45). Burns argues that the two seemingly contradictory aspects to Hegel's thought, namely, his commitment to the natural rights constitutive of the free will on one hand, and his defense of the Aristotelian conception of ethical community, on the other, is best understood in terms of his development of Aristotelian natural law. Our aim here is not to engage in any depth in the debate about whether or not Hegel can be seen as a natural law theorist; rather, by drawing out Burns's argument regarding the complex nature of Hegel's natural law theory, our aim is to specify the relationship Hegel develops between natural right and the state. For Hegel, freedom of the will is not merely external, as in the immediacy of the right to property, nor is it to merely subjective, as in moral self-consciousness. Both of these moments of the development of the will are abstractions; their truth lies in the ethical dialectic in which the universal concept of the good (immediate right) and the particularity of subjectivity (moral self-consciousness) are united (Dallmayr, 1989). The ethical mediation of the abstract and particular dimensions of the will, in turn, is structured on the institutional plane. It is this dialectic that Burns argues Hegel develops in his Aristotelian conception of natural law wherein the precepts of natural law, and the individual rights embodied therein, may only be interpreted by the laws of the political community or in positive law.

It must be stated from the outset that Hegel is not antagonistic to individual freedom. On the contrary, Hegel is deeply committed to the development of subjective freedom. Hegel's profound contribution to the question of selfhood consists in his claim that the freedom of the will, or selfhood's capacity for self-recognition is not immediate; it requires an institutional mediation in order for its own practices as a family member, as a worker, and as property owner and as citizen to be recognized and thus for its freedom to become *objective to itself.* It is in light of the cultural and political process through which this self-recognition, this objectification of the will's particularity in light of its civic-institutional figuration, that the state is to be understood. Shlomo Avineri has argued that it is this civic-institutional figuration of selfhood that Hegel has in mind when he develops his notion of rational freedom:

> The state, then, is based on rational freedom, organized in such a way as to enable each to realize his freedom in conjunction with others, while in civil society one can realize one's ends only by disregarding everyone else's aims. Hence the purely individualistic concept of freedom, which maintains no limits on one's arbitrary choice, has to be superseded by the ethical order which makes my freedom dependent on that of the other. The state is 'freedom universal and objective'. (Avineri, 1972: 179)

The sheer particularity of the will, then, entails a certain ethical blindness on the part of all particular wills to the moral and social facts constitutive of selfhood. That is to say, in the realms of immediate right and moral self-consciousness, there is no sociological standard of judgment through which practice may be submitted to ethical evaluation; rather, these spheres of particularity are constituted precisely by the absence of ethical evaluation. The morality of the state, then, consists in the continual labor of drawing these particularities or differences out in the form of ethical, social, political, and economic knowledge. Burns, like Smith, underscores Hegel's commitment to subjective freedom. At the same time, Burns argues, Hegel rejects modern natural law theory's emphasis on individualism central to the social contract. The natural rights which emerge from the social contract, Hegel argues, are abstract and lack the developmental dynamism of Ethical Life (Burns, 1996: 53). Thus, for Hegel, there is a distinction between subjective freedom or the development of individuality and individualism (MacPherson, 1964). It is for this reason that Hegel rejects the modern natural law tradition. While for Hegel there are certain inalienable human rights, yet these rights cannot be asserted *against* the state, for their objective development occurs within and through the civic institutions and laws of the state. The actualization of right cannot be discerned outside of its objective development within Ethical Life:

> It follows that within Hegel's system *although individuals do indeed possess certain natural rights these rights are not rights against the state as such.* These rights have an abstract character. They require definition and interpretation, and for Hegel it is positive law that should define them. Positive rights, for Hegel, are natural rights, in so far as the latter have been concretely defined. Hence natural law and natural rights cannot, as a consequence, provide the individual with a means of questioning the moral validity of positive law. (Burns, 1996: 64, my emphasis)

Natural rights exist as moments of Ethical Life; it is for this reason that their explication is only possible in terms of the rational development of the philosophy of the rational state. Thus, the normative status of right is reflexively developed in the state's knowledge of itself as social law. We have interpreted the Golden Rule, or the norm of reciprocity on the institutional plane in terms of the continual demand for the civic inclusion of all citizens. The Golden Rule underwrites the normative dimension of Hegelian-Aristotelian natural law and in this respect, the classical natural law tradition is close to the formal natural law tradition articulated by Kant. There is, however, an important difference in the way that these two traditions actualize the norm of reciprocity. As we have been arguing, when we interpret the norm of reciprocity in terms of the ethical aim of wanting to live well with and for others in just institutions, one's rights depends on those civic institutions that guarantee the rights of each. Without this institutional figuration of right, the norm of reciprocity remains abstract.

While the Golden Rule may indeed provide the Kantian categorical imperative with a content, this content itself remains abstract precisely because it has no way of ethically determining its content. While the Golden Rule expresses the norm of reciprocity, what this reciprocity means and how it is related to the ethical aim of treating others as ends in themselves is not clarified in the categorical imperative. The same holds true for the Hobbesian version of natural law: the law remains formal because its content is itself an abstraction. The Golden Rule or the norm of reciprocity requires an institutional context, namely, the state's reflexive knowledge of itself as a social law, for its actualization. This is precisely what the Hegelian-Aristotelian conception of natural law provides.

Both Burns and Smith argue that Hegel's defense of subjective freedom and his argument for the *objective* figuration of subjective right is in a large part due to his appreciation of the tradition of practical philosophy in Aristotelian natural law. Burns's argument is that what Hegel rejects is the doctrine of modern natural law, not natural law as such. In order to understand Hegel's relationship to natural law, we must understand Hegel's indebtedness to the Aristotelian conception of natural law (Burns, 1996: 53).

In particular, Burns argues, Hegel turns to the classical Aristotelian conception of law in response to the individualism in modern natural law and its corresponding presuppositions on the state of nature and the social contract. In the Aristotelian tradition, the first principle of natural law is that the polis is prior to the individual in terms of which Hegel develops his conception of ethical nature (Burns, 1996: 53).

In the Aristotelian-Hegelian conception of natural law, there is no opposition between natural law and positive law; positive law complements natural law. For Hegel, like Aristotle, the positive laws of particular communities represent the concretization of the general ideals or principles of law. Different communities will have different ways of determining the general principles of law in their codes of positive law; how different ethical communities are constituted through these differences in the institutionalization of positive law rests solely in their particular cultural and political organization (Burns, 1996: 59–60). In order to understand the Aristotelian-Hegelian claim that positive law and natural law are not in opposition to each other, Burns argues that we must understand Hegel's critique of formal Kantian morality. Hegel's argument is that the formal principles in Kantian moral philosophy gain their substantial content through the conscience of the individual, and thus the substantive realization of the formal principle may be filled by caprice, so long as it is conscientiously done. In the Aristotelian-Hegelian version of natural law, beneath the formal principle are substantive principles that provide the formal principle with its objectivity. Such substantive principles include the prohibition against lying, stealing, murder, and so on. At the same time, these substantive principles remain abstract because while they have the form of a prohibition, they cannot tell us when and whether we are dealing with a particular instance of the general law. Thus, we further require practical principles of application in order to clarify and apply the formal and abstract principles of justice (Burns, 1996: 61). These practical principles that interpret the formal principles of natural law are constituted by the ethical system of the polis, not by the conscience of the individual will. In Kantian natural law tradition, the formal principles of justice are applied and realized by the individual will; in the Aristotelian natural law tradition, it is the laws and institutions of the ethical community that carry out the interpretation of the formal principle of justice through *phronēsis* or practical wisdom (Burns, 1996: 62).

Phronēsis, when applied on the institutional plane, signifies public deliberation on civic institutional practices. This civic deliberation is structured by the norm of reciprocity. The justice norm informs civic deliberation on the institutions and practices constitutive of an ethical community. Taken together, the institutions and practices of an ethical community constitute positive law.

The norm of reciprocity understood as the principle of *civic inclusion*—which Burns argues constitutes the principle of justice in the Aristotelian-Hegelian conception of natural law—informs reflexive public deliberation on the principles of positive law. Burns illustrates this point with a Hegelian interpretation of the prohibition against theft. In following the primary principle of natural law, articulated by the principle of reciprocity, Hegel argues, we are obliged to recognize the prohibition against committing theft. Thus, the prohibition against theft is a subsidiary principle in relation to the principle of reciprocity. The prohibition against theft, however, remains abstract because it does not tell us that we have a right to property or how we can recognize when someone has committed theft. We thus require institutional modes of interpretation in order to specify the abstract or formal prohibition: "To carry out this task is the principle function of the positive law of the ethical community in which we live" (Burns, 1996: 63). The transcendental basis for society, then, is a commitment to social justice as it is formulated in the Golden Rule. Hegel is close to Kant in this respect. However, this transcendental basis understood as the norm of social justice constitutes the self-reflexivity of the norm's relationship to itself. That is to say, for Hegel, the norm is the self-reflexive state which continually gains knowledge of itself and thereby becomes objective to itself through its civic practices and institutions. In developing the idea of the self-reflexivity of the state norm, we shall argue that the state norm is the justice norm whose ethical aim it is to establish reciprocity wherever reciprocity is lacking and thus entails the sociologization of judgment.

Locating the Self: Hegel's Civic Narrative

The civic narrative constitutive of the ethical aim draws out the interrelationship between the three planes of the ethical aim: the acting and speaking self, dialogic intersubjectivity, and civic institutions. *Phronēsis* or public deliberation, then, traverses the evaluative axis of ethical aim through which each of these planes are brought into relation with one another. In this way, *phronēsis* or practical-public deliberation is not separated from the evaluative practices of society; rather, *phronēsis* is constitutive of ethical evaluation. Thus, the recognitive dimension of selfhood, or the rights-bearing individual citizen, depends upon the distributive figuration provided by civic narrative. I read Hegel's concept of ethical necessity as a civic narrative through which both the recognitive and redistributive dimensions of selfhood are developed. It is by virtue of this civic narrative that the individual may be said to be capable of the kind of moral self-evaluation constitutive of Kantian self-consciousness. It is for this reason that we cannot think moral self-consciousness outside of its figuration in the system of ethical necessity or civic narrative with the rational state.

Hegel argues that the problem with "the good," as it presents itself in moral self-consciousness, is that it is abstract; that is to say, it has no basis upon which to recognize itself. At the same time, subjectivity, as it is presented in immediate right, that is, in the possession of private property as such, is equally abstract because its mode of universality is not self-conscious; its mode of self-objectification is undifferentiated. Hegel describes the two-fold "determining principle" through which the good and subjectivity are brought into relation with one another in the following way:

> That is to say, in their one-sidedness, when each is bent on declining to have in it what is in it implicitly—when the good is without subjectivity

> and a determinate character, and the determining principle, subjectivity, is without what is implicit within it—and when both build themselves into independent totalities, they are annulled and thereby reduced to moments, to moments of the concept which becomes manifest as their unity and, having acquired reality precisely through this positing of its moments, is now present as Idea—as the concept which has matured its determinations to reality and at the same time is present in their identity as their implicit essence. (Hegel, 1967: Remark to §141)

At the same time, the abstract nature of both of these moments—the universal good and particular subjectivity—is drawn out precisely because they are themselves moments of determinate or substantial freedom or as moments of Ethical Life. Hegel articulates the development of freedom in the following way: Freedom is first embodied in terms of the immediacy of right. This immediate right is then sublimated, by right's self-reflection, into self-consciousness as the good. In the third stage, the subjectivity of the first two moments, namely, in the immediacy of right and in the self-consciousness of the good, are brought into a dialectical relationship with the objectivity inherent in these subjective moments, namely, in the form of right and good. This third stage is Ethical Life, which is the truth of both subjective and universal or objective moments of right: "Ethical Life is a subjective disposition but one imbued with what is inherently right" (Hegel, 1967: Remark to §141). It is important to note that Hegel distinguishes Ethical Life from Morality by arguing that in Ethical Life both the objective and subjective moments of freedom are brought together (Hegel, 1967: §141). What Hegel means here is that both sides of freedom are rendered determinate by being brought into relation to one another. I want to explore the nature of this determinacy as it relates to Hegel's idea of substantive freedom. Specifically, I want to bring this Idea to bear on our preceding discussion on the relationship between human capacity, practice, and its institutional context. Freedom, Hegel argues, is substantiated through a two-fold principle of determination through which subjective and objective freedom are actualized:

> For the good as the substantial universal of freedom, but as something still abstract, there are therefore required determinate characteristics of some sort and the principle for determining them through a principle identical with the good itself. For conscience similarly, as the purely abstract principle of determination, it is required that its decisions shall be universal and objective. If good and conscience are each kept abstract

> and thereby elevated to independent totalities, then both become the indeterminate which ought to be determined. (Hegel, 1967: §141)

This reflexive actualization is not possible in the realm of morality precisely because subjective freedom and objective freedom are kept distinct and thus remain abstract (Hegel, 1967: §140–41). Thus, subjective morality requires an ethical-political structure for its actualization. This is Ricoeur's argument as well. It is this two-fold figuration of the good life, considered in both its universal and particular guises that I wish to trace here.

Hegel's critique of morality is that because it resides solely in the will, it is one-sided. In morality, the good is conceived as something distinct from the particular will, as something *abstract*. Because the (Kantian) sphere of morality privileges the self-determination of the will such that the maxim of the will ought not to be contradictory, the determination of specific duties is not possible (Hegel, 1967: §135). Thus, the sphere of determination is transcended for the sphere of the unconditioned (Hegel, 1967: Remark to §135). And at the same time, the Kantian will has no way of sublimating these contradictions. That is to say, it has no way of actualizing its distinctions between natural necessity, or particularity, and the demand of the universal or the categorical imperative. All the moral subject can do is will freedom, but even this willing is empty precisely because the act of willing is rendered impossible. Such is the predicament of the Beautiful Soul, as developed by Hegel in the *Phenomenology of Spirit*. We need some way of mediating between subjectivity and the good such that the terms are not collapsed into one another. Freedom is the *concept* of subjectivity but we require a determining principle that Hegel describes in terms of "ethical necessity" to *realize the concept of freedom in a way that is adequate to the concept itself* (Hegel, 1967: Remark to §152)[7]:

> The right of individuals to be subjectively destined to freedom is fulfilled when they belong to an actual ethical order, because their conviction of their freedom finds its truth in such an objective order, and it is in an ethical order that they are actually in possession of their own essence or their own inner universality. (Hegel, 1967: §153)

Another way of saying this is that the moral subject requires the institutions of Ethical Life for its actualization as a universal will. The universal will is actualized within a system of ethical relations made possible by the state and its institutions. That is to say, the universality of moral subjectivity is actualized within a system of ethical necessity comprised of society's institutions. Without this mediation, Hegel argues, subjectivity remains distinct from universality. It is for this reason that the subject of morality, whose concept is freedom, cannot actualize this freedom. The moral subject has no basis on which to act, because it cannot render itself determinate without contradiction. That is to say, the form of subjectivity found in morality seeks to find the ground or justification within itself: this subjectivity seeks to both embody or actualize the good and also to be the sole judge of the good. Here, the two sides of the good, namely, acting and judging, are performed by one and the same subject in her infinite self-reflection (Hegel, 1967: Remark to §139). But because both the foundation and the end of action are to be found in the subject's infinite self-reflection, both the self and the action are negated:

> The culminating form of this subjectivity which conceives itself as the final court of appeal—our topic here—can be nothing except what was implicitly present already in its preceding forms, namely, subjectivity knowing itself as the arbiter and judge of truth, right, and duty. It consists within in this, *that it knows the objective ethical principles, but fails in self-forgetfulness and self-renunciation to immerse itself in their seriousness and to base action upon them.* Although related to them, it holds itself aloof from them and knows itself as that which wills and decides thus, although it may equally well will and decide to do otherwise. (Hegel, 1967: Remark to §140, my emphasis)

What this subjectivity fails to realize, however, is that it requires a structure of determination in order to make itself the author of its actions. That is to say, the subject of morality cannot will the universal because it stands in opposition to the universal, and thereby becomes merely particular. The realization of freedom in a way that is adequate to the concept of subjective freedom requires the mediation of an objective ethical order through which the subjective and objective moments are brought together.

Hegel argues that it is in fact the case that moral self-consciousness has attained self-reflection and so can be said to possess infinite subjectivity. But this self-reflection disintegrates and becomes something like solipsism precisely because the moral subject tries to determine the objective grounds of action from within itself:

> This type of subjectivism not merely substitutes a void for the whole content of ethics, rights, duties, and laws—and so is evil, in fact evil through and through and universally—but in addition its form is a subjective

> void, i.e. it knows itself as this countless void and in this knowledge knows itself as absolute. (Hegel, 1967: Remark to §140)

From this point of view, the specification of duties is impossible. Here, both the universality of duty and the universality of the subject are conflated and thereby undermined and thus, there is no context in which right may be articulated.

The self cannot ground itself precisely because it cannot recognize itself in abstract duty. Hegel's argument is that the subject is not to be found in the realm of morality; rather, universal subjectivity makes its first appearance in the realm of need and its modes of satisfaction. At first, it is this particularity of need and its satisfaction that comprises the universal moment. Universal subjectivity continues to be determined by the principle of Objective Mind; however, at the stage of civil society we are concerned with the development of the universal as it appears in the sphere of particularity:

> Individuals in their capacity as burghers in this state are private persons whose end is their own interest. This end is *mediated* through the universal which thus *appears* as a *means* to its realization. Consequently, individuals can attain their ends only in so far as they themselves determine their knowing, willing, and acting in a universal way and make themselves links in this chain of social connexions. (Hegel, 1967: §187, original emphasis)

In the context of particularity, however, the individual is related to society through *necessity* only, through her particular needs, and thus the unity of the whole and the part is not yet based upon freedom (Hegel, 1967: §186). That is to say, this purely natural necessity has not yet been sublimated into an ethical necessity. Yet, even here, Hegel argues, we can discern the figuration of objective mind:

> In these circumstances, the interest of the Idea—an interest of which these members of civil society are as such unconscious—lies in the process whereby their singularity and their natural condition are raised, as a result of the necessities imposed by nature as well as of arbitrary needs, to formal freedom and formal universality of knowing and willing—*the process whereby their particularity is educated up to subjectivity*. (Hegel, 1967: Remark to §187, my emphasis)

That is to say, individuals' accidental relationship to one another arising from the network of needs is raised to the level of formal subjectivity, insofar as meeting one's own needs requires the coordination and recognition of others.

Thus, subjectivity first arises through the socialized attempt at dealing with the proliferation of need. Acting in accordance with one another allows us the first glimpse at universal freedom. However, this freedom whose basis is the satisfaction of need is still not genuine universality. This is so because it is the satisfaction of need that is the immediate impetus for coordinated social action. There are two points worth noting here with respect to Hegel's characterization of the nature of the universal and coordinated action as it applies to his conception of subjectivity. First, subjectivity is determined through the objective Idea. It is by virtue of this figuration that individuals are raised beyond the level of need and can be said to be knowing and willing subjects. Thus, the universal moment is implicit even in extremely particularity. It is through this principle of figuration that "particularity is educated up to subjectivity" (Hegel, 1967: §187). The nature of this ethical relation is becoming clear: genuine universality is only possible when natural necessity is sublimated and the unity tying members of the state together is ethical rather than natural. The first instance of this is found in the corporation. Hegel argues that the corporation in many ways fulfills the same ethical functions as the family on the level of civil society insofar as it is responsible for the protection of its members from the effects of natural contingency through the redistribution of wealth and through the provision of education to its members (Hegel, 1967: §251). Moreover, the very actualization of particular right requires that the abstract articulation of this right be structured so as to reflect the ethical obligations underlying these rights. Hegel's conception of mind refers precisely to this inward figuration.

The movement from family to civil society is first observed through the emergence of the form of right. Hegel's argument will be that "receiving one's share," that is, receiving goods in terms of education and welfare, is a necessary counterpart to "articulating one's right.". Thus, as long as rights language remains abstract, that is, differentiated from the good, from a concern with just distribution, it cannot be realized. Thus rights language is necessarily contextualized within an obligatory context. Just as the self-subsistent individual necessarily arises from the context of the family, it continues to rely on those very institutions first articulated in the family, namely education and private property, for its very differentiation from the family. Thus, dissolution of the self-subsistent family does not imply the complete dissolution of the institution of the family, nor does it result in the formation of the completely self-subsistent individual.

While the self-subsistent individual can no longer ground itself solely in the family, this subjectivity continues to rely on the institutions of education, welfare, and private property. It is precisely through the education provided by the family and the dissolution of commonly held property through inheritance into private property that the particular or differentiated individual is first articulated (Hegel, 1967: §175–178). This form of individuality is not to be found in the immediacy of the family. But the membership that is felt in the family requires a new civic-cultural context for its determination. This membership based on feeling is ethical in nature precisely because the substantiality of the family is based upon love (Hegel, 1967: §158). Moreover, the ethical nature of the family is in fact articulated in terms of each of its ethical aspects. Thus, the family is itself differentiated even within its immediacy, which is why it is an *ethical* institution. *That is to say, the very particularity enjoyed by the individual in the Family is owed to the differentiated nature of the family*. Even at the level of feeling and immediate attachment of the family, we can discern the differentiation within this immediacy both in terms of capital and education (Hegel, 1967: §170–§181). Hegel explicates the workings of the institutions of property and education in the ethical development of the ethical institutions of the family, the corporation, and the state. Each of these institutions develop from their immediacy and are differentiated and brought into relation with the other institutions through the workings of the distribution of property and through education which are, in turn, structured through the interrelations between these institutions. Thus, the differentiated, autonomous subject whose workings we observe in civil society is itself structured by the institutions of Ethical Life, whose interdependency Hegel refers to in terms of an "ethical necessity."

Hegel's argument is that the individual in civil society *cannot exist as such unless a network of obligations makes it possible for him to differentiate his labor precisely through the imposition of limits on production and the mediation of need.* Unless this mediation of need and inequality is possible, there is no individuality. This is so because without this civic mediation, there is no possibility for the individual's self-recognition as a worker or as a citizen:

> In the Corporation, the family has its stable basis in the sense that its livelihood is assured there, conditionally upon capability, i.e. it has a stable capital. In addition, this nexus of capability and livelihood is a *recognized* fact, with the result that the Corporation member needs no external marks beyond his own membership as evidence of his skill and his regular income and subsistence, i.e., *as evidence that he is a somebody*. (Hegel, 1967: §253, original emphasis on "*recognized*," my emphasis thereafter)

By being freed from the dehumanizing effects of such contingencies, the individual is thus related to the universal or the state precisely through her cooperation and participation in the institutionalized practices embodying social obligation:

> It is also recognized that he belongs to a whole which is itself an organ of the entire society, and that he is actively concerned in promoting the *comparatively disinterested end of this whole. Thus he commands the respect due to one in his social position* (Hegel, 1967: §253, my emphasis).

Hegel's explicit argument is that there can be no recognition of individuality outside of a network of social obligation which serves to protect the individual from the interrelated effects of both poverty and unlimited consumption. Civic recognition, then, entails the recognition of citizens' differential circumstances and their membership in a common ethical community. Individuality, then, is only possible if appetitive desire or the universal indifference characterizing the universal particularity in civil society is structured by institutional life.

Returning once again to the family, then, we can see that the familied subject is differentiated insofar as the family is itself differentiated by virtue of its interrelationships with the corporation or the workers' guilds and the state: it is through these interrelationships that the family forms its relationships to its property and to the education of its children. Thus, when Hegel speaks of the dissolution of the family, this dissolution is not absolute; the institution of the family is itself integral to the working of Ethical Life. What dissolves is the self-subsistence of the family or the family's alienation from its civic grounding. Thus, Hegel refers to the dissolution of the family as an "ethical dissolution" in which the family is returned to its civic figuration:

> The *ethical dissolution* of the family consists in this, that once the children have been educated to freedom of personality, and have come of age, they become recognized as persons in the eyes of the law and as capable of holding free property of their own and founding families of their own . . . (Hegel, 1967: §177, my emphasis)

The internal differentiation of the family is in fact the result of the broader figuration of societal practices and institutions. This is so because the family itself is a central social institution through which the state organizes and recognizes itself. Thus, we are required to rework the cultural context for these practices of care such that they become civic practices of obligation. An instance of this is found in the corporation, which in many ways functions as the family in the sphere of civil society.

The absolute dissolution of the self-subsistent family would in fact correspond to its separation from its civic grounding. Such a dissolution, in turn, corresponds to the formation of self-sufficient universal undifferentiated particularity. It is precisely the self-sufficiency of particularity, Hegel argues, that leads, on the level of civil society, to severe inequality and the proliferation of need, and on the level of morality, to evil. Both, I argue, are fascist expressions of the alienated self. Hegel's argument is that both the extreme poverty marking the immediate stage of civil society and the evil characterizing the purely moral have the same structure, namely, undifferentiated particularity. This undifferentiated particularity is itself a moment or a manifestation of universality, but in such a way that the universal remains external to the particular. What both of these moments have in common is that they fall outside of institutional life. That is to say, both are modes of individualism that refuse society. Unstructured particularity, or universal particularity, as it is manifested in the self-sufficient particularity of civil society and the self-determining will of morality, then, are expressions of fascistic subjectivity, at both its "macro" and "micro" levels. The Hegelian argument is that fascism is always articulated at both the societal-political level and at the level of individual psychic life as it is manifested in the family and in consumption practices (O'Neill, 2004). Fascism, for Hegel, is nothing other than unmediated universal necessity whose truth is slavery. In both morality and in civil society, modes of slavery are presented as modes of freedom. Hegel's response to fascism, then, must be understood in terms of his two-fold figuration of individual and society. That is to say, Hegel's response to fascism is to argue that the self is unrecognizable outside of an institutional context that works to differentiate or to structure universal particularity.

What Hegel argues is that obligation is itself differentiated in nature; that is to say, we transform difference due to contingency into ethical difference, or what Hegel refers to as recognition. For recognition to be possible, we must be able to mediate appetitive desire. Thus, recognition is a culturally and institutionally grounded concept. That is to say, it makes possible differentiated individuality thanks to its civic figuration structured nature. The same is true of need and inequality. Thus, differentiated individuality is not the same as individualism. For Hegel, individualism is in fact undifferentiated particularity. For, as we have already seen, Hegel argues that subjectivity, or what is the same thing, differentiated individuality, is the product of a cultural *Bildung* that is practiced and realized within society's institutions.

The corporation is that body through which the particularity of need is returned to its universal context; that is to say, the contingency attaching to need is sublimated in terms of social obligation. It is only when contingency is in this way sublimated that the individual is recognized as such:

> The so-called "natural" right of exercising one's skill and thereby earning what there is to be earned is restricted within the Corporation only in so far as *it is therein made rational instead of natural.* That is to say, it becomes freed from personal opinion and contingency, saved from endangering either the individual workman or others, recognized, guaranteed, and at the same time elevated to conscious effort for a common end. (Hegel, 1967: Remark to §253, my emphasis)

It is within the corporation that the particularity of need and its modes of satisfaction are brought together. *Another way of saying this is that the desire for recognition is in fact first formulated in this institutional context.* Thus, both right and need are substantialized within the corporation. Outside of the social/class status recognition afforded by the corporation, the isolated worker is continually exposed to the contingencies of free-range capitalism and the corresponding inequalities in health and well-being:

> Unless he is a member of an authorized Corporation (And it is only by being authorized that an association becomes a Corporation) an individual is without rank or dignity, his isolation reduces his business to mere self-seeking, and his livelihood and satisfaction become insecure. Consequently, he has to try to gain recognition for himself by giving external proofs of success in his business, and to these proofs no limits can be set. (Hegel, 1967: Remark to §253)

Thus, Hegel's project cannot be about totalization, when it is concerned at each level with ethical differentiation. Hegel's argument is that both the substance and the mediation of this differentiation is made possible through institutions of cultural obligation. That is to say, both the differentiation of the individual, namely, the development of the individual with rights, and the universal nature of this right, that is, the assertion of a right as a claim on the state, is made intelligible through the social institutions articulated by Hegel.

Another way of saying this is that the recognition politics underlying rights claims presuppose a redistributive framework embodied in society's institutions. Thus, Hegel's explication of the differentiated subject maps onto his explication of the inward differentiation of the state as such. As we saw with Ricoeur, what a teleological narrative of the state shows is that there is no necessary opposition between the individual and the state. Both individual and state are developed through their institutionalized modes. It is only when we conflate the twofold differentiation of individual and state that we can arrive at the idea of the Monarch or absolute subjectivity.

The Hegelian Conception of Civic Duty

Where the Kantian deontological tradition articulates the infinite freedom of universal subjectivity, Hegel's argument is that this universal subjectivity is actually a reflexive identity articulated in objective mind, or the state. He argues that the concept of right is itself unintelligible unless it is understood in terms of those institutions through which citizens are able to recognize, legally and politically, their right in terms of their identity as citizens. That is to say, the concept of right must be actualized in order for it to be meaningful to citizens. The actualization of right in turn refers to the institutions of society, namely the family and the corporation or worker's guilds:

> Now in the family and civil society they acquire their right in the first of these respects directly and in the second indirectly, in that (i) they find their substantive self-consciousness in social institutions which are the universal implicit in their particular interests, and (ii) the Corporation supplies them with an occupation and an activity directed on a universal end. (Hegel, 1967: §264)

The concept of right is for Hegel to be understood as the actualization of the citizen body. If right is itself structured, so too is the subject, insofar as the two are inherently connected for both Kant and Hegel. Where Kant attempts to ground right in abstract duty, Hegel argues that because right is structured in objective mind, that is to say the state, it is in the state that duty or obligation is actualized.

Right, insofar as it articulates the subject, requires a state-institutional context. "Ethical Life is a subjective disposition, but one imbued with what is inherently right" (Hegel, 1967: Remark to §141). What is "inherently right" is for Hegel that which is both necessary and objective. That is to say, the objective ground of right is not to be found within the subjective will because this will cannot actualize itself. Hegel brings together subjective and objective freedom by explicating the conceptual movement of right. Hegel, then, is not concerned with empirical subjectivity but rather with the concept of citizenship itself, insofar as the citizen is to be understood conceptually in relation to the state (Houlgate, 2001). Moreover, because Hegel is concerned with the *concept* of citizenship, his explication is focused on those institutions through which citizenship is engendered. Another way, then, of thinking about Hegel's concept of the self-conscious and self-actualizing monarch, then, is to think instead about the way in which for Hegel, the state is the realm through which self-conscious subjectivity is made possible. This becomes clear when Hegel argues that what distinguishes Ethical Life from morality is that while both are manifestations of infinite subjectivity, the former attains self-consciousness while the latter lacks the foundation for the development for the reflexive self (Hegel, 1967: §142–144). Such a foundation is made possible by society's legal-institutional context. Duty, then, appears to be external to subjectivity; it is related to a substantial-rational end, that is, the state. Right, on the other hand, expresses the particularity, the freedom, of subjectivity. Right and duty, therefore, appear to refer to distinct ethical-practical realms. Right and duty, citizen and state, are brought together through the ethical inter-relationships of the institutional moments of Ethical Life through which the state becomes objective to itself and subjectivity realizes its freedom in its relationship to this reflexive objectivity: "In the state, as something ethical, as the inter-penetration of the substantive and the particular, my obligation to what is substantive is at the same time the embodiment of my particular freedom" (Hegel, 1967: Remark to §261).

What Hegel means here is that when the citizen makes a claim to a right, what she is in fact doing is making a claim on the state's obligation to protect or to endorse her right. Thus, Hegel understands subjective freedom primarily in terms of the status of citizenship. The status of citizenship has a twofold meaning, then. That is to say that the subject actualizes her universality in the state, her freedom gains meaningful determinacy through her status as a citizen of the state. Unless the status of citizenship is specified or determined in this way, the universal status of right remains entirely abstract (Hegel, 1967: §155). It is because this particularity is missing in the abstract civil right and morality and thus right remains formal in those contexts. That is to say, right in those contexts is not substantial precisely because it lacks the moment of differentiation. Obligation or duty, then, cannot be understood outside of this differentiation that is made possible through a language of universal determination made possible by the state and its institutions. That differentiation is at the heart of both right and duty is made apparent through the working of social institutions. This is what Hegel means when he says that mind cannot know itself unless this internal differentiation through its moments is possible. Moreover, this internal differentiation becomes objective precisely because particularity exhibits its differentiation through the mediating influence of society's institutions, namely, the family, civil society, and finally the constitution of the state (Hegel, 1967: §157). Ethical necessity, then, is to be understood fundamentally as a system of obligation. It is institutionalized obligation that makes possible the differentiation or the reflexive self-knowledge of the universal.

It is through the determination of the objective and subjective aspects of freedom are understood as moments within a system of ethical necessity in which they are actualized through their mediation within this system:

> That is to say, in their one-sidedness, when each is bent on declining to have in it what is in it implicitly—when each is bent on declining to have in it what is in it implicitly—when the good is without subjectivity and a determinate character, and the determining principle, subjectivity, is without what is implicit within it—and when both build themselves into independent totalities, they are annulled and thereby reduced to moments, to moments of the concept which becomes manifest as their unity and, having acquired reality precisely through this positing of its moments, is now present as Idea . . . (Hegel, 1967: remark to §141)

This twofold determination between individual and society through the establishment of a common cultural-political commons is the work of the institutions of the state. The negation of the realms of absolute right and absolute duty such that they are brought together in ethical necessity is accomplished through society's institutions.

The otherness of individual and state are superseded through the workings of these institutions. The ethical necessity at the heart of infinite subjectivity, then, is not to be found in a particular subject, that is, in the Monarch, but in Hegel's teleological conception of the state. It is through these institutions that Ethical Life achieves objectivity, or what is the same thing, substantiality. Through civic institutions, individuals in their particular ends are reconciled with the public good and it is through the institutions of the public good that their individuality is both developed and preserved. This objectivity has a two-fold determination, namely that of particularity and ideality; it is precisely the interrelation of these terms that Hegel argues constitutes right. Right, then is understood teleologically.

That is to say, right is structured through the institutions of the state, which serve to articulate the common ends of the citizen and state:

> These institutions are the components of the constitution (i.e. of rationality developed and actualized) in the sphere of particularity. They are, therefore, the firm foundation not only of the state but also of the citizen's trust in it and sentiment towards it. *They are the pillars of public freedom since in them particular freedom is realized and rational, and therefore there is implicitly present even in them the union of freedom and necessity.* (Hegel, 1967: §265, my emphasis)

Such a teleological reading refocuses our attention on Hegel's politicization of Ethical Life within the state and its institutions. A teleological reading of the relationship between the state, Ethical Life, and the citizen has the further advantage of drawing out the implicit rationality or universality of each of these moments of the ethical system. It is this implicit rationality that Hegel sets out to explicate systematically.

Thus, the good and subjectivity are brought together in a double-determination in which their abstract nature is transcended. That is to say, both the good and subjectivity are only actualized in terms of their mediation. Note the twofold play of action:

> Ethical Life is the Idea of freedom that on the one hand it is the good become alive—the good endowed in self-consciousness with knowing and willing and actualized by self-conscious action—*while on the other hand self-consciousness has in the ethical realm its absolute foundation and the end which actuates its effort.* Thus Ethical Life is the concept of freedom developed into the existing world and the nature of self-consciousness. (Hegel, 1967: §142, my emphasis)

Here, Hegel's argument is that there can be no action, no actuality, and no subjectivity in morality and civil life because they lack those institutions that make the twofold determination/figuration necessary for self-consciousness. Self-consciousness, then, is articulated in the twofold movement of duty and right. This point of reflection is made possible by society's institutions, which is missing in the spheres of purely personal rights and purely moral self-consciousness. In these contexts, rights cannot be actualized because the relationship between right and duty stands outside the embodiment of right in the state, that is say, is external to the system of ethical necessity. Thus, there is only a formal identity between right and duty between isolated individuals detached from the state. Thus, rights owe their content to the rational state. The proliferation of rights is itself only possible from within the state and its institutions. Because rights owe their content to this substantive basis, we can say that they are in fact necessitated by this substantive foundation. This substantive basis is the good, through the ethical relation that has been actualized.

Thus it is from the perspective of the good that the relationship between right and duty is to be understood. The particularity of the content of rights does not result in the atomism of individualism precisely because the content of right can only be determined from within the state. This is what Hegel means when he says that particularity must always be returned to its universal foundation:

> The *isolated* individual, so far as his duties are concerned, is in subjection; but as a member of *civil society* he finds in fulfilling his duties to it protection of his person and property, regard for his private welfare, the satisfaction of the depths of his being, the consciousness and feeling of himself as a member of the whole; and, in so far as he completely fulfils his duties by performing tasks and services for the *state*, he is upheld and preserved. (Hegel, 1967: Remark to §261, original emphasis)

It is only to the abstract or indeterminate subjectivity that duty is felt as an external coercion and thus as a limitation on its freedom. As we have seen, however, it is through duty that the indeterminate subjectivity of civil society is freed from the contingencies of hunger, unemployment, and the unmediated competition of the market. Similarly, the abstract subjectivity of the moral realm finds its freedom in its capacity to determine its action, and thus, by actualizing itself, to become objective to itself: "In duty the individual acquires his substantive freedom" (Hegel, 1967: §149).

Here, indeterminacy is confused with universality, when the universal is in fact a structured concept through which particularity is educated in accordance with the structure of freedom. That is to say, the actualized ethical order that is the state is made possible through a process of cultural education, or Bildung. Hegel's understanding of Bildung is that process of objectification through which the part and whole are structured reflexively, that to say, self-consciously. *This self-conscious or reflexive actualization of the state is made possible through a teleological investigation of its moments*:

> Since the state appears as a result in the advance of the philosophic concept through displaying itself as the true ground [of the earlier phases],

> that show of mediation is now cancelled and the state has become directly present before us. *Actually, therefore, the state as such not so much the result as the beginning.* (Hegel, 1967: Remark to §256, my emphasis)

We have argued that the *Philosophy of Right* must be read teleologically. A teleological investigation of right, or the concept of freedom, is concerned primarily with the conditions for the actualization of freedom, and thus with the figuration of freedom:

> It is within the state that the family is first developed into civil society, *and it is the Idea of the state itself which disrupts itself into these two moments.* Through the development of civil society, the substance of Ethical Life acquires its infinite form, which contains in itself these two moments: (1) infinite differentiation down to the inward experience of independent self-consciousness and (2) *the form of universality involved in education, the form of thought whereby mind is objective and actual to itself as an organic totality in laws and institutions which are its will in terms of thought.* (Hegel, 1967: Remark to §256, my emphasis)

Thus, the figuration of freedom, mind made objective, is understood pedagogically, that is, in terms of the work of the mediating institutions of the state.

Aristotle Contra Hobbes: Ewald's Sociological Interpretation of the Norm of Reciprocity

In Chapter 2, we argued that the articulation of the categorical imperative requires, for its very articulation, a recognition of the fact of inequality. This was demonstrated through the reflexive mirroring by Ricoeur of the norm. Thus far, we have been developing the philosophical context of our argument, namely, that the respect owed to persons may only be realized within the context of redistributive justice. In this way, we have been challenging the Hobbesian solution to the dilemma posed by the state of nature, i.e., to replace the redistributive context of reciprocity, that would require a common measure, with the form or the law of reciprocity, in which the judgment each makes about himself and with others may be regulated through the principle of equality. In Hobbes the *phronēsis* underlying proportional equality gives way to equality as the rule of justice (Ewald, 1987: 104). Because equality becomes the very rule of justice, that is to say, becomes synonymous with law, individualism is thereby preserved. This is so because once equality takes the form of justice, social relationship is transformed into pure relationship (Ewald, 1987: 103). It is the very form of the law of reciprocity that counts. Hobbes is in this way able to preserve both the individualism of judgment characterizing the state of nature and its social formulation through the law of the Gospel: "Do not that to another, which you wouldest not have done to yourself" (Hobbes, 1947: 103). Reciprocity constitutes the form of this commandment. Because the commandment has the form of reciprocity, there arises a new objectivity of judgment, which resides in the law of equality itself. Because the very objectivity of judgment about oneself and about others resides in the principle of equality, the fact of inequality vanishes. The very conditions of objectivity, of judgment, are only possible through the principle of equality. As we shall see, the limits of social knowledge are inscribed therein, precisely because the objectivity of judgment is circumscribed within the law itself.

The principle of equality functions as the rule of justice in the state of nature in the following way. The propositional form of "do not do unto others. . ." may be agreed upon by all without thereby imposing a particularized judgment upon anyone. This is so because the force of the law resides in the form of reciprocity itself:

> How could a common judgment be possible that was domination of some particular judgment? The proposition: "do not do unto others . . .", which has immediately the legal form of a commandment, testifies to this possibility and indicates its form and style: there, one has a rule whose characteristic is to be able to be imposed on all without imposing anything in particular on anyone. What is it then, that gives it its power? The fact that it has no other content than to state a form: *reciprocity*. (Ewald, 1987: 103, original emphasis)

Precisely because the very form of the law is constituted by the principle of equality, the law becomes self-justifying. That is to say, the otherness of the other is negated through the very principle of equality. If the form of law is reciprocity, equality is the rule of justice. Here, then fact is conflated with law: Acting as if an-other is equal to myself immediately negates the question as to whether or not the other is in fact equal or unequal to me. Equality no longer needs to be configured, for it is presupposed (Ewald, 1987: 103). Because the principle of equality constitutes the rule of justice, self-other knowledge is rendered unnecessary. Ewald notes that

Hobbes provides two justifications for rendering this kind of socio-knowledge unnecessary; the first is factual, the second, legal. The factual reason consists in this, that the differences between men are never so great as to prevent each from being able to kill the other. And even if natural differences between men did exist, no one would accept this fact of inequality because there is no measure with which to render this inequality objective (Ewald, 1987: 104).

In this way, the very objectivity afforded by law works to separate the rational aspect of law from its factual aspect:

> Hence the formula keeps coming up, that men must "*regard themselves as being (and not are) naturally equal to each other*". The objectivity thus conquered derives less from a finding of what is than from a pure decision: one will act *as if*. Equality is thus very exactly posited as a *rule of judgment*. What characterizes it is the reintroduction into legal and political judgment of the objectivity that the consideration of nature is no longer capable of supplying. (Ewald, 1987: 104, original emphasis)

However, if the rule of justice is determined by the principle of equality, this equality cannot be said to constitute the conditions of objectivity, and thus of a rule of justice, precisely because it prohibits knowledge of the other by oneself and knowledge of oneself vis-à-vis others (Ewald, 1987: 104). The question of the relationship between law and social knowledge arises, however, with the founding problematic for natural law, namely, that the polis, far from being naturally given, is deeply problematic and cannot be said to constitute a coherent whole. The question of the foundation, of the origin of law, was a critique of the teleological or natural law conception of the polis and of law. However, as we have been demonstrating, classical natural law theorists grounded the laws of the polis in "prudence," in collective *phronēsis*. This means that the norm, or the state, rests upon critical (as opposed to naïve) agreement or *phronēsis*. Here, the socio-knowledge rejected by modern natural law theorists is constitutive of the law itself

It is this idea of critical agreement, or prudence, that is radicalized by modern natural law theorists. What we have tried to demonstrate the norm of reciprocity cannot be self-founding; is constituted by virtue of a civic prudence, a collective *phronēsis*, through which socio-knowledge is both produced and incorporated into law in the name of social justice. The principle of equality, as a rule of judgment, requires not the separation of law and fact, but their reconciliation by the norm. This reconciliation of fact and law occurs through the sociologization of the norm, through the investigation and development of law and social policy in response to economic and sociological facts of inequality.

Ewald develops this claim by treating the problematic nature of the state, emphasized by both classical and modern natural law theorists, in terms of socio-knowledge; that is to say, by reframing the Hobbesian worry with the founding laws of the state with the problem of social knowledge.[8] Here Foucault's influence on Ewald's methodology in the study of power and knowledge is here apparent:

> The norm has a very different epistemological structure: it is supposed to be experimental; it keeps to the facts whose differences, divergences and hierarchies it privileges. It multiplies inequalities and brings them out wherever it takes hold: inequalities in face of death, in face of sickness and knowledge etc. It does so not so much because the norm reveals a particularly inegalitarian society, but because it "unequalizes", because it is set up on the basis of its capacity to locate the most minimal disparities (Ewald, 1987: 107).

Ewald develops Foucault's emphasis on the importance of pursuing and investigating the particular histories of "subjugated knowledges" in his lectures that appear in *Power/Knowledge: Selected Interviews and other Writings* (1977: 81). Against unitary or systemized institutional hierarchies of systematized knowledge, Foucault seeks out a methodology of critical inquiry into what he refers to as "local" or "low-ranking" knowledges (Foucault, 1977: 82). In order to be drawn out, subjugated knowledges must be brought into explicit conflict with objective systems of knowledge (Foucault, 1977: 85). It is only in this way that the historical aspect of the struggles against state forms of domination through its techniques and institutions for the discipline of the body may be drawn out and genuine democracy pursued. That is to say, the mechanisms of discipline through which the operation of law in the institutions of democracy itself reproduces relations of inequality between subjugated knowledges and histories and codified systems of scientific knowledge (Foucault, 1977: 105).

Foucault refers to subjugated knowledges that serve to draw out the specifically historical aspect of struggles against the domination of knowledge systems as genealogies (Foucault, 1977: 83). Ewald emphasizes the historicity of the sociological and economic facts of inequality and thus rejects the merely formal principle of equality that prevails in the Hobbesian state of nature. While he rejects the sovereignty of law embodied in Hobbes's Leviathan, he seeks to refigure the modern natural law tradition's emphasis on the particularities of the conflict and the role of *phronēsis* in the constitution of a common measure of justice emphasized in the classical law tradition. In this way, Ewald develops the reflexivity of the law or of the state norm. The state, then, is not to be conceived in terms of the law or in terms of sovereign power, but in its capacity for its reflexive development as social law. Particular individuals, then, are not related to the sovereign or to law in terms of the disciplinary body. Understood in terms of social law, the state norm continually reconciles itself with the sociological and economic facts of inequality by understanding these facts in terms of social justice.

In order to understand the difference between Foucault's and Ewald's conception of law, we will need to understand the relationship that Foucault traces between monarchial or sovereign power and the disciplinary techniques and institutions of the modern state. Foucault conceives of modern right, or the juridical aspect of the state, in terms of a continuation of sovereign right or sovereign power. While sovereign power may have been sublimated into collective or democratic power, its underlying structure of domination has remained in tact and appears in terms of the state's disciplinary practices and institutions (Foucault, 1977: 107). Where Ewald argues for the perpetual search for the socioeconomic particularities of inequality and their reconciliation with law, or with the state norm that makes possible the production of *social knowledge*, that is to say, reinforces the reflexivity or the sociality of the law, Foucault rejects such a possibility through the opposition he articulates between hierarchalized and institutionalized knowledge systems with the "local" or "low-ranking" forms of subjugated knowledge or the sociological and economic facts of inequality (Foucalt, 1977: 82).

In Ewald's argument, the practices of repression or subjection are by definition subject to review and scrutiny by the laws of the state. Thus, he rejects Foucault's binary between "science" and "subjugated knowledge" and his argument that the disciplinary measures and techniques of the state work to reinforce sovereign right by perpetuating the domination of the sovereign through the myriad techniques and institutions of discipline found in the modern state. Whereas Ewald is concerned with the development of social knowledge in the investigation of the sociological and economic facts of inequality, Foucault's concern lies with bio-knowledge, or the disciplinary body: "Let us ask, instead, how things work at the level of on-going subjugation, at the level of those continuous and un-interrupted processes which subject our bodies, govern our gestures, dictate our behaviours, etc." (Foucault, 1977: 97).

Thus, Foucault interprets the particularity of the wills in the Hobbesian state of nature on the bodily level: these particular bodies are constituted by the power of the sovereign will or the state; in this way, they remain peripheral to the centralized power of the state. Like Hobbes, Foucault rejects the reflexive capacity of the law: law, or right, always refers to the domination of the sovereign will, even where the sovereign will has been sublimated into the collective will in the modern state. In the modern state, the power of domination by the sovereign is carried out through its coercive practices and institutions of the body. What we need, argues Foucault, is a way of studying the practices of power which discipline these peripheral bodies such that they legitimize the central power of the sovereign will or the state. Thus, Foucault is interested not in the centralized, objective forms of power, but in the specific institutions and practices of the state which subjugate the body (Foucault, 1977: 99). The regressive nature of Foucault's rejection of the reflexive capacity of the law lies in this, that his critique of punitive state practices in bodily discipline cannot be translated by the state norm into the social knowledge that arises from its investigation of its punitive practices.

While accepting the centrality of conflict in the contestation of state power, Ewald argues that the very articulation of these conflicts is not to be uncovered in the separation of the state and the socioeconomic particularities of inequality; rather, it is the reflexivity of the state norm that constitutes a context of solidarity that permits the continual search for the facts of inequality.

Ewald's method consists in mediating the *phronēsis* emphasized by classic natural law with the radical problematization of the state emphasized by modern natural law. He does so by historicizing and sociologizing the conflict central to modern natural law theory, such that the historical and social character of the conflict is not separated from the civic narratives which render these conflicts intelligible. That is to say, the actors of natural law and social law are very different: the individualism of natural law is sublimated in social law by the historical and social conflicts of groups and collectives which nevertheless submit their conflicts to civic-solidaristic modes of investigation and debate. In social law, then, "conflict and solidarity are like heads and tails" (Ewald, 1987: 106). If social law recognizes both conflict and mutual dependency, it must constitute an objectivity, a rule of justice that grounds *phronēsis* in its very self-reflexivity. To say that the law must be self-reflexive is to say that its evaluative measures have social justice as their object. Economic and sociological facts must be subject to juridification; fact must be reconciled with law through the norm's capacity to draw out the facts of inequality:

> Correlatively, the equality to which the norm refers back does not correspond to anything in reality: an average man exists no more than does a normal man. *The norm is a pure instrument of comparison, a yardstick that society equips itself with in order to follow its own transformations, and that transforms itself, and this is the point, along with the transformations that it describes.* (Ewald, 1987: 107, my emphasis).

It is by highlighting and thereby transforming the socioeconomic facts of inequality into law that the norm produces social knowledge, that is to say, constantly transforms itself and articulates itself in light of these transformations.

Hegel's Socialization of the Moral Norm: The Investigative Practices of the Modern State and the Development of Moral Personhood

In his study of the relationship between Hegel and Marx on the history and politics of state intervention, MacGregor argues that Marx's *Capital* reveals Marx's deep appreciation for the Hegelian conceptualization of the social state in the centrality he accords to the Factory Inspectorate appointed by the English government. In the course of its commissions, the inspectorate constituted a regulatory counterforce to capitalist production through their investigations on the conditions of the working classes:

> [The Factory Inspectorate] are the ones who ferret out the clues of the crime, i.e. gross exploitation of women, children and men in the factories and mills, the degradation of humanity in noisy factories filled with deadly cotton dust, the retailing of infants and children in big city flesh markets. Factory Act bureaucrats pursue the wrong-doers and bring them to justice, while ridiculing capital's powerful accomplices in the ranks of political economy. *Most important, the Inspectorate is a leading force behind the solution to overwork and unsafe working conditions in industry: factory legislation.* (MacGregor, 1996: 57, my emphasis).

In the course of its commissions, the Inspectorate documented specific aspects of working conditions under industrialism, such as child mortality, sanitation, and the length of the working day. By recording the social facts characterizing the lives of the working masses in the form of social statistics the Factory Inspectorate provided the basis for social reform.

MacGregor notes that Marx was referring to the reports made by medical commissioners and Factory Act inspectors even prior to his treatment of them in *Capital* (MacGregor, 1996: 60). In his address on "the English Factory Act," Marx notes the twofold significance of the reports produced by the Inspectorate which, precisely through their systematic production of social statistics chronicling the working class's conditions made possible what Marx referred to as "the working man's measure," which constituted a *comparative measure* of the distinct political economies of the middle class and the working class. Marx explicates the significance of this working measure in his discussion of the debate over shortening the length of the working day:

> The struggle about the legal restriction of the hours of labour raged the more fiercely since, apart from frightened avarice, it told indeed upon the great contest between the blind rule of the supply and demand laws which form the political economy of the middle class, and social production controlled by social foresight, which forms the political economy of the working class. (MacGregor, 1996: 61)

In other words, through the constitution of a working man's measure, the absence, and thus the necessity, for social regulation is made objective. The education for children and the protection of children and other vulnerable members of society from overwork arises directly out of the codification of the absence of the necessary political economy and social conditions that make this possible.

It is helpful here to recall Ewald's emphasis on the "economic and sociological positivities" that underlies solidaristic societies. Because solidarity, or civic membership, depends upon collective negotiation and deliberation upon these positivities, it is this very negotiation that centers around these economic and sociological positivities that constitution the norm:

> The norm is the *common measure* whereby, in societies based on solidarity, each can assess his value, his identity and his respective place in society. In a quasi-experimental manner, the norm solves the problem of judgment of oneself by oneself raised by Aristotle: *it confers on it the objectivity of the statistical procedures that allow its definition. The norm socializes judgment and identities* (Ewald, 1987: 108, my emphasis).

The "sociologization" of judgment results in the creation of social policy. When the norm takes the shape of a regulatory or social state, social reason is provided with social force (MacGregor, 1996: 60).

The social state's regulatory measures necessarily extend beyond its experimental or investigative practices. In this respect, MacGregor observes that government inspectors figured centrally in the Victorian state whose Hegelian account Marx provides in his description of the inspectors' role in the actual implementation of statutes relating to the regulation of the working day (MacGregor, 1996: 205). By conferring statistical objectivity to the working conditions of the masses, MacGregor argues, the Factory Inspectorate, employed by the state, constructed a "social barrier between labor and capital" (MacGregor, 1996: 217). This barrier required the regulation of free-range capitalism through the implementation of health, safety, and education standards. The implementation of the Factory Act of 1833 was made possible by the involvement of the Victorian interventionist state through which the Factory Inspectorate was administered:

> Most historians agree that the most far-reaching aspect of the 1833 legislation was the appointment of factory inspectors, "paid professionals employed by a central agency" (Roberts 1960: 103). These "guardians" of the law, Marx (1976: 349) observed, are placed "directly under the Home Secretary, and their reports are published every six months by order of Parliament. They therefore provide regular and official statistics of the voracious appetite of the capitalists for surplus labour". *Assisted by superintendents (later called sub-inspectors) the factory inspectors were responsible for supervision not only of working hours of restricted persons and the health and safety provisions applying to them, but also for implementing the education sections of the Act.* (MacGregor, 1996: 217, my emphasis).

Here MacGregor notes Marx's comment that the implementation of Labor Laws prior to 1833 had failed because of the absence of a regulatory state to ensure their enforcement. Thus, the structure of the regulatory state made possible both the critical investigations of the Factory Inspectorate in the course of which standards of health, length of working days, and educational requirements for children were established and enforced.

Thus far, we have been concerned with the narrative figuration of selfhood. We turn to Hegel at this juncture because it is Hegel who demonstrates that the self cannot recognize itself *qua* subjectivity through his narrative of spirit in the *Philosophy of Right* (1967). The argument that we are developing here is that Hegel's philosophical conceptualization of the modern social state is a demonstration of both Ricoeur's articulation of the ethical aim and Rawls' deontological defense of the distributive conception of selfhood, by drawing out the kind of civic *phronēsis* that these two traditions, traditionally thought to be opposed to one another, enables. With Rawls and Ricoeur, Hegel argues that Kantian moral self-consciousness is only able actualize its universality by virtue of its civic membership within the institutions of the state. In the course of our argument, we have developed a specifically civic-institutional practices of *phronēsis*, thereby preparing the way for our subsequent studies on another of Ricoeur's themes, namely, the *imputation* of action to agent. Hegel and Ricoeur develop a civic or public-spirited conceptualization of Aristotelian *phronēsis*. It is through the civic institutions constituting Ethical Life that the citizen recognizes him or herself as the author of his or her practices as worker, as family member, as property owner and as citizen.

Chapter 6

The De-Penalization of Responsibility: A Genealogy of Enfranchisement in the Modern Welfare State

The Civic Configuration of Capability

Rawls has taught us that full autonomy—the capability of persons to recognize themselves as having authored their own lives—is configured by the unfolding of each life trajectory, from childhood, youth, adulthood, and old age within a civic narrative of reciprocity, of trust. We have argued that the social view of morality developed by Rawls' proceduralism is a demonstration of the norm of reciprocity, or the rule of proportionality, that guides Ricoeur's ethical development of the capable subject. For it is by virtue of the norm of reciprocity, embodied in the public culture of society, that the capabilities of *one*-self for literacy, health, housing, employment, and familial, communal, and cultural membership are recognized in similar capabilities for an-*other*. In short, the social view of morality articulated by redistributive justice teaches us that the very capability for constitutive selfhood has a redistributive grounding. As Hegel has shown us, it is through the institutionalization of a civic-cultural narrative of redistribution that citizens are able to exercise self-recognition and the rights that attach to this self-recognition. It is only when we are able to control the contingencies of hunger, disease, and lack of social welfare that we can speak of the individual and his/her rights at all. Thus, individual rights are inextricably tied up with a civic narrative that articulates individuals' lives in terms of their civic membership within the institutions of the state. Because civic membership *mediates* the effects of the contingencies attaching to hunger, disease, lack of education, and unemployment by furnishing citizens with the necessary material and social basis for the development of their capabilities, these capabilities are also protected from being undermined to an unjust extent through, for example, extreme forms of criminal punishment such as disenfranchisement and the death penalty.

In this chapter, I want to apply the social view of morality advanced by Rawls, which underwrites Ricoeur's conception of a civic liberalism, to the issue of punishment in the modern civic state. We shall argue that it is the distributive interpretation of the least advantaged member, developed by Ricoeur and Rawls, that underwrites the development of the public institutions of society. It is our history of sharing advantage and disadvantage, embodied in the public culture of society, that underwrites citizens' capabilities for self-recognition—or what Ricoeur refers to as the capability for imputation—even in the context of our practices of holding someone accountable for an action that is punishable by law. For beneath the yoke of retribution lies the person who must be capable of recognizing herself as the author of her action. It is by returning the evaluative axis of practice and of capability to its redistributive grounding that we prevent the *recognitive* aspect of selfhood, or the *imputation* of an act to its author, from being equated with *retribution*, with punishment. In this way, the *capability* for imputation dear to Ricoeur is preserved. The issue of redistribution and recognition is related to the problem of punishment in the following way: through a civic narrative of redistribution, we interpret the capabilities for selfhood not only along *evaluative* lines, but along *distributive* lines. That is, we understand issues of poverty and crime along social and public lines and thus we treat these problems not along *individualized*, or to use Ricoeur's terminology, moralized lines, but rather in terms of social issues for public policy, that is, as issues of social justice.

In this chapter, I want to apply Ricoeur's theory of action to the moral and juridical conceptualizations of responsibility, as they are developed in *The Just* (2000). My aim is to elaborate upon his conceptualization of the capability for action as it is manifested in the philosophical, juridical, and political contexts of self-designation. By examining self-designation in these contexts, I want to draw out Ricoeur's claim that the question of *responsibility* is necessarily tied up with the author's very *capability* for self-designation. Now, it is the nature of this self-designation that requires clarification. Ricoeur's argument will be that the capability for self-designation, for imputation, should not become synonymous with responsibility, taken in both the philosophical and the juridical sense of the term (Ricoeur, 2000: 20). The Kantian model of imputation, as is well known, is articulated in the categorical imperative. The result is a *moralization* or a *penalization* of the very concept of responsibility such that, in the juridical realm, responsibility becomes synonymous with retribution (Ricoeur, 2000: 20).

The crux of the matter here will be to link together considerations of the civic narrative that we have been outlining through which a capable subject emerges with juridical notions of responsibility. Juridical notions of imputation must be able to take account of a broader civic narrative through which the both the subject of rights and the subject of responsibilities emerges. This civic narrative forges a dialectic between the terms of Kant's antinomy—freedom and responsibility—by broadening the very grounds of that antinomy along cultural-political lines. It is here that the social view of morality advanced by Rawls joins with Ricoeur's articulation of the ethical intention: the norm of reciprocity governing the ethics of oneself as another has a deontological figuration, because it is realized in a society of moral strangers. *A society that is not founded as an association or as a particular community is itself an ethical society.* A just society is one in which persons are not viewed as possessing, or being constituted by, their fortune or misfortune; it is a society in which the moral worth any one person may not be reduced to her fortune or to her misfortune. In a public society, what matters is not persons' associational or constitutional commitments, which they are nonetheless presumed to have, but rather the background or the public institutions of cooperation, which include every-*one* through the sharing or the distributing both fortune and misfortune, thereby extending the capability for moral authorship, for imputation, to every-one. That is, the background institutions of a political society establish a *just* distance between persons and their constitutive commitments, and thus persons themselves, so that all may affirm their membership in the public culture of society. It is in this way that we preserve the "who" of action, speech, and narration, or to borrow Kant's deontological language, the person as an end in herself.

Conversely, if we regard persons as possessing, or as being constituted by, their misfortune, we risk punishing them for their arbitrary luck. It is in this context that we turn to examine the *sociologization* of the Kantian conception of responsibility through the distribution of capabilities and disabilities in historical development of the modern welfare state. We shall consider the narrative of progressive enfranchisement traced by sociologist T.H. Marshall. Specifically, we shall in seeing how this historical narrative of the welfare state informs the Oakes test analysis used by the Supreme Court of Canada in its judgment that the political disenfranchisement of prisoners constitutes an unjust form of punishment by regressing on the historically developed norms of reciprocity from which the subject capable of imputation emerges. We shall begin, however, by considering one of the first philosophical articulations, advanced by Kant, on the relationship between the concept of responsibility and capability for imputation.

De-Penalizing Responsibility

In his essay, *The Concept of Responsibility: An Essay in Semantic Analysis*, Ricoeur traces the relationship between the well-established use of the term responsibility on the juridical plane on one hand, and the underdevelopment of the concept of responsibility on the other (Ricoeur, 2000). In the civil law tradition, responsibility is understood as the obligation to compensate for the tort inflicted through one's actions, and in the penal law tradition, responsibility is understood as the obligation to undergo punishment. In contrast to these well-established figurations of responsibility in the juridical field, a certain vagueness prevails on the conceptual plane: thanks in part to the radical extension of the concept of responsibility in a modern society that is characterized by precarity and risk, the meaning of obligation in moral philosophy has come to overflow that of compensation to such an extent that obligation has become—as in the philosophy of Emmanuel Levinas—a principle unto itself: "This overflowing runs in many directions, thanks to the chance assimilation encouraged by the polysemy of the verb 'to respond'—not just in the sense of 'to answer for' . . . but also as 'to respond to' (a question, an appeal, an injunction, etc." (Ricoeur, 2000: 13). This overflowing of the concept of obligation on the plane of moral philosophy, then, has an affinity with the juridical preoccupation with the obligation to compensate, but here the reference to the author of the action, or even to the patient of the action, seems to have become overwhelmed by the very principle of obligation itself. It is for this reason that Ricoeur prompts us to trace the juridical concept of responsibility back to another tradition in moral philosophy, one that can be said to precede the concept of responsibility. In following this trajectory, he argues, we are able to revitalize the significance of the norm of reciprocity governing the relationship between the agent and the patient of action both on the juridical plane and in the moral figuration of responsibility.

In tracing the origins of the concept of responsibility, Ricoeur argues, we must make our way even further back than the preoccupation on the moral plane with the verb "to respond"—to an injunction, a demand. The moral conception of responsibility or of obligation is itself grounded within the conception of imputation, of which the idea of obligation to offer compensation or to undergo punishment constitutes only a part. The verb "to impute" in turn figurates, or gives an account of, the moral agent capable of recognizing herself as the author of her actions. Here, Ricoeur appeals to the definition of imputation found in the dictionary. To impute is "to put on the account to someone a condemnable action, a fault, therefore an action initially marked by an obligation or a prohibition that this action infringes or breaks" (Ricoeur, 2000: 13). This definition reveals the twofold narrative structure of the verb to impute. In one direction, beginning with the prohibition against some action, passing by way of an injunction, the judgment of imputation leads to retribution, that is, the obligation to offer compensation or to undergo punishment. But this path from imputation to retribution belies the inverse trajectory, which carries us from the idea of retribution to the idea of imputation. Here, Ricoeur cites the *Dictionnaire de Trévoux*, the text referred to by the *Robert*: "to impute an action to someone is to attribute it to its actual author, to put it, so to speak, on his account and to make him responsible for it" (Ricoeur, 2000: 14). What underwrites retribution—the obligation to offer compensation or to undergo punishment, is the *attribution* of an action to an agent. This capability for attribution figurates—by way of an *account*, a *narrative*—the "who" of responsibility.

This twofold movement between retribution and attribution is articulated by Kant's conception of imputability, which is located at the conjunction between the attribution of an action to an agent, and the moral, and thus negative, tenor of that action: "The *Metaphysics of Morals* defines *Zurechnung* (*imputatio*) in the moral sense as the judgment by which someone is regarded as the orginator [*Urheber*] (*causa libera* [free cause]) of an action [*Handlung*], which is then called a 'deed' [*Tat*] (*factum*) and stands under laws" (Kant, 1996: §Ak, A, 6, 227 quoted in Ricoeur, 2000: 16). But to appreciate the aporetic relationship between the conjunction in Kant between the agent of action and the moral law of freedom, we must go as far back as the *Critique of Pure Reason*, in the third "cosmological Antinomy" of the Transcendental Dialectic:

> Thesis: Causality in accordance with laws of nature is not the only causality from which the appearances of the world can one and all be derived. To explain these appearances it is necessary to assume that there is also another causality, that of freedom.
>
> Antithesis: There is no freedom; everything in the world takes place solely in accordance with the laws of nature. (Kant, 1965: §A444-45, B472–73)

The priority of this absolute spontaneity of the cause has the effect of at once concealing and holding in abeyance the source of imputation, namely the author of the action. The concept of transcendental freedom conceals the moment of imputation to an author, and at the same time, it preserves, on the cosmological plane, the very capability for the imputation of an action to an agent: "On the one side, the concept of transcendental freedom remains empty, waiting for its connection with the moral idea of a law. On the other, it is held in reserve as the cosmological root of the ethico-juridical idea of imputability" (Ricoeur, 2000: 18). This paradox is resolved by Kant through the dialectic of the moral law of freedom, in which freedom and the law coincide, but this very coinciding eclipses the *agent* of the action altogether: "It is here that the second *Critique* introduces the decisive connection, that between freedom and law, a connection in virtue of which freedom constitutes the *ratio essendi* of the law, and the law constitutes the *ratio cognoscendi* of freedom. Only now do freedom and imputability coincide" (Ricoeur, 2000: 18, original emphasis). Once the agent of action has been eclipsed in this way, the imputation or the attribution of an action to an agent is displaced with the obligation—or the punishment—to compensate for the damage the action has caused, or to suffer the penalty. In short, the cosmological grounding of freedom, by virtue of which we are able to impute an action to an agent, undergoes "a complete moralization and juridicalization" (Ricoeur, 2000: 19).

Ricoeur seeks to "demoralize" our understanding of imputation so as to be able to think of imputation in terms of self-recognition, or the capability of an actor to recognize him/herself as the author of his/her actions:

> If the enterprise were to succeed, the concept of responsibility, which ended up by displacing that of imputability to the point of becoming its synonym and even of replacing it in contemporary vocabulary, it might again become available for new adventures, which would not exclude new attempts to remoralize responsibility, but in other ways than in terms of obligation, in the sense of a moral or internalized constraint. (Ricoeur, 2000: 20)

We prevent the moralization of responsibility by relating our evaluative practices with our distributive ones through a civic narrative in which the capabilities of citizens are articulated and preserved. It is useful to recall here Hegel's critique of the Beautiful Soul as it is articulated in the *Phenomenology of Spirit* (1977), namely, that moral subjectivity lacks any basis upon which to *act*. While the *concept* of subjectivity is freedom, it requires the institutions of ethical life for its adequation, or, to put it in Ricoeur's terms, for the actualization of the subject of rights. That is, the Beautiful Soul requires a civic institutional narrative for its very objectivity, for its actualization.

This juridification of (individual) responsibility brings us to the twofold Aristotelian concern with *proportionality*, and the practice of *phronēsis*, or wise deliberation. Judgment is not limited to the question of individual responsibility, but instead represents a meditation on the two aspects of imputation that we have been considering above, namely, imputation as capability on the one hand and imputation as responsibility on the other. If we hold, with Ricoeur, that a central aspect of imputation is the capability for action, then we are already in the domain of distributive justice. Let us recall here our argument about the distributed self, namely that the practiced or evaluative self is already *distributed*: One-self is here no longer the strictly practiced self, "one" implies "any-other"; at the same time, another refers not only to the distributed self but also to the singular, practiced self. The cultured or practiced individual, then, is so by virtue of his or her membership in a culture, in society. Thus, the strictly evaluative aspect of imputation, the result of which is always retributive, must always be mediated by the distributive aspect of imputation, such that our retributive policies should not translate into disenfranchisement, to the exclusion or to the sacrifice of members from public life. Here, we understand disenfranchisement in terms of the history of civic inclusion and exclusion developed by the classical historian of citizenship, T.H. Marshall (1992). Marshall's historical analysis in *Citizenship and Social Class* (1992) of civic exclusion and inclusion speaks to the intersection between the redistributive and the evaluative or the juridical dimensions of selfhood by tracing a trajectory that demonstrates the way in which social democracies have historically balanced their redistributive or egalitarian aims with the competitive and individualizing demands of the market. What underlies the *civil* rights characterizing the market are the *social* rights that constitute citizenship as such, that is, those rights that everyone is entitled to by virtue of their status as citizens (Marshall, 1992: 26). Ricoeur and Rawls' socialization of the Kantian principle of the inviolability of persons demonstrates that moral prescriptions only make sense from within cultural and political recognition of the public character of the capability for imputation. Our retributive policies, then, must not violate this public recognition of the capability for imputation.

T.H. Marshall's Narrative of Civic Inclusion/Exclusion

In order to understand the principle of inclusion that funds the capability for imputation, it is helpful to understand the historical trajectory Marshall traces in the development of the institution of citizenship: Civil rights developed first in the eighteenth century, followed by the development of political rights in the nineteenth century and finally social rights in the twentieth century. Civil rights are defined in terms of those rights necessary for individual freedom, such as the right to liberty, to free speech, to free association, the right to own property, and the right to access justice. The institution that corresponds to civil rights is the court of law. Political rights are comprised by the participation of members of a society in the organization and operation of the political authority. The corresponding institution to political rights is parliament. Social rights are constituted by the right to a social wage, and the corresponding right to avail oneself of those institutional resources necessary for a standard of well-being that reflects society's historical *Bildung* of civic inclusion. In addition to minimum economic security, access to public education and social services constitute the institutional presuppositions for the realization of social rights.

Prior to the industrial revolution, civil, political, and social rights were intertwined: there were no strict differentiations between the court of law, government, and legislative assembly. Furthermore, access to these institutions of justice—that is, access to social rights—was dependent upon individuals' social status. Membership in society was determined by status; differences in status were not determined from within the equality of citizenship:

> But the status was not one of citizenship in our modern sense. In feudal society status was the hallmark of class and the measure of inequality. There was no uniform collection of rights and duties with which all men—noble and common, free and serf—were endowed by virtue of their membership in society. There was, in this sense, no principle of equality of citizens to set against the principle of the equality of classes. (Marshall, 1992: 8)

Citizenship was bound up with the particular status differentiations which made up specific polities and communities.

However, with the economic reorganization resulting from the shift from feudalism to industrialization the institutions of civil, political and social rights were subject to increasing differentiation and thus may be said to have distinct historical developments. The first manifestation of a universal conception of citizenship may be traced to the development of civil rights in the eighteenth century, which coincided with industrialization and the proliferation of the economic freedoms of the individual

(Marshall, 1992: 11). In the realm of the economy, civil rights most significantly referred to the right to work and the right to freedom of occupation. By the nineteenth century, "the principle of economic freedom was accepted as axiomatic" (Marshall, 1992: 11). The principle of economic freedom defined the meaning of citizenship; that is, one's status as a citizen was fundamentally tied up with one's freedom to participate in the market. Stratification due to status, then, no longer determined the civil right to participate in the market or to own property, nor did it determine the capability for citizenship.

Civil rights, insofar as they defined the principles of the freedom of the individual, lent substance to the idea of general citizenship. Political rights were, in their inception, tied up with the universal freedom expressed in the right to participate in the market. Thus, they did not create new rights but extended the franchise to sections of the population that had heretofore been excluded. The franchise was extended in terms that were compatible with nineteenth-century capitalism; that is, group monopoly of the franchise still existed, however, it was "a monopoly which could, with some degree of plausibility be described as open and not closed" (Marshall, 1992: 12).

Access to the franchise was opened to those who could provide sufficient proof of success through their participation in the market. The expansion of the franchise in accordance with the civil freedom of the right to work meant that a citizen's *capability* for civic participation was no longer determined by his *status* but rather signaled a recognition of this capability as such: "He was free to earn, to save, to buy property or to rent a house, and to enjoy whatever political rights were attached to these economic achievement. His civil rights entitled him, and electoral reform increasingly *enabled* him, to do this" (Marshall, 1992: 12, my emphasis). Thus, political rights were, in the nineteenth century, derivative of civil rights. By the twentieth century, however, political rights were detached from their grounding in the civil rights of the individual; following the enactment of manhood suffrage in 1918, political rights were attached to the status of citizenship as such—although women did not yet enjoy the right to vote.

This grounding of political rights in the status of citizenship in the twentieth century brings us to the development of social rights. In order to understand the significance of social rights, then, it is important to note that the logic of social rights is not to be found in the freedom of the individual. The social rights attaching to membership in local communities and workers' associations gave way to the Poor Law and an infrastructure for wage regulation. The system for wage regulation was in turn weakened by the political and economic changes of industrialization and the strengthening of the civil rights attaching to the market—wage regulation contradicted the principles of freedom which allowed individuals to freely contract into work.

In this way, social rights became detached from membership in local communities and instead became dependent upon individuals' market participation. In this context, the Poor Law no longer represented a program for social security implemented into the wage structure: "The Poor Law treated the claims of the poor, not as an integral part of the rights of the citizen, but as an alternative to them—as claims which could be met only if the claimants ceased to be citizens in any true sense of the word" (Marshall, 1992: 15).

The status of full citizenship, then, depended upon individuals' capability to exempt themselves from social security measures. Marshall refers to the civic exclusion of vulnerable members of society as a result of their inability to participate in the market as the "*disability of disenfranchisement*" (Marshall, 1992: 15, my emphasis).

However, the development of public education in the nineteenth and twentieth centuries reveals the re-institutionalization of social rights within the development of citizenship itself. The development of social rights, such as access to public education, represents the historical *Bildung* of a society that recognizes the organic relationship between the civil rights of the individual citizen and the social obligations underlying the development of healthy and educated citizenry who may then exercise its civil rights.

> It was increasingly recognized that, as the nineteenth century wore on, that political democracy needed an educated electorate, and that scientific manufacture needed educated workers and technicians. The duty to improve and civilize oneself is therefore a social duty, and not merely a personal one, because the social health of a society depends upon the civilization of its members. (Marshall, 1992: 16)

The existence of public education, then, signifies re-establishment of social rights in the development of citizenship. The significance of the development the institutions of social rights cannot be explained solely by reference to the development of the free individual; the emergence and development of social rights instead speak to the institutional narrative of the reflexive development of citizenship itself.

Membership in civic institutions, Ricoeur notes, entails both the idea of *sharing* in those institutions and in receiving one's *share* in those institutions.

Civic membership implies a twofold understanding of the principle of inclusion that we have been developing with Marshall, and which Ricoeur refers to as "proportional equality" (Ricoeur, 1992: 201). Drawing together Marshall and Hegel, we can say that redistributive justice makes possible the mediation of the civil rights of the market by the social rights afforded by the status of citizenship, thus tempering the vast inequality characterizing the market through civic membership that is not premised on the market value of any individual citizen. We can say that it is this mediation by the institutions of redistributive justice that makes possible differentiated individuality, through the solicitous extension of social rights to each citizen.

In Marshall's argument, inequalities in social democracies are dynamic in one sense and not dynamic in another. By sufficiently divorcing social rights from market demands and the civil rights attaching to them through the provision of public education, health care, housing and social transfers, we have removed, or greatly reduced, the contingencies attaching to extreme poverty, such as homelessness and sickness, on the one hand, and the privileges attaching to heredity on the other (Marshall, 1992: 38). What this has meant is that the motivation for upward mobility comes not from a sense of *exclusion* from the status of citizenship that poverty has historically entailed, but from *within* the institutions of citizenship itself. Thus, for example, access to education is based upon the principles of equality, and at the same time, because education is always related to the demands of employment, it must operate on the basis of a "planned stratification" through which students are differentiated according to their abilities through legitimate standards of evaluation within the institution of education:

> The right of the citizen in this process of selection and mobility is the right to equality of opportunity. Its aim is to eliminate hereditary privilege. In essence it is the equal right to display and develop differences, or inequalities, the equal right to be recognized as unequal. In the early stages of the establishment of such a system the major effect is, of course, to reveal hidden equalities—to enable the poor boy to show that he is as good as the rich boy. *But the final outcome is a structure of unequal status fairly apportioned to unequal abilities.* The process is sometimes associated with ideas of *laissez faire* individualism, but within the education system it is a matter, not of *laissez faire*, but of planning. (Marshall, 1992: 38–39, my emphasis)

The *contingent* nature of inequality is thus transformed into a legitimate form of inequality. But it is not contingent inequality that is legitimized;

the effects of poverty and privilege are mediated through the institution of education, which then opens the way for legitimate forms of evaluation. Such evaluations, even while they take place within a context of equal opportunity, nonetheless legitimize the inequalities of ability, which is commensurable with the diverse demands of the market for professionals, technicians, service workers, and so on. Thus, opportunity becomes unequal from within those institutions, such as education, which are developed according to the principles of social justice.

Precisely because education is always linked to the qualifications required for different kinds of work, it will inevitably restrict opportunity for some groups while creating opportunity for others. That is, because individual children are subject to a process of "assimilation" according to the demands of the market, differences between children within groups become less and less significant, and the differentiation between groups gains significance. In this way, social classes are created. However, Marshall argues, all "fluid" societies develop in this way (Marshall, 1992: 39). That is, the inequalities produced through this balancing of social justice and market demands are organized according through a socioeconomic concept of "status," which itself has a twofold meaning:

> We are not aiming at absolute equality. There are limits inherent in the egalitarian movement. But the movement is a double one. It operates partly through citizenship and partly through the economic system. In both cases the aim is to remove inequalities which cannot be regarded as legitimate, but the standard of legitimacy is different. In the former it is the standard of social justice, in the latter it is social justice combined with economic necessity. (Marshall, 1992: 45)

Everyone enjoys the status of citizenship. What this means is that everyone has the right to the institutions attached to citizenship, such as the right to vote, the right to an education, and the right to health care. On the other hand, status is also a differentiated concept. While this differentiation does not apply to the substantial rights attaching to citizenship, it nonetheless develops from within the institutions of citizenship. This is so because the state and citizenship are not divorced from the market, nor is the working of the market separated from the state.

The disenfranchisement, or the sacrifice of members from public life in the civic commons, that results from the punitive interpretation of imputation represents a regression in the Marshallian account of the civic covenant. The civic narrative articulates our cultural and political responses to various guises of disenfranchisement, namely, economic, social, and political exclusion, such as the right to vote and the development of trade unions, to name a few. What we receive from this civic [hi]story of disenfranchisement is that no-one must be excluded from membership in civic-institutional life because any-one can find him or herself in a position of vulnerability in the form of mental or physical illness, unemployment, disability, poverty, and so on. The moralization of imputation is exclusionary and invokes an individualization of responsibility at the price of society. Marshall's historical narrative of our solicitous responses to vulnerability, inequality, and contingency represents the preservation of an inclusive and public-spirited society, over and against the temptation for vengeance and sacrifice. Thus, the distributive aspect of imputation must continue to inform the evaluative dimension of imputation in order for the distinction between justice and vengeance to hold.

[Dis]Enfranchisement and the Civic Narrative

Thus far, we have been discussing philosophical and juridical conceptions of imputation and responsibility as they are developed by Ricoeur in *The Just* (2000), against the backdrop of the essay that opens that collection and our own work here, namely, "Who is the Subject of Rights?" As we have seen, Ricoeur examines the philosophical development of the concept of imputability in *The Concept of Responsibility: An Essay in Semantic Analysis.* He begins his meditation on the philosophical origins of imputation with the Kantian notion of responsibility, which he argues has become synonymous with the notion of retribution, and argues that we must preserve a notion of imputation that is not necessarily reducible to retribution or punishment. As we have seen, the ability of an actor to recognize herself as the author of her actions, and the erosion of this capability by the contingencies of poverty, poor health, illiteracy, and lowered living standards, is central to Ricoeur and Rawls's sociological rendering of the Kantian principle of the inviolability of persons. In another essay from *The Just* that we shall now consider entitled "Sanction, Rehabilitation, Pardon" Ricoeur considers the implications of the pair imputation-as-retribution and imputation-as-capability on the juridical plane. He demonstrates that this capability for imputation is central to the very goals of punishment. That capability is central to a juridical analysis of imputation becomes clear in the distinction that informs trial process, namely, that between justice and vengeance.

What we shall add to this analysis is a demonstration of the pair imputability-capability by drawing out an implicit claim in Ricoeur's argument that the Kantian pairing of imputation-retribution and the subsequent juridical emphasis on punishment is realized in the *exclusion* of actors from a broader civic narrative through which they would gain self-recognition. We have appealed to Marshall's historical narrative of citizenship at this juncture precisely in order to draw out the relationship between imputation-as-capability and imputation-as-retribution. We noted above that Marshall traces the narrative of civic membership in terms of the history of disenfranchisement and enfranchisement of citizens in terms of civil, political and social rights in his *Citizenship and Social Class* (1992). His argument is that it is in terms of the development of civil, political, and social rights that the institutionalization of citizenship is to be understood. By bringing Marshall's narrative of the institutionalization of citizenship to bear on the pair imputation-capability, we will be explicating the very cultural standards through which we deliberate upon issues of justice, understood in its relation to both the development of civic capabilities and to the objectives of punishment in a free and democratic society. That is, whenever we are thinking about imputation in terms of responsibility, or respect for the law, we are at the same time referring to the law of reciprocity, to our shared capabilities for civic membership. It is important to understand the way in which the very capability for civic responsibility must remain central to the objectives of punishment precisely because the justness of the punishment loses its validity when it undermines the status of membership of those convicted of a crime. By examining the relationship between imputation and the status of citizenship in this way, we will apply the conceptual pairing of imputation-capability proposed by Ricoeur and by Rawls.

That the status of citizenship is central to understanding the twofold conceptualization of imputation becomes clear if we recall Ricoeur's conceptualization of *self-esteem* as it is developed in *Oneself as Another* (1992). We are returning to the concept of self-esteem precisely because it is what underlies the twofold development of imputability: the figure of self-respect marking the realm of morality is only realized through respect for *others*. That is, the *universality* characterizing the categorical imperative must be expressed along *institutional* lines, which we have argued is nothing other than those cultural narratives of redistribution through which the figure of self-respect, the *one-self*, becomes genuinely universal, that is, becomes *an-other*. Respect is owed not to the universal norm, but to that which the norm *figures*, namely, the respect that is owed to *others*. This universal figuration of respect is achieved through the principle of equality informing institutional life (Ricoeur, 1992: 202). Respect for the norm must extend to respect for *others*, which itself remains incomplete unless the one offering respect to the other understands him/herself *as an-other*, that is, as a *distributed* self:

> It results from this that self-respect, which on the moral plane answers to self-esteem on the ethical plane, will reach its full meaning only at the end of the third stage, when respect for the norm will have blossomed into respect for others and for "oneself as another", and when respect will be extended to anyone who has the right to expect his or her share in an equitable distribution. (Ricoeur, 1992: 203–4)

The distributed self is not a less meaningful or substantial self than the evaluative self belonging to the realm of respect, of the categorical imperative. Rather, the distributed self ought to be understood in the Marshallian sense, namely as the *progressively enfranchised* self, whose esteem is understood in terms of that trajectory of civic inclusion along civil, political, and social dimensions. Self-esteem, then, is intimately tied to citizens' membership in society. In the last analysis, then, self-esteem is not understood individualistically, but according to that civic narrative through which each citizen understands himself or herself as an-other citizen. That is, the development of the institution of citizenship is not to be understood as distinct from the rights of individual citizens. It is helpful to recall here Ricoeur's theory of narrative, in which he demonstrates that the character in a story is not to be understood apart from the process of emplotment, or through narrative.[1] In an important sense, characters are themselves plots. When we apply this to the realm of redistributive justice, we say that citizens cannot be interpreted apart from their membership in society. This membership, in turn, is instituted in terms of a just scheme of redistribution. Herein lies the project of respect: "when respect will be extended to anyone who has the right to expect his or her just share in an equitable distribution" (Ricoeur, 1992: 203). Outside of this civic membership, there is no possibility of self-respect. Self-respect, then, develops not in terms of the categorical imperative, but is narrativized through a civic *Bildung* of membership. Thus, when we *exclude* citizens from this civic *Bildung*, by denying access to health care, education, to old age and disability pensions and through criminalization, we undermine the institution of citizenship itself. Given that each of us enjoys the status of membership, we cannot undermine others' membership without violating the very principles of equality upon which our status as citizens rests. What this historical narrative of disenfranchisement and enfranchisement teaches us is that capability is fundamentally understood as the capability for the civil, political, and social participation of citizens in society. (Marshall, 1992: 8). Disenfranchisement, then, is a disabling of the civic narrative itself insofar as it is through the development of civic, political, and social capacities of citizens that modern societies have developed.

The issue of disenfranchisement, of the exclusion of persons from the civic commons, is no less pressing on the juridical plane, where the civic capability of those held responsible of an infraction or a crime ought not to be overwhelmed by the stated objective of a given punishment. That punishment is not synonymous with disenfranchisement is demonstrated by the judicial practices of deliberation, of *phronēsis* that are invoked when the constitutionality of a law is in question. The example that we will consider here is the Oakes Test, which is employed by the Supreme Court of Canada in the cases that come before it which require clarification on the issue of the justification of the limitation of the rights and freedoms enshrined in the *Charter of Human Rights and Freedoms*. The laws and corresponding punishments outlined in the Canadian Criminal Code are subject to Section 1 of the *Charter*, which states that the rights and freedoms articulated in the *Charter* are guaranteed and subject to only those limitations that can be justified in a free and democratic society. When the constitutionality of a law is called into question, the onus is on the state to prove that the sanction in question does not infringe upon citizens' rights and freedoms in a disproportionate way, that is, such that the very meaning of citizenship of the accused, and of the convicted, is thrown into serious question, thereby undermining the meaning of the punishment itself. The main purpose of the Oakes Test is to determine the *proportionality* of the law in question with respect to the objectives of the government in designing the punishment. My argument will be that what the Oakes Test aims to establish is a meaningful tie between the concerns of the state in punishing offenders, the centre of which is the concern for security and the threat of recidivism, and the rights of prisoners as rights-bearing citizens whose claims to recognition as members of society rest on the progressive enfranchisement institutionalized in documents such as the Charter.

From these preliminary considerations, we should already be able to discern the twofold play of the pair imputation-capability and imputation-retribution, namely, the way in which the concern for security and the threat of recidivism cannot be treated separately from the concern with the exclusion of inmates from meaningful membership in society. Herein lies the essence of the Oakes Test, which, when used as a tool for deliberation by judges, is exemplary of Ricoeur's Aristotelian conceptualization of practical wisdom, or *phronēsis*, where wise judgment consists in the discerning of the most appropriate means for the objective(s) in question, for the clarification of our cultural-political objectives in a given situation (Ricoeur, 1992: 175). There is a second aspect, or level, to this practical wisdom. Ricoeur's claim is that narrative theory makes possible the sublimation of action-chains into cultural-political practice (Ricoeur, 1992: 170). Ricoeur argues along Hegelian lines that wise deliberation on the conflicts over the laws of the state necessarily occurs at the institutional level:

> [. . .] by carrying the sword of conflict first to the plane of institutions, we are immediately confronted by the Hegelian plea in favor of *Sittlichkeit*, the actual and concrete morality that is held to take over from *Moralität*, from abstract morality, and which has its center of gravity in the sphere of institutions and, crowning all others, in the state. If we were to succeed in showing that the tragedy of action deploys some of its exemplary figures in this sphere, we could thereby remove the Hegelian hypothesis concerning practical wisdom instructed by conflict. *Sittlichkeit* would then no longer denote a third agency, higher than ethics and morality, but would designate one of the places in which practical wisdom is exercised, *namely, the hierarchy of institutional mediations through which practical wisdom must pass if justice is truly to deserve the name of fairness.* (Ricoeur, 1992: 250, my emphasis)

We can quarrel with Ricoeur's claim here about whether Hegel conceives *Sittlichkeit* or Ethical Life as standing over and above morality and civil society and does not instead posit a system of ethical necessity through which abstract morality and civil society gain actuality, or to use Ricoeur's terminology, practicality, through the institutions of *Sittlichkeit*, without which the state could not become objective to itself, or know itself and gain the status of mind.[2] However, what we wish to retain here is simply Ricoeur's Hegelian claim that practical wisdom plays itself out on the institutional plane. Thus, *practical* nature of *phronēsis* already has to do with the cultural-political narrative through which the *capability* for civic membership develops. Because *phronēsis* is defined in terms of the narrative of practice, the exercise of wise judgment always involves a consideration of civic membership.

Having defined *phronēsis* in its relation to a civic narrative of justice, I want to turn now to apply it specifically to the interplay of the two senses of imputation that we have been developing thus far, namely, imputation-capability and imputation-retribution. In so doing, I want to examine how practical judgment enacts a "just" separation between these two pairs of imputation. It is for this reason that I have chosen the application of the Oakes Test in judicial decision making; in determining the constitutional limits of punishment, we are skirting the delicate line between imputation-capability and imputation-retribution. It is fruitful to spend some time examining the mode of reasoning used by the judges of the Supreme Court of Canada in their application of the Oakes Test. In order to do this, I have chosen to explicate the application of the Oakes Test to *Sauvé*, the 2002 Supreme Court case which challenged s. 51(e) of the Canadian Elections Act, which stated that prison inmates serving a sentence of two years or more do not have the right to vote (*Sauvé* § 2). I have chosen *Sauvé* for my analysis of the relationship between imputation-capability and imputation-retribution because in *Sauvé, imputation-retribution and imputation-capability overlap to such a degree that the former is substituted for the latter.* The challenge in *Sauvé* is to determine whether civic exclusion through disenfranchisement is a legitimate form of punishment. Thus, the application of practical wisdom in accordance with the Oakes Test offers us an opportunity to test Ricoeur's Rawlsian claim that the heart of *phronēsis* is a concern with redistributive justice, or equality. In what follows, we shall read the Court's application of the Oakes Test in conjunction with Ricoeur's semantic analysis in *The Just* of imputation and retribution as it applies to the trajectory sanction-rehabilitation-pardon. Our emphasis here will be on the relationship between sanction and rehabilitation, where pardon figures a civic forgiveness which mediates the retributive aims of punishment. Pardon restores the capabilities of those who have undergone punishment, and is in this sense the spirit of rehabilitation. Returning once more to the Kantian problematic of self-respect, we shall be able to demonstrate Ricoeur's argument that self-respect can only be saved through recourse to the institutional plane. It is this institutionalized memory that provides us with what both Ricoeur and Rawls refer to as a "*sense of justice*" (Ricoeur, 1992: 201, note 48). Thus, it is important to keep in mind that it is the state that is required to demonstrate the justifiability of limiting fundamental rights and freedoms (Sauvé: § 90). Where the *constitutionality* of a given law is in dispute, proportionality is determined with reference to the narrative or history of the institutionalization of the respect owed to all persons. It is the exclusion from participation in civic institutions that results in the loss of dignity of citizens. In order to discern a violation of this dignity, and to thus render dignity or self-respect public and objective, we appeal to the "sense of justice" institutionalized in the Canadian Charter of Rights and Freedoms.

The Demoralization of Responsibility in the Social State

We will read *Sauvé* alongside Ricoeur's essay "Sanction, Rehabilitation, Pardon" from his collection *The Just* (2000). In so doing, we will be explicating a *just distance* between imputation-capability and imputation-retribution. The aim here is to supply Ricoeur's *semantic* differentiation of the two senses of imputation, as it is developed in "*The Concept of Responsibility*," with a redistributive context that is grounded in a historical narrative of civic membership. We shall limit our considerations to the majority's treatment of the Oakes Test and their subsequent decision. What we shall show is that there is no strict division between sanction and rehabilitation, and in fact, both of these moments are interconnected such that the last stage of the trajectory, pardon, is presupposed by the interplay of sanction and rehabilitation in the sense that the aim of punishment is not to enact vengeance upon the accused and the convicted through an exclusion of citizens from society, but rather to promote civic membership, or justice, even whilst promoting the aims of punishment.

To this end, Ricoeur argues that the distinction, or more accurately, the *distance* between justice and vengeance is presupposed in the trial process as it unfolds within the state. To recognize the accused or the convicted as an actor is to recognize him or her in terms of his or her civic membership. This civic cohesion, this public membership, cannot be undermined through the objectives of punishment without contradiction. Drawing from Hegel and Kant, and I would add, Durkheim, Ricoeur argues that sanction is owed, not just to the victim, to public opinion and to the condemned person, but to law itself:

> Kant and Hegel join hands on this point with the idea that the sanction *restores* the law. For the one as for the other, the law expresses the body of moral conventions that assures the minimal consensus of the political body, a consensus summed up in the idea of order. With regard to this order, every infraction is an attack against the law, something that upsets order. We can give a religious reversion to this idea, where one ties the law to an immutable, divinely guaranteed order. *However, a profane version has bit by bit been substituted for the idea of an offense against the gods and taken the form of a secularized idea of a disturbed social order, of a threatened public peace. In both versions of such transgression, the punishment has as its first function to mend a public disorder, in short, to reestablish order.* Hegel gives this process the dialectical form of a negation of negation. To the disorder that negates order responds the negation of disorder that reestablishes order (*Philosophy of Right*). (Ricoeur, 2000: 137, my emphasis)

Sanction restores the law insofar as the law reflects a political consensus. We recall here Rawls' Durkheimian emphasis not on individual laws but on the collective conscience (Durkheim, 1938). If sanction is owed to the law, then *sanction cannot take the place of the law, whose spirit is public and collective.* In this regard, it is important to note that on the semantic level, sanction refers not only to punishment but also to consent as it relates to *authorization.* The meaning of sanction is to be understood through its civic-public trajectory through which the wrong done to the victim may be recognized as such only by virtue of the separation of justice from vengeance.

The object of civic *phronēsis* is to determine a proportionate—a just—sanction by returning the evaluative moment of sanction to its solicitious grounding. The trial process institutes a break between justice and vengeance such that mimetic rivalry is sublimated in terms of the recognition afforded by membership in civic institutions:

> [The trial process] consists in establishing a *justice distance* between the hideous crime that unleashes private and public anger, and the punishment inflicted by the judicial institution (original emphasis). *Whereas vengeance short-circuits the two forms of suffering, that undergone by the victim and that inflicted by the avenger, the trial process gets interposed between these two, instituting the just distance we have just spoken of.* (Ricoeur, 2000: my emphasis)

It is this through this sense of public order that crimes and corresponding punishments are instituted, and thus must not be undermined but preserved in order for the victim and the accused or the convicted to be given their due recognition. It this *sense of pubic order* that sublimates the mimetic rivalry of the victim and avenger, in which there can be no responsibility, with an institutional context in which the capability for responsibility remains connected to the very idea of punishment itself. It is within the institution of the state, which is separate from civil society, which makes possible genuine recognition of individual actors. That civil society ought to be kept distinct from the state is emphasized by Hegel in his teleological conception of the state. Civil society is indeed part of the state, but is configured by the institutions of the state. This is so because the civil society is unable to differentiate itself and thus, its members cannot recognize themselves as human beings. Hegel characterizes members of civil society in terms of their undifferentiated particularity. Hegel's argument is that it is only when civil society, or the market, is brought into relation with civic institutions such as education and unions that individuality (and the corresponding human rights) develops. In Chapter 5, we argued that without the structuration of civil society and the development of genuine individuality, we attain not a differentiated society, but a fascist one. It is for this reason that the legitimate use of violence presupposes a distinction between civil society and the state. Following Marshall, however, we shall reaffirm that while the state is distinct from civil society or the market, it is not wholly divorced from it. This is a more faithful reading of what we have referred to as the principle of differentiation developed by Hegel in the *Philosophy of Right* (1967). It is because the state is characterized by this principle of differentiation that Ricoeur can characterize it as a "third party," and which consequently works to "demoralize" juridical notions of responsibility (Ricoeur, 2000: 135).

The sublimation of vengeance by justice, then, depends upon the distinction between the state and civil society. The very institutionalization of law depends upon a civic narrative, of the kind we have been attributing to Hegel, through which individuality is developed along redistributive lines. It is this redistributive narrative, the solicitous story, that renders *proportionality* as an essential measure in the rendering of human justice in questions of *individual* responsibility:

> Our third party does not find himself set in the required non-partisan position except when backed by a juridical system consisting essentially of written laws, *their inscription and conservation representing a considerable cultural acquisition thanks to which state power and judicial power are conjointly established. It is up to the laws on the one hand to define crimes, and on the other to establish a proportion between crime and punishment.* The first operation contributes to bringing about a distance from violence by making possible the use of the qualification "crime" *as applied to infractions defined and named in the most unequivocal way possible.* Furthermore, the establishment of a double scale of crimes and punishments, *on the basis of a rule of proportionality*, when added to the qualification of what counts as a crime, allows any incriminated act to be situated with the greatest possible precision, not just on the chart but also on the scale of crimes. (Ricoeur, 2000: 135, my emphasis)

It is the mediation of individual responsibility by the law of proportionality that characterizes justice. In this way, the issue of the moralization of responsibility finds its antidote in those redistributive civic institutions through which, as Hegel has argued, citizens develop the capability to recognize themselves as the authors of their conceptions of the good, or to borrow Sandel's language, to be constituted by their conception of the good.

By mediating the moralization of responsibility, the rule of proportionality makes possible the *separation* of the protagonists to the conflict. The moralization of responsibility cannot account for this separation precisely because it eclipses imputation-capability with imputation-retribution. As we have already seen, the notion of imputation as capability requires a civic context, a context that the retributive understanding of imputation overwrites. This denial of the civic context of imputation entails a denial of the separation of justice from vengeance, and thus, the separation of the parties of conflict. Imputation-as-retribution precludes civic membership by striking at the fiduciary basis of language, namely, public institution. On the other hand, it is the differentiation of actors in a conflict and the presupposition of their political and cultural-linguistic membership in a society that makes judgment meaningful:

> The gap set up by this basic unity of the hearing transforms the flesh-and-blood victim, as well as the presumed guilty party, into "parties in the trial process", into accuser and defendant. But we have not yet spoken of what is most essential. It is important that the hearing be oral and confrontational, and established as such by a known procedure imposed on every protagonist in the hearing. *In this way the hearing presents itself as a war of words: argument against argument, the arms being the same and equal on both sides.* (Ricoeur, 2000: 136, my emphasis)

Because the terms of the conflict depend upon a shared language and culture, the nature of judgment itself takes on a distributive character. It is because the very context of judgment takes place within a context of redistributive justice, that the passive recipient of judgment is recognized as an actor, as a member of society: "Finally, we must not omit underlining that the passive subject of our first approximation—someone is judged—is promoted by the hearing into an actor in the trial process" (Ricoeur, 2000: 136, original emphasis). The very notion of rehabilitation, or the reintegration of those convicted of crimes into society, is not to be understood as being externally added to the objective of punishment, but rather as arising from the very institutionalization of punishment itself.

Thus far, we argued that both imputation-retribution and imputation-capability are grounded in the redistributive institutions of society. Let us turn now to examine how the concern for proportionality figures in the Supreme Court of Canada's deliberation on questions of constitutionality. What these deliberations will reflect is Marshall's claim that civil rights or the rights of the individual have historically developed in terms of *social* rights, in concordance with the principles of social justice. Thus, the right to vote, which is a constitutional right, and thus applies to *each* citizen, cannot be denied to some citizens without the public culture of society being undermined. What is wrong with the idea that a constitutional or civic right can be denied to some class of individuals is that, in effect, it reframes the question of civic membership in terms of individual responsibility, i.e., it moralizes the very idea of citizenship.

Sauvé Versus *Canada*

Sauvé challenged Section 51(e) of *Canada's Elections Act*, which denies the right to vote to "[e]very person who is imprisoned in a correctional institution serving a sentence of two years or more" (quoted from *Sauvé* headnote). The constitutional basis of the challenge to Section 51(e) of the *Canada's Elections Act* is that the Act infringes on the democratic rights of citizens expressed in Section 3 of the *Charter*, which protects the right to vote and the equality provisions expressed in Section 15(1) of the *Charter*. These constitutional infringements could not be saved under Section 1 of the *Charter*, which states that all guaranteed rights and freedoms are subject to limitations that can be shown to be consistent with the values and aims of a free and democratic society.

Let us briefly describe the two-part analysis that constitutes the Oakes Test before considering its application by the government in *Sauvé*. In the first step of the analysis, the government is required to identify and, if necessary, clarify, the objectives of the government in limiting a constitutional right (*Sauvé*: § 20). Having identified its objectives, the government is then required to deliberate on the proportionality of the law through a threefold analysis. In the first stage of the proportionality test, the crown must be able to discern a *rational connection* between the limitation of the constitutional right and the government's objectives; that is, the limitation of a constitutional right must be shown to further the government's objectives. In the second stage of the analysis is the *minimal impairment test*, in which it must be demonstrated that the punishment achieves the government's stated goals such that the impairment to constitutional rights is minimal. In the last level of the analysis, it must be shown that the benefits of the rights infringement are greater than its deleterious effects through the *proportionate effects test* (*Sauvé*: §27).

In their treatment of the Oakes Test, the majority first states the government's objectives in denying prisoners the right to vote. The majority noted that the government's objectives were aimed not a specific problem but rather two broad considerations, namely, to promote "civic responsibility and respect for the law" (*Sauvé*: §21). The broadness of these objectives raises concerns for delineating a meaningful connection between the punishment and individual culpability through which those being punished would be able to recognize themselves as actors, a connection that is dear to Ricoeur. We shall return to this concern in our consideration of the minimal impairment test.

Having stated the government's objectives, the majority begins the second part of the Oakes Test, namely, the proportionality test. The first phase of the proportionality test is the rational connection test. Here, the majority must analyze the government's three-fold aim in denying the right to vote: denying the right to vote serves a pedagogical function by communicating the respect for the law to inmates and citizens alike; denying the right to vote also serves a moral objective because allowing inmates to vote "demeans" the political system; finally, disenfranchisement is, generally speaking, a legitimate form of punishment, irrespective of the nature of the specific circumstances of individual offenders (*Sauvé*: §29).

With respect to the first aspect of the government's aim, namely, the pedagogical value of the denial to vote to inmates, the majority reasons that this aim fails precisely because the denial of the right to vote enforces a break between the [individual] obligation to obey the law and the civic membership that is entailed in the making of law through elected representatives. The power of the state to create laws flows from the *participation* of citizens in the state through voting. That is, it is the right to vote that ultimately authorizes the state to create laws and corresponding sanctions:

> This delegation from voters to legislators gives the law its legitimacy or force. Correlatively, the obligation to obey the law flows from the fact that the law is made by and on behalf of the citizens. In sum, the legitimacy of the law and the obligation to obey the law flow directly from the right of every citizen to vote. As a practical matter, we require all within our country's boundaries to obey its laws, whether or not they vote. *But this does not negate the vital symbolic, theoretical and practical connection between having a voice in making the law and being obliged to obey it.* This connection, inherited from social contract theory and enshrined in the *Charter*, stands at the heart of our system of constitutional democracy. (*Sauvé*: §31, my emphasis)

In order for citizens to have respect for the law, then, it is not sufficient to emphasize that aspect of the sanction that is expressed in terms of punishment at the expense of the very civic authorization of the citizen body that provides the state with the legitimacy to enforce the punishment. The aim of punishment becomes contradictory if its civic grounding becomes hidden beneath the weight of its punitive aspect: "Reflecting this truth, the history of democracy is the history of progressive enfranchisement. The universal franchise has become, at this point in time, an essential part of democracy" (*Sauvé*: §33). Historically, citizens were excluded from the franchise on the basis of class, race, and gender, thereby limiting the right to vote to the elite. Canada's history of progressive enfranchisement has resulted in the universal right of all citizens to vote. What this history of progressive enfranchisement entails, then, is a *progressive demoralization* of the status of citizenship:

> As Arbour J.A. observed in *Sauvé No. 1, supra*, at p. 247: . . . the slow movement toward universal suffrage in Western democracies took an irreversible step forward in Canada in 1982 by the enactment of s. 3 of the *Charter*. *I doubt that anyone could now be deprived of the vote on the basis, not merely symbolic but actually demonstrated, that he or she was not decent or responsible.* By the time the *Charter* was enacted, exclusions from the franchise were so few in this country that it is fair to assume that we had abandoned the notion that the electorate should be restricted to a "decent and responsible citizenry", previously defined by attributes such as ownership of land or gender, in favour of a pluralistic electorate which could well include domestic enemies of the state. (*Sauvé*: §33, my emphasis)

Ricoeur raises the possibility of the demoralization of imputation in his discussion of the moralization of responsibility:

> We may speak, in an opposite sense, of a process of demoralization of the root of imputation to characterize attempts to restore the concept of a "capability" to act, hence of "imputability", whose place we have seen among natural law jurists. If this enterprise were to succeed, the concept of responsibility, which ended up by displacing that of imputability to the point of becoming its synonym and even of replacing it in contemporary vocabulary, might again become available for new adventures, which would not exclude new attempts to remoralize responsibility, but in other ways than in terms of obligation, in the sense of a moral or internalized constraint. (Ricoeur, 2000: 20)

Ricoeur here is referring to a remoralization of responsibility along civic lines. It is this idea of civic responsibility that Amartya Sen underscores in his *Commodities and Capabilities* (1985) in developing his argument for what Ricoeur refers to as social capability or the social-institutional configurations that make individual liberty and well-being possible in the first place (Ricoeur, 2005: 141). Sen's argument is that economic theory has traditionally tended to frame well-being in utilitarian terms, namely, in terms of the advancement of self-interest either in terms of satisfaction or happiness or as desire-fulfillment (Sen, 1985: 2). While Sen's own conceptualization of well-being is rooted in the utilitarian tradition, it expands upon the classical utilitarian understanding of right. Where utilitarians view rights as means to the attainment of other goods, Sen's argument is that "rights" refer not simply to the actual attainment of well-being, but rather to the opportunities or capabilities that the person has, compared to others, to achieve well-being (Sent, 1985: 5). Sen refers to the capability to make use of commodities in terms of functionings: "In getting an idea of the well-being of the person, we clearly have to move on to 'functionings', to wit, what the person succeeds in doing with the commodities and characteristics at his or her command" (Sen, 1985: 10). This expanded notion of right, which includes the capability for well-being, Ricoeur argues, connects together the individual liberty emphasized in economics with the institutional preconditions for civic responsibility, that underwrite individual liberty.[3]

As we argued in Chapter 2, the norm of reciprocity which articulates the dignity of each person as an end in him or herself is expressed in terms of civic inclusion on the plane of institutions. Because membership in the civil, social and political institutions of citizenship extends to *each* citizen, denial of this membership to discrete groups undermines the civic structure assuring the dignity of each citizen: to borrow Rawls' language, it undermines the public culture of society through which the Kantian principle of the inviolability of persons is recognized. In this way, the majority argues that the denial of the right to vote is overly broad:

> More broadly, denying citizens the right to vote runs counter to our constitutional commitment to the inherent worth and dignity of every individual . . . *the fact that the disenfranchisement law at issue applies to a discrete group of persons should make us more, not less, wary of its potential to violate the principle of equal rights* and equal membership embodied in and protected by the *Charter.* (*Sauvé*: §36, my emphasis)

Denying the right to vote to discrete groups, then, entails a failure to re-moralize responsibility along civic lines. Our civic responsibility to include *all* citizens in the right to vote is reflected in the *Charter's* explicit language around the constitutional protection of prisoners' right to vote (*Sauvé*: §38).

The moral objective the government hopes to fulfill by demonstrating that those convicted of crimes ought to be excluded from the franchise because they "demean" the political process is thus rejected by the majority precisely because of its own moralistic interpretation of responsibility, of citizens' capability for imputation. The exclusion of inmates from the franchise on the grounds that this group is morally unworthy undermines the principle of the inviolability of persons through its rejection of the publicity requirement. In other words, the government's rationale in denying inmates the right to vote itself demeans the dignity of the institution of citizenship: "The government's novel political theory that would permit elected representatives to *disenfranchise a segment of the population finds no place in a democracy built upon principles of inclusiveness, equality, and citizen participation*" (*Sauvé*: §41, my emphasis).

The last argument the government offers in its demonstration for rational connection is that denying inmates the right to vote is a legitimate form of punishment. The majority responds by questioning whether the denial of a constitutional right is a legitimate form of punishment. The denial of the right to vote to a discrete group of persons represents a moral and civic exclusion from the constitutional protections constitutive of a democratic society. Furthermore, the punishment is not tailored to the particular individual offender's crime; all inmates, regardless of the nature of their criminal conduct, are excluded from a central civic institution (*Sauvé*: §50). Again, what this means is that the punishment is overly broad; it catches too many people in the broadness of its scope.

Because the punishment is overly broad, it cannot speak to the moral culpability of the actor. As a punishment, disenfranchisement does not speak to the personal, social, or political circumstances of those to whom it is applied. We return here to the distinction between justice and vengeance with which we began our discussion. Where justice presupposes those civic institutions through which the capable subject, that is, the subject capable of self-recognition emerges, vengeance *severs* the actor from his or her civic membership, thus negating the possibility for self-recognition. This divorce results in the moralization of responsibility in the form of punishment that which at the same time fails to recognize the actor's stats as a moral person:

> Retribution in a criminal context, by contrast [to vengeance], represents an objective, reasoned and measured determination of an appropriate

> punishment which properly reflects the *moral culpability* of the offender, having regard to the intentional risk-taking of the offender, the consequential harm caused by the offender, and the normative character of the offender's conduct. (*Sauvé*: §50, original emphasis)

As a punishment, the deprivation of a constitutional right does not recognize the agency of the actor.[4] Such a punishment cannot enact justice; when a punishment undermines the public figuration of the inviolability of persons consists, it is restricted to the domain of vengeance. In this way, the very legitimacy of the punishment in terms of its potential for retribution or denunciation becomes questionable.

Thus, the government fails to establish a rational connection between Section 51(e) and its stated goals of promoting respect for the law and in enforcing legitimate punishment. The majority's reasoning with respect to the remaining two aspects of the proportionality test, namely, the minimal impairment test and the proportionate effect test flows directly from its treatment of the rational connection test. Because the Section 51(e) failed the rational connection test, it also fails to pass the rational impairment test and the proportionate effect test because it is, as we have already noted, too broad. Not only do the deleterious effects of the punishment far outweigh any benefits reached in furthering the government's stated goals, it renders the objectives themselves unintelligible insofar as the publicity requirement which would make the government's objectives relevant to the punishment, is undermined.

Retribution, Redistribution, and Recognition

Dear to Marshall, then, are those institutions, such as education and social services, such as social transfers and wage regulation, which develop a citizen-body that has the capability for responsible membership within the state. Thus the capability for freedom of the citizen-body presupposes a national cultural heritage in which the very right, to use Marshall's language to become "civilized," or gain genuine membership into society, presupposes a national cultural heritage embodied in institutions such as education and social transfers. This national narrative articulates the recognition of a society that its well-being rests on the enfranchisement of its citizens (Marshall, 1992: 16). With respect to *Sauvé*, the right to vote refers not only to a political right exercised by an individual or a group of individuals. The significance of enfranchisement refers, rather, to voters' inclusion in the status of citizenship and the principle of equality upon which it rests. It is in this light that we are to understand the Supreme Court's contention that the denial of the right to vote to a group of citizens results in a loss of dignity for those citizens. This loss of dignity cannot be explained merely by reference to individual rights, but to the denial of access to the institution of citizenship:

> Citizenship is a status bestowed on those who are full members of a community. All who possess the status are equal with respect to the rights and duties with which the status is endowed. There is no universal principle that determines what those rights and duties shall be, but societies in which citizenship is a developing institution create an image of an ideal citizenship against which achievement can be measured and towards which aspiration can be directed. *The urge forward along the path thus plotted is an urge towards a fuller measure of equality, an enrichment of the stuff of which the status is made and an increase in the number of those on whom the status is bestowed.* (Marshall, 1992: 18, my emphasis)

The denial of the right to vote, then, represents a regression in Marshall's teleology of citizenship and human dignity. That is, a retributive understanding of imputation represents a regression on the development of an inclusive citizenship through which the dignity of personhood, or imputation understood as capability, has historically developed. As we have seen, the institution of citizenship rests on the principle of civic inclusion through which the dignity of each citizen is insured through civic membership in public institutions of health, welfare, social transfers, and pensions. When we undermine the civic rights of a group of citizens, as the government attempts to do in Sauvé, we are violating the principle of civic inclusion through which the government gains its legitimacy. The government's argument that the denial of the right to vote only applies to those serving a sentence of two years or more is not an adequate response to the charge that the punishment is both overly broad and disproportionate in its deleterious effects on civic rights: "The fact that the disenfranchisement law at issue applies to a discrete group of persons should make us more, not less, wary of its potential to violate the principles of equal rights and equal membership embodied in and protected by the Charter" (*Sauvé*: §35, my emphasis). The civic exclusion of inmates from the right to vote, then, undermines the institution of citizenship as such.

As Rawls and Ricoeur have argued, the equality afforded by the status of citizenship is constituted by a framework of just redistribution, wherein the dignity, or to use Kant's language, respect, attaching to personhood is extended to any-one who has the status of citizenship. That is, the violation of the right to vote is a violation not of an individual right but a violation of the principle of equality upon which the institution of citizenship has historically developed. The principle of equality articulated by Marshall above flows from the institution or the status of citizenship and thus is self-evidently not to be found in individual citizens. What this means is that individual citizens cannot be excluded from the principle of equality, central to civic practices such as voting, either. The government's position in *Sauvé* attempts to negate the principle of substitutability underlying the equality provisions in the Charter guarantee of the freedom by treating these civic rights along individualistic lines. The majority's response to the government's position is to argue that once certain groups of people are disenfranchised, the principle of equality is undermined.

Punishment in the form of civic-moral exclusion of offenders from central institutions of society is incompatible with the democratic ideals of any criminal justice system (Lacey, 2007). In her work, legal theorist Nicola Lacey is concerned with explicating the institutional preconditions for moderation in punishment in modern liberal societies so that punishment does not become synonymous with civic exclusion and the loss of the capability for citizenship in democratic societies. Lacey's argument is that we must go beyond cultural analyzes of the history of criminal justice systems compatible with democratic society and look more broadly to the socio-economic and political institutions constitutive of different welfare state regimes. Her focus on the differential structuration of socioeconomic and political institutions in welfare state regimes is prompted by their differences in exclusionary and inclusionary practices of certain social groups, not only in terms of punishment, but in terms of membership in the socio-political and economic institutions of the state. This requires a twofold analysis: First, we must appreciate the differential institutional structuration of different liberal welfare state regimes. Second, we must understand how these differences in institutional interrelationships help us to understand how different liberal-democratic states have come to exhibit such varying degrees of commitment to the democratic-civic inclusion of criminal offenders (Lacey, 2007: 6). Here, I just want to briefly note Lacey's argument that the differential capabilities for the rehabilitation, reintegration, and inclusion in liberal-democratic systems of criminal justice is best explained through a political and economic analysis that explicates the political and economic institutions of citizenship, such as the development of civic institutions of education, employment, and a public and professional bureaucracy that reflects the co-ordination of these civic institutions in its evaluations and recommendations in the form of public policy (Lacey, 2007: 27).

Lacey argues that the degree of the development of coordination of these civic institutions and public bureaucracy helps us to distinguish between liberal market democracies such as the USA and Britain on one hand, and Scandinavian countries, and to a lesser degree, Canada, on the other. While Scandinavian countries exhibit high degrees of what Esping-Andersen (1990) refers to as cross-class coalition building through highly coordinated civic institutions of education, welfare provision, sickness and disability pensions, such cross-class solidarity is missing in residual welfare regimes, whose social security measures remain tied to the market. In her work, Lacey observes the relationship between the politicization and consequent moralization of crime in her comparison of coordinated market economies and liberal market economies. Lacey's observations center upon the relationship between the role of bureaucracy and the development of public policy. The relative independence of the civil service on questions of public policy on, for example, state approaches to crime rates and the punishment of offenders, has to do in part with the capability of coordinated market economies for cross-class coalition building. The institutional framework underlying cross-class solidarity, coupled with a proportionally representative electoral system, makes possible a comparatively less divisive climate in coordinated market economies than that of liberal market economies. This, she argues, prevents the politicization and moralization of issues such as crime and the treatment of prisoners. Liberal market economies, such as the USA, on the other hand, whose electoral systems are not based upon a proportionally representative system but rather on a "first-past-the-post, winner-takes-all" model and where political parties tend to choose their own political advisors, end up creating a highly politically and morally divisive atmosphere in which public opinion ends up heavily influencing governments' harsh stance on crime and criminals: "Once a professional bureaucracy is undermined, one of the main tools for depoliticizing criminal justice is removed" (Lacey, 2007: 19).

The Social State as the Third Party: The Neuter in Civic Liberalism

We have developed Ricoeur's defense of civic liberalism, grounded in the ethical institutions of the third party through Rawls' proceduralist demonstration of the public society. In so doing, we have argued that Rawls' theory of distributive justice, far from being anti-communitarian, constitutes a profound defense of the mutual society, a virtue emphasized by Aristotle in his *Nichomachean Ethics*. The *ethical* significance of the institutional figuration of the third party lies in the refusal of the social state to separate capability from disability through the distribution of both advantage and disadvantage in the public culture of society, and in this way, articulates an ethics of *oneself as another*. It is the distribution—the sharing—of capability and disability that is defended by Rawls' theory of justice. We illustrated Ricoeur and Rawls' theory of civic liberalism—a liberalism that is figurated by the third party—through Hegel's principle of differentiation, whose historical narrative is articulated by Marshall, and have argued that the dignity of each person depends upon the development of the institutions of citizenship in the social state, or the modern welfare state. Membership in the modern state engenders the differentiation necessary for the genuine individuality or, phrased in terms of modern discourses on citizenship, for the dignity of each citizen. Hegel's argument about the development of individual dignity is that that those institutions of the state, such as the provision of social transfers and education that mediate class inequality do so by first recognizing that class exists, and that class inequality exists. Thus, it is not by denying class inequality that individual dignity is engendered. It is precisely this denial that underlies the market ideology of free-range capitalism. It is the state's recognition of social and economic inequalities through the mediation of civic institutions that engenders individual dignity. The mediation of civic institutions, by intervening on the indifference of the marketized desire and need, prevents the usurpation of individual dignity through the contingencies of disease, poverty, crime, unemployment, single motherhood, disability, and old age. We are here reminded of Ricoeur's prayer in the opening lines of *The Just*:

> . . . citizens who issue from this institutional mediation can only wish that every human being should, like them, enjoy such political mediation, which when added to the *necessary* conditions stemming from a philosophical anthropology becomes a sufficient condition for the transition from the capable human being to the real citizen. (Ricoeur, 2000: 10, original emphasis)

Notes

Introduction

[1] See Molly Harkirat Mann (2009) "The Course of Recognitive *Phronēsis*: Ricoeur's Response to the Moralization of Inequality," *Philosophy Today: Selected Studies in Phenomenology and Existential Philosophy* 2009 (53): 201–206.

[2] Canadian Census, 2005.

[3] David Olive, "David Olive on the census: A country divided" *The Toronto Star*, May 2, 2008.

[4] David Olive, "David Olive on the census: A country divided."

[5] François Ewald, "Justice, Equality, Judgment: On 'Social Justice'" in *Juridification of the Social Spheres*, ed. Gunther Teubner (New York: Walter de Gruyter): 91–110.

[6] John Rawls, *A Theory of Justice: Revised Edition* (Cambridge: Cambridge University Press, 1999).

[7] Paul Ricoeur, *Oneself as Another*, trans. Kathleen Blamey (Chicago: The University of Chicago Press, 1992).

[8] Michael Ignatieff, *The Needs of Strangers* (London: Hogarth Press, 1984).

[9] Jean-Pierre Dupuy, "Les paradoxes de 'Théorie de la justice': Introduction à l'oeuvre de John Rawls," *Esprit* 134 (January 1988): 72–84.

[10] Paul Ricoeur, "Is a Procedural Theory of Justice Possible: John Rawls's *Theory of Justice*?" in *The Just*, trans. David Pellauer (Chicago: The University of Chicago Press, 2000): 36–57.

[11] Jonathan Wolff and Avner De-Shalit, *Disadvantage* (Oxford: Oxford University Press, 2007), 7.

[12] Paul Ricoeur, *The Just*.

[13] In this book, I will be interested in developing Ricoeur's distinct contribution to a distributive theory of capability justice, which will entail a careful analysis of the relationship Ricoeur draws between recognition justice and redistributive justice. My argument will be that Ricoeur develops a theory of recognition justice, one that is intimately tied up with his theory of distributive justice, long before the appearance of *The Course of Recognition* (2005), and for this reason, I will focus on Ricoeur's treatment of recognition justice in the writings that precede his work on recognition proper.

[14] Paul Ricoeur, "The Concept of Responsibility: An Essay in Semantic Analysis" in *The Just*, 11–35.

[15] In this respect, it is interesting to note the important role that Nozick's libertarianism plays in Walzer's argument for the constitutive self. See Robert Nozick, *Anarchy, State, Utopia* (New York: Basic Books, 1974).

[16] Martha Nussbaum, *Women and Human Development: The Capabilities Approach* (Cambridge: Cambridge University Press, 2000).
[17] Martha Nussbaum, *Women and Human Development*, 81.
[18] Jonathan Wolff and Avner De-Shalit, *Disadvantage*.
[19] Ibid., 21.
[20] Michael Walzer, *Spheres of Justice: A Defense of Pluralism and Equality* (Oxford: Basil Blackwell, 1989); David Miller and Michael Walzer, *Pluralism, Justice and Equality* (Oxford: Oxford University Press, 1995).
[21] *Disadvantage*, 10.
[22] *Disadvantage*, 10, my emphasis.
[23] "Is a Procedural Theory of Justice Possible?", 53.
[24] I am here applying the distinction Ricoeur draws between the Kantian idea of the 'attribution' of an action to an agent, which implies the agent's capacity for self-recognition, and 'responsibility' that an agent has for his or her actions, to the problem of the moralization of inequality. In his critique of Kant, Ricoeur argues that we must be careful not allow the concept of responsibility to eclipse the capacity for attribution, or the imputation, of an action to an agent. It is important that we do this, Ricoeur argues, in order to safeguard the very meaning of the Kantian law of freedom, or the categorical imperative. See Paul Ricoeur, 'The Concept of Responsibility: An Essay in Semantic Analysis' in *The Just*, 11–35.
[25] *Disadvantage*, 167.
[26] The idea of corrosive disadvantage is another way of expressing the clustering of disadvantage. See *Disadvantage*, 166.
[27] Arjumand Siddiqi and Clyde Hertzman, "Towards an Epidemiological Understanding of the Effects of Long-Term Institutional Changes on Population Health: A Case Study of Canada Versus the USA," *Social Science and Medicine* 64 (February 2007): 589–603.
[28] Ibid., 599.
[29] See Gøsta Esping-Andersen, "Distribution Regimes in the Power Structure" in *The Three Worlds of Welfare Capitalism* (Cambridge: Polity Press), 105–143.
[30] "Towards an Epidemiological Understanding of the Effects of Long-Term Institutional Changes on Population Health: A Case Study of Canada Versus the USA," 599.
[31] *Oneself as Another*, 172, original emphasis.
[32] Paul Ricoeur, "Débat sur l'identité narrative," *Esprit* No. 8 (August 1988): 295–314.
[33] G.W.F. Hegel. *Phenomenology of Spirit*, trans. A.V. Miller (Oxford: Oxford University Press).
[34] Paul Ricoeur, "Débat sur l'identité narrative," 308.
[35] Paul Ricoeur, "Autonomy and Vulnerability" in *Reflections on the Just*, trans. David Pellauer (Chicago: The University of Chicago Press), 73.
[36] Eric Nelson, "From Primary Goods to Capabilities: Distributive Justice and the Problem of Neutrality," *Political Theory*, 36 (February 2008): 93–122.
[37] I am self-consciously using the term *equality* refer to Rawls's political principles and his economic principle in contradistinction to Nelson's argument that Rawls endorses moral and economic *egalitarianism*.

[38] Eric Nelson, "From Primary Goods to Capabilities: Distributive Justice and the Problem of Neutrality," 115. Nelson is here referring to the capability theories developed by Amartya Sen and Martha Nussbaum. See Amartya Sen, *Commodities and Capabilities* (Oxford: Elsevier Science Publishers B.V., 1985); Martha Nussbaum, *Women and Human Development: The Capabilities Approach* (New York: Cambridge University Press, 2000).

Chapter 1

[1] Kymlicka has also argued, though along very different lines, that Rawls's theory of justice is not a debate about the priority of the right over the good, but rather an argument for the equal consideration of each person's good. Despite Rawls's confusion of moral and amoral conceptions of utilitarianism, Kymlicka argues, his conception of equality stands. See Will Kymlicka, "Rawls on Teleology and Deontology," *Philosophy and Public Affairs* (1988): 173–190. In his own work on the relationship between the right and the good in modern welfare states, Kymlicka endorses a Rawlsian position that redistributive and recognitive policies are interconnected and cannot be pursued in isolation from one another. See Keith Banting and Will Kymlicka, eds. *Multiculturalism and the Welfare State: Recognition and Redistribution in Contemporary Democracies* (Oxford: Oxford University Press, 2006).

[2] This argument has received its strongest articulations in communitarian critiques of liberalism and in pluralist conceptions of justice, such as Sandel (1982, 1984), Walzer (1989), Taylor (1994), Honneth, Nussbaum (2000). In Chapters 3 and 4, we shall argue that paradoxically, the very structure of some of the major communitarian arguments which characterize Rawls's conception of justice ultra-individualistic itself has neo-liberal implications.

[3] In Chapter 6, we shall consider how the historical and educative character of the basic structure of society shapes persons' capabilities to recognize themselves as the authors of their actions in our discussion of the political right to vote, and whether it is just to deny this vote to incarcerated individuals. The historical and the educative character of the basic structure of society is emphasized by the court in the Canadian case which challenged the constitutionality of the denying prisoners who are serving sentences of two or more years the right to vote.

[4] We shall consider in some detail major attempts to personalize the historical development of the neuter bond in Chapters 3 and 4. These attempts are grounded in misreadings that characterize Rawls's efforts to preserve the thoroughly social character of the neuter bond simultaneously as anti-social and anti-communitarian on one hand, and as an attack on individual autonomy on the other. As we traverse these critiques of Rawls's theory of distributive justice, we will be better able to understand how these two seemingly opposed positions can be asserted at once.

[5] It is noteworthy that Ricoeur includes Hegel, along with Aristotle, Marx, and Arendt, as part of the philosophical history of civic liberalism in contradistinction to the "political atomism" of the ultra-individualism defended by Robert

Nozick, and grounded in the work of Locke and Mill. See Paul Ricoeur, "The Fragility of Political Language," *Philosophy Today* 31(1987): 35–44.

6 Axel Honneth has most recently confused Rawls's conception of full autonomy with arbitrary individualism in his *Pathologies of Individual Freedom: Hegel's Social Theory* (2010). By failing to appreciate the role of the background institutions of society in the configuration of individual autonomy, Honneth also misses the Hegelian character of Rawls's conception of distributive justice. Honneth argues that Hegel's social figuration of personhood is nowhere to be found in individualist conceptions of justice, such as Rawls's. In contrast, our argument will be that Rawls's starting position, like Hegel's, is not the individual, but rather the role of the background social institutions of society in the development and the preservation of autonomous selfhood. Our close reading of Rawls's argument that individual autonomy develops from within the social institutions of society will serve to draw out the historical implications of his proceduralist argument: the social institutions of society develop over time, and as such, it is necessary to take a long-term view when thinking about these institutions. As Hegel has argued, the state does not develop linearly, but rather self-reflexively through the historical development of the social institutions which engender the development of autonomous, self-determining citizens. Through its civic institutions such as the family, education, unions, and social transfers, the state thinks itself, that is, continually renders itself objective to itself. This objectification, however, is not totalizing; quite the opposite, in continually rendering itself objective to itself, the civic state continually investigates the social and economic inequalities affecting citizens' capabilities for autonomy. Rawls refers to the state's capacity to think itself, to render itself objective to itself, through its public institutions, when he refers to Hegel's *Philosophy of Right* to articulate his conception of a properly "philosophical point of view," which allows us to regard our public institutions rationally. The rational development of our public institutions belies their historical character:

> [P]olitical philosophy may try to calm our frustration and rage against our society and its history by showing us the way in which its institutions, when properly understood from a philosophical point of view, are rational, and developed over time as they did to attain their present, rational form. This fits one of Hegel's well-known sayings: "When we look at the world rationally, the world looks rationally back." He seeks for us reconciliation—*Versöhnung*—that is, we are to accept and affirm our social world positively, not merely to be resigned to it. See John Rawls, *Justice as Fairness: A Restatement*, ed. Erin Kelly (Cambridge, MA: Harvard University Press, 2001), 3.

We shall develop Rawls's Hegelian conception of the modern welfare state in chapter three and we shall consider the development of citizens' capabilities for political participation and for health, central to autonomous personhood, in relation to the historical development of the social institutions of the modern welfare state in Chapter 6.

7 In this regard, Jean-Pierre Dupuy notes that the Rawls's entire proceduralist exercise is an effort to return to the utilitarian's sacrificial victim the status of membership: "Tout l'effort de Rawls consist alors à prouver que le détenteur de la position la moins favourable est, dans l'utilitarisme, une victim sacrificielle, mais

que la coneption de la justice qu'il defend en fait un sociétair à part entière. Ce qui suffit à prouver la supériorité de cette dernière" (Dupuy, 1988: 83).

8 On the relationship between the demonstration of collective deliberation by the social contract and the preservation of the membership of the least advantaged member, see Jean-Pierre Dupuy:"L'argument de Rawls est le suivant: les sociétaires ne sont pas des décideurs isolés, ce sont des associés qui s'engagent les uns par rapport aux autres à respecter un contrat selon des principes defines publiquement et acceptés unanimement. Le contrat crées des liens et l'engagement, des contraintes" (Dupuy, 1988: 83).

Chapter 2

1 Axel Honneth's contribution to Axel Honneth and Nancy Fraser, *Redistribution or Recognition?: A Political-Philosophical Exchange* (New York: Verso, 2003). Also see Nancy Fraser, "Recognition without Ethics" pp. 21–42 in Scott Lash and Mike Featherstone, ed. *Recognition and Difference: Politics, Identity, Multiculture* (London: Sage, 2002) and Axel Honneth, "Recognition or Redistribution?: Changing Perspectives on the Moral Order of Society," pp. 43–55 from the same collection.

2 Charles Taylor, "The Politics of Recognition," in Amy Gutmann, ed. *Multiculturalism* (Princeton: Princeton University Press, 1994), p. 28.

3 While Fraser has most recently defended this position in her exchange with Axel Honneth in *Redistribution or Recognition? A Political-Philosophical Exchange* (2003), earlier arguments for redistributive justice can be found in arguments for the welfare state advanced by R.H. Tawney and Richard Titmuss. See R.H. Tawney, *Equality* (New York: Barnes & Noble, 1965) and Richard Titmuss, *The Gift Relationship: From Human Blood to Social Policy* (New York: New York Press, 1997), *Income Distribution and Social Change: A Study in Criticism* (London: George Allen & Unwin, 1962), *The Right to Welfare and Other Essays* (London: Heinemann Educational Books Ltd., 1981).

4 See Herbert Spiegelberg, "A Defense of Human Equality," *The Philosophical Review*, Vol. 53, No. 2, pp. 101–124 and D. Daiches Raphael, "Justice and Liberty," *Proceedings of the Aristotelian Society*, Vol. 51, pp. 167–196.

5 In her otherwise admirable analysis of the conception of otherness in Aristotle and Ricoeur, Gaëlle Fiasse fails to appreciate the reflexive relationship between the solicitous preservation of otherness on the plane of friendship and on the plane of just institutions. See Gaëlle Fiasse, *L'autre et l'amitié chez Aristote et Paul Ricoeur: analyses éthique et ontologiques* (Louvain: Louvain-la-Neuve Editions de l'Institut supérieur de philosophie, 2006).

In this way, she risks moralizing the otherness of the other. This risk was highlighted in her recent paper on the "fragile other," exemplified in, for example, the figure of the disabled other. A fully ethical or solicitous preservation of otherness, especially in the case of disability, just conjoin the figuration of disability, which does not reside *in* an individual as such, with social, political, and economic figuration of disability within the institutions of health care, education, social transfers, transportation, and old age and disability pensions. This prevents the individualization—and thus moralization—of the figure of the "fragile other." Fiasse made this argument in a paper entitled "Soi-même comme un autre fragile chez Paul Ricoeur" at the Society for Ricoeur Studies Annual Meeting, November 6, 2010.

6 Aristotle's emphasis on persons' capabilities for self-determination will play an important role in the way Martha Nussbaum defines a "fully human life" in her theory of capability, which we shall examine closely in Chapter 4.

7 In *After Virtue* (1981), MacIntyre defends a pre-modern conception of the virtues wherein virtues may only be discerned within the context of a unitary life: "And the unity of a virtue in someone's life is only intelligible only as a characteristic of a unitary life, a life that can be conceived and evaluated as a whole" (MacIntyre, 1981: 191). That is, we require the organizational structure of narrative in order to be able to give an account of ourselves, and thus for our life, taken as a whole, to achieve an *appreciative* dimension: "How, indeed, could a subject of action give an ethical character to his or her own life taken as a whole, if this life were not gathered together in some way, and how could this occur if not, precisely, in the form of a narrative?" (Ricoeur, 1992: 158). This ethical integration of a life under the aegis of goodness, of a good life, however, presupposes an organization, an *evaluation* that is itself shaped by ethical reasoning appropriate to ethical evaluation. Ricoeur, following MacIntyre, underscores the ethical realm of evaluation on the practical plain through his emphasis on the "standards of excellence" (Ricoeur, 1992: 176). The ethical character of these standards of excellence is that they are constitutive of those evaluative and normative precepts in view of which we may appraise and recognize a good practitioner, such as a good teacher, a good doctor, etc. However, where MacIntyre's analysis focuses on the stories told and enacted in everyday activity, Ricoeur argues that the ethical significance of stories lies in the separation between the literary realm and the stories enacted in everyday life. Drawing on Aristotle's conception of emplotment, Ricoeur argues that the relationship between action and agent is easiest to perceive in the story, and at the same time, this relationship may be submitted to potentially endless imaginative variances. This two-fold structure of emplotment enables profound self-reflection in real life (Ricoeur, 1992: 158–159). See Richard Kearney, *On Paul Ricoeur: The Owl of Minerva* (Aldershot: Ashgate Publishing, 2005) and John Wall, *Moral Creativity: Paul Ricoeur and the Poetics of Possibility* (New York: Oxford University Press, 2005).

8 Michael Ignatieff. 1984. *The Needs of Strangers*. London: Hogarth Press.

9 We discuss Michael Sandel's defense of communitarianism and constitutive selfhood in Chapter 3.

10 See notes 7 and 8 in Chapter 1.

11 I first made this argument in Molly Harkirat Mann (2009) "Ricouer's Principle of Civic Inclusion: An Aristotelian Interpretation of Rawls' Theory of Justice" *Philosophy Today* (Spring 2009): 44–57. Also see Gary Foster, "Rawls and Ricoeur on Reconciling the Right and the Good: An Overlapping Consensus or an Ethical Aim?" Philosophy Today (Summer 2007): 159–176. For an account of the complex nature of practical wisdom developed by Ricoeur, see David Pellauer, "At the limit of Practical Wisdom" Richard A. Cohen and James L. Marsh,

eds., *Ricoeur as Another: The Ethics of Subjectivity* (Albany: SUNNY Press, 2002), pp. 187–201.

[12] We shall note the relationship between the capability for self-recognition, and the idea of merit in Chapter 3 where we will consider the background social, political and economic conditions that enable agents' self recognition as the author of their actions.

[13] See Henry Sidgwick, *The Methods of Ethics* (Chicago: Chicago University Press, 1962).

[14] See Paul Ricoeur "Le Cercle de la demonstration" *Esprit* No. 2 (1988): 305–314.

[15] In what is the only sustained reflection on Ricoeur's political thought, Bernard Dauenhauer notes Ricoeur's debt to Rawls' conception of distributive justice. However, although he mentions the lexical relationship among the principles of justice, he overlooks the ethical significance Ricoeur attaches to the lexical ordering of Rawls' principles of justice, concluding that ". . . [Rawls'] principles, taken singly or jointly, are too abstract to implement in actual social practice, especially in judicial practice". See Bernard Dauenhauer, *Paul Ricoeur: The Promise and Risk of Politics* (New York: Rowman & Littlefield Publishers, Inc.), p. 180.

Chapter 3

[1] Ricoeur, in noting the ethical significance of Rawls's theory of justice, cites Jean-Pierre Dupuy's article, "Les paradoxes de "Théorie de la justice": Introduction à l'oeuvre de John Rawls". *Esprit*. No. 8 (January), in which Dupuy emphasizes the anti-sacrificial character of Rawls's principles of justice. See notes 7 and 8 in Chapter 1.

[2] Charles Taylor, "The Politics of Recognition" in *Multiculturalism*, ed. Amy Gutmann (Princeton: Princeton University Press, 1994): pp. 25–73.

[3] Throughout *Liberalism and the Limits of Justice* (1982), Sandel refers to the constitutive self as the "radically situated self."

[4] Sandel owes his conception of the constitutive or the radically situated self to Robert Nozick's criticism of Rawls's argument that natural talents and capabilities are, morally speaking, arbitrary. Nozick argues that Rawls's distributive figuration of capability, which regards natural talents as common, rather than a possessive, asset, runs against the deontological emphasis on the distinction between persons:

> People will differ in how they view regarding natural talents as a common asset Some will complain, echoing Rawls against utilitarianism, that this 'does not take seriously the distinction between persons'; and they will wonder whether any reconstruction of Kant that treats people's abilities and talents as resources for others can be adequate. The two principles of justice . . . rule out even the tendency to regard men as means to one another's welfare.' Only if one presses *very* hard on the distinction between men and their talents, assets, abilities and special traits. (Nozick, 1974: 228, original emphasis).

5 The capability approach in its classical articulation was of course first advanced by Amartya Sen. Nussbaum, while crediting Sen's approach to capability justice as the foundation of her own theory of capability, distinguishes her approach from Sen's by virtue of its "irreducibly" pluralist character. We return to Sen and Nussbaum's capability approach to social in Chapter 4.

6 Wolff and De-Shalit also credit Martha Nussbaum's pluralist approach to capability justice in their figuration of advantage and disadvantage. Nussbaum's approach to capability justice, I shall argue, is in turn informed by Walzer's resourcist critique of Rawls's theory of distributive justice. See Chapters 3 and 4.

7 I first made this argument in an article entitled "The Course of Recognitive *Phronēsis*: Ricoeur's Response to the Hyper-Moralization of Inequality", *Philosophy Today* (*Selected Studies in Phenomenology and Existential Philosophy*), vol. 34 (2009), pp. 201–206.

8 Wolff and De-Shalit here cite Richard Wilkinson and Michael Marmot (eds), *The Social Determinants of Health: The Solid Facts* (World Health Organization, 2003). It is significant that Wolff and De-Shalit do not make reference to Wilkinson and Marmot's emphasis on the role of class inequality in population health outcomes. We will return to the role of socio-economic stratification in population health outcomes in social epidemiological research in Chapter 4.

Chapter 4

1 See "Introduction".

2 See Molly Harkirat Mann, "Civic *Phronēsis*: Rawl's Anti-Sacrificial Ethics for Capability Justice," *Philosophy and Social Criticism* 37 (2011): (forthcoming) for an earlier articulation of this argument.

3 See Chapter 3, "The Sacrificial Ethics of Constitutive Communitarianism".

4 See Chapter 3.

5 See also Martha Nussbaum and Amartya Sen, eds. *The Quality of Life* (Oxford: Clarendon Press, 1993).

6 Eric Nelson, "From Primary Goods to Capabilities: Distributive Justice and the Problem of Neutrality," *Political Theory* 36 (2008): 93–122.

7 Paul Ricoeur, *Oneself As Another*, trans. Kathleen Blamey (Chicago: University of Chicago Press, 1992).

8 The possessive or the individualistic interpretation of liberal democratic thought, as C.B. Macpherson has taught us, has been with us since at least the 17th century, and be traced as far back as Hobbes's political thought, which sought to extract political rights and obligations from the needs and interests of the individual: "It's [modern liberalism's] possessive quality is found in its conception of the individual as essentially the proprietor of his own person or capacities, owing nothing to society for them. The individual was seen neither as a moral whole, nor as part of a larger social whole, but as an owner of himself. . . . *The individual, it was thought, is free inasmuch as he is proprietor of his person and capacities. The human essence is freedom from dependence on the wills of others, and freedom is a function of possession. Society becomes a lot of free equal individuals related to each other as proprietors of their capacities and of what they have acquired by*

their exercise. Society consists of relations of exchange between proprietors." See C.B. Macpherson, *The Political Theory of Possessive Individualism* (Oxford: Oxford University Press, 1963), p. 3.

[9] Jean-Pierre Dupuy, "Les paradoxes de 'Théorie de la justice': Introduction à l'oeuvre de John Rawls," *Esprit* 134 (1988): 72–84.

[10] Martha Nussbaum, *Women and Human Development: The Capabilities Approach* (Cambridge: Cambridge University Press, 2000), 5.

[11] It is in this respect that Sen's theory of capability departs in an important way from Nussbaum's. Sen and Nussbaum both agree that the focus of justice ought to be on the capabilities of persons to be able to do certain things—such as becoming able to be adequately nourished and clothed and to be capable of good health—but where Nussbaum takes the argument further and argues that the Rawlsian figuration of distributive justice is opposed to the "principle of each person's capability," Sen views capability justice as a "natural extension of Rawls's concern with primary social goods, shifting attention from goods to what goods do to human beings". See Amartya Sen, "Equality of What?" in *The Tanner Lectures on Human Values*, Volume 1, ed. Sterling M. McMurrin (Salt Lake City: University of Utah Press, 1980), 197–220. That Sen is able to substitute Rawls's primary social goods with capabilities implies that Rawls' distributive configuration of moral autonomy—structured by the lexical ordering of the principle of moral equality and the principle of distribution—already contains an account of capability, insofar as it recognizes that capabilities for moral dignity are *shared capabilities*. This observation of Sen's civic understanding of capability accords with his earlier writings on the social-institutional figuration of natural disasters. See Amartya Sen, *Commodities and Capabilities* (Oxford: Elsevier Science Publishers B.V., 1985).

[12] For Nussbaum's full explication of her list of capabilities, see Nussbaum, *Women and Human Development*, 78–80.

[13] Ibid., original emphasis.

[14] Nussbaum emphasizes that capability justice requires "affirmative material and institutional support," and in this way constitutes a response to the neo-liberal emphasis on "negative liberties," wherein moral autonomy is only ensured through the prohibition of state action. But her own theory of liberty, while insisting on the "principle of the capabilities for each person", lacks the institutional figuration for a distributive understanding of capability, itself falls prey to her own lengthy critique of neoliberal attacks on the capabilities of our most vulnerable citizens. See Martha Nussbaum, "Capabilities as Fundamental Entitlements: Sen and Social Justice," *Feminist Economics* 9 (2003), 33–59, esp. 38–39.

[15] Consider, Nelson argues, the capability for showing concern for other people: "Moreover, the prospect of direct coercion remains present: in the case of something like 'showing concern for other people' (where having the capability and exercising it are presumably inseparable), the misanthrope will never conceive that he has an incapacity and so will not seek state assistance for socialization therapy. In that case, since we have already identified it as an 'essential human functioning', we are not committing ourselves to the view that no one functioning properly would decline to pursue it, and, therefore, that the man in question

ought to be put into therapy 'for his own good' (or, more precisely because if he were 'acting rationally' he would voluntarily submit)?" Nelson, "From Primary Goods to Capabilities," 100.

16 Nussbaum has explicitly argued that Rawls does not have a theory of capability because his primary goods do not shape the overall ends of human life. See Martha Nussbaum, "Human Functioning and Social Justice: In Defense of Aristotelian Essentialism," *Political Theory* 20 (1992): 202–246. Rawls, however, never discusses the primary social goods outside of the normative configuration of our least advantaged citizens. While rights and liberties are always equally distributed, income and wealth are to be distributed so as to raise the index of our least advantaged citizens: "If we know how the distribution of goods to the more favoured affects the expectations of the most disfavoured, this is sufficient. The index problem largely reduces, then, to that of weighting primary goods for the least advantaged. We try to do this by taking up the standpoint of the representative individual from this group and asking which combination of primary social goods it would be rational for him to prefer." Rawls, *A Theory of Justice*, 80. Thus, it is the recognitive expectations or capabilities of our least advantaged citizens that determines the distribution of the primary social goods. It is by indexing the recognitive expectations of our least advantaged citizens that Rawls solves the problem of how to determine a decent social minimum in a way that overcomes the challenge of arbitrariness faced by Nussbaum's argument for the establishment of the social minimum through her conceptualization of two distinct capability thresholds: the first threshold of capability which, when achieved, signifies that a person has the most basic capabilities constitutive of a human life, and a second threshold of capability which, when achieved, signifies that a person is living a good human life. See Richard Arneson, "Perfectionism and Politics" *Ethics* 111 (2000), 37–63. For Nussbaum's threshold argument, see Nussbaum, "Human Functioning and Social Justice: In Defense of Aristotelian Essentialism", 221 ff; Nussbaum, *Women and Human Development*, 75 ff; Martha Nussbaum, "Aristotle, Politics, and Human Capabilities: A Response to Antony, Arneson, Charlesworth, and Mulgan" *Ethics* 111(2000), 102–140.

17 H.L.A. Hart has argued against Rawls that liberty cannot be distributed because once distributed, it is not clear that the liberties chosen from behind the veil of ignorance would survive the test of what rational self-interested persons would want once the veil of ignorance is lifted. That is, it is impossible to calculate from within the original position what the costs to *one's self* would be if the liberties enjoyed by oneself were to be extended to all others, since it is impossible to know how others will choose to exercise these liberties. Rawls, Hart argues, fails to appreciate the difficulties a rational person will encounter in determining what kinds of disadvantages her or she will be exposed to through the general distribution of liberty. Nelson adopts Hart's competitive gloss on the distribution of liberty through this opposition between the good of one-self to that of an-other. See H.L.A. Hart, "Rawls on Liberty and Its Priority" in *Reading Rawls*, ed. Norman Daniels (Stanford, CA: Stanford University Press, 1989), 230–252.

18 "More generally, it turns out to be a proxy for the question 'Do you desire a situation in which entitlements and obligations are generated for your actual self by a collection of abstracted selves in a specified imaginary environment?' Had he known his idea of the good, Nozick would not have answered these implied

questions in the affirmative. Notice that this is *not* a complaint that depends on knowledge of Nozick's particular position in the 'natural lottery' and social world (i.e., that he was a very talented, relatively well-off professional academic); to take the objection seriously would not, therefore, be to allow morally arbitrary factors to influence the selection of the principles of justice. Nozick could formulate his complaint if he knew nothing other than his idea of the good. We can therefore conclude that the very act of generating a list of primary goods is non-neutral in a way that is impermissible on Rawls's own account." Nelson, "From Primary Goods to Capabilities," 113.

[19] Michael Ignatieff, *The Needs of Strangers* (London: Hogarth Press, 1984).

[20] Here I am in agreement with Norman Daniels's argument that the Rawlsian conception of fair equality of opportunity, which is an argument for distributive justice, implies an argument for recognitive justice. That is, justice as fairness implies that each member of the political community must be able to enjoy a "normal opportunity range," or have the capability to recognize him or herself as a member of his or her community, as a neighbor, as a parent, as a care-giver, as a worker. Daniels argues that the Rawlsian ideal of fair equality of opportunity cannot be satisfied where some citizens are excluded from the opportunity for these recognitive capacities due to, for example, poor health. The satisfaction of health care needs such that citizens are capable of recognizing themselves as members of a civic community are thus an essential feature of distributive justice. See Norman Daniels, "Health Care Needs and Distributive Justice," *Philosophy & Public Affairs* 10 (1981), 146–179.

[20] Ricoeur, *Oneself as Another*, 194.

[21] Ibid., 195; Paul Ricoeur, "The Model of the Text," in *Hermeneutics and the Human Sciences: Essays on Language, Action and Interpretation*, trans. John B. Thompson (Cambridge: Cambridge University Press, 1981), 197–221; Paul Ricoeur, "Is a Procedural Theory of Justice Possible?: John Rawls's *Theory of Justice*" in *The Just* trans. David Pellauer (Chicago: University of Chicago Press, 2000), 36–57.

[22] In his *The Three Worlds of Welfare Capitalism*, Gøsta Esping-Andersen identifies three welfare state regime types: the "social democratic" model exemplified by the Scandinavian countries, the "Conservative" model found in countries such as Italy, Germany, France, and Austria and the "Liberal" model of the USA, Canada, the United Kingdom, and Australia. See Gøsta Esping-Andersen, *The Three Worlds of Welfare Capitalism* (Cambridge: Polity Press, 1990).

[23] G.W.F. Hegel, *Philosophy of Right*, trans. T.M. Knox (Oxford: Oxford University Press: 1967). The *telos* of the state, according to Hegel, is the continual development of its self-knowledge, or the objectification of Mind. When the fable of consequentialism is applied to Hegel's theory of the social state, the *reflexive* aim of the social state is reduced to totalitarianism. We shall instead adopt an historical approach to the development of the reflexive knowledge practices of the social state, such as the one advanced by David MacGregor in his Hegel, Marx, and the English State (Toronto: University of Toronto Press, 1996) in Chapter 6.

[24] Paul Ricoeur, *Time and Narrative*, Volumes 1 and 3, trans. Kathleen McLaughlin and David Pellauer (Chicago: University of Chicago Press, 1994).

[25] See *The Three Worlds of Welfare Capitalism*, Chapter 5 entitled "Distribution Regimes in the Power Structure, pp. 105–143.

[26] David Coburn, "Income Inequality, Social Cohesion and the Health Status of Populations: The Role of Neoliberalism", *Social Science & Medicine* 51 (2000): 135–146.

[27] Nancy A. Ross, Michael C. Wolfson, James R. Dunn, Jean-Marie Berthelot, George A. Kaplan, John W. Lynch, "Relation between Income Inequality and Mortality in Canada and the United States: Cross-Sectional Assessment using Census Data and Vital Statistics," *British Medical Journal* 320 (2000): 898–902; Vicente Navarro, "Health and Equity in the World in the Era of 'Globalization'" pp. 109–119 in *The Political Economy of Social Inequalities: Consequences for Health and Quality of Life*, ed. Vicente Navarro (New York: Baywood Publishing Company, Inc., 2002); David Coburn, "Beyond the Income Inequality Hypothesis: Class, Neo-Liberalism, and Health Inequalities," *Social Science & Medicine* 58 (2004): 41–56; Arjumand Siddiqi and Clyde Hertzman, "Towards an Epidemiological Understanding of the Effects of Long-Term Institutional Changes on Population Health: A Case Study of Canada versus the USA," *Social Science & Medicine* 64 (2007): 589–603.

[28] For a discussion on how the Rawlsian principle of equality may be used to justify the methodological consideration of the relationship between access to health-promoting resources and socio-economic status, see Antoine Bommier and Guy Stecklov, "Defining Health Inequalities: Why Rawls Succeeds Where Social Welfare Theory Fails," *Journal of Health Economics* 21 (2002): 497–513.

[29] Paul Pierson, "Big, Slow-Moving and. . .Invisible: Macrosocial Processes in the Study of Comparative Politics," pp. 177–207 in *Comparative Historical Analysis in the Social Sciences,* eds. James Mahoney and Dietrich Reschemeyer (Cambridge: Cambridge University Press, 2003).

[30] Nancy Adler, Thomas Boyce, Margaret A. Chesney, Sheldon Cohen, Susan Folkman, Robert L. Khan, Leonard S. Syme, "Socioeconomic Status and Health: The Challenge of the Gradient" *American Pyschologist* 49 (1994): 15–24.

[31] Vicente Navarro, ed. *The Political Economy of Social Inequalities: Consequences for Health and Quality of Life* (New York: Baywood Publishing Company, Inc., 2002).

[32] *A Theory of Justice*, pp. 244–245. See Rawls on "Background Institutions" in *A Theory of Justice*, pp. 242–251.

Chapter 5

[1] It is significant that Ricoeur cites Hegel's conception of relationship between individual and state, along with Aristotle and Marx, in his philosophical narrative of civic liberalism. See note 5 in Chapter 2.

[2] For a comparative account of Rawls' and Hegel's theories of the state, see Stephen Houlgate "Hegel, Rawls, and the Rational State" pp. 249–274 in Robert R. Williams, ed. *Beyond Liberalism and Communitarianism: Studies in Hegel's* Philosophy of Right (New York: State University of New York Press, 2001).

[3] In her argument for the necessity of both universal norms and the absolute singularity of self and other, Butler tries to reconcile Levinasian and Hegelian ethics. While Butler makes an argument for the reflexive self, this reflexivity is constituted at the limits of a twofold exteriority, at the intersection of universal

or "impersonal" norms and the irreducible singularity of both self and other. The reflexivity of self, then, is articulated in terms of its "exceptionality" to institutional structuration. Butler's position is a defense of a nonstructured subjectivity whose ethical responsibility unfolds in this state of exceptionality or singularity[1] Butler's assumption is that the demand for recognition is a demand for the other to be *like me, to be the same as me.* She goes on to put forward the typical argument that this demand for sameness by the totalizing mirror is violent.

There is, after all, always the tacit operation of the mirror in Hegel's concept of reciprocal recognition, since I must somehow see that the other is like me, and see that the other is making the same recognition of our likeness. There is lots of light in the Hegelian room, and the mirrors have the happy coincidence of usually being windows, as well. *This view of recognition does not encounter an exteriority that resists a bad infinity or recursive mimesis.* There is no opacity that shadows these windows or dims that light (Butler, 2005: 39, my emphasis).

This classical misreading of Hegel misses the *reflexive* nature of the Hegelian mirror. In the Hegelian argument we have been developing, self-other recognition is made possible through the mediation of appetitive desire by society's institutions. It is precisely the reflexive structure of the Hegelian mirror that interrupts the linear time of appetitive desire or "bad infinity." It is worthwhile to consider the workings of the Hegelian mirror in the master/slave dialectic.

The "misreading" of Hegel as a thinker of sameness results from Butler's misreading of the Hegelian mirror in the master/slave dialectic. Whereas Butler reads Hegel's mirror as the mechanism for the generation of the self-same other, I shall argue that the Hegelian mirroring works as a reflexive concept for the figuration of the self. It is because Butler fails to appreciate the reflexive nature of the Hegelian mirror that she can claim that "This [Hegelian] view of recognition does not encounter an exteriority that resists a bad infinity or recursive mimesis" (Butler, 2005: 39). In the *Phenomenology* (Hegel, 1977), the master/slave dialectic is preceded by Desire. Desire is indeed a mirrored consciousness insofar as it is a reflected consciousness that is able to apprehend its object in a way that immediate sense certainty cannot. Because Desire apprehends its object in terms of a reflection, the object has a double significance:

Consciousness, as self-consciousness, henceforth has a double object, one is the immediate object, that of self-certainty and perception, which however *for self-consciousness* has the character of a *negative*; and the second, viz. *itself*, which is the true *essence*, and is present in the first instance only as opposed to the first object [original emphasis]. *In this sphere, self-consciousness exhibits itself as the movement in which this antithesis is removed, and the identity of itself with itself becomes explicit for it* [my emphasis] (Hegel, 1977: §167).

It is important to spell out the structure of the double-significance of the object for self-consciousness, since this will have implications for the duplication of self-consciousness itself. There is in fact a four-fold movement in the duplication of the object, such that the significance of the object changes as we move from consciousness to self-consciousness. Specifically, it is the object that structures self-consciousness' reflection into itself. Thus, the object plays a crucial role in making self-certainty adequate to its truth, that is to say, in the development of self-consciousness as such: "But now there has arisen what did not emerge in these previous relationships, viz. a certainty which is identical with its truth; for the certainty is to itself its own object, and consciousness is to itself the truth" (Hegel, 1977: §166). Thus, when Hegel says that the object is no longer the 'mere being' of self-certainty and perception, what he means is that we are now dealing not with sensory objects of consumption. Rather, what is revealed in self-certainty, perception and force and the understanding, is that the object is now to be understood as a mode of objectification through which self-consciousness comes to know itself. We have now to see how self-consciousness experiences its mode of objectification, that is to say, we have to observe self-consciousness as desire. It is in this light that we are to understand the role of the negative. We can already see that the Hegelian mirror cannot be understood as a tool of reflection for self-same consciousness. Rather, the mirror serves as a conceptual tool through which 'we' follow self-consciousness' experience of its four-fold constitution.

The four-fold movement of the doubled object of Desire may be broken down in the following way:

1] a] In the first instance, self-consciousness apprehends its object in its *immediacy*, as mere being. This is the object of self-certainty.

1] b] This object is *for self-consciousness a non-object*, or a non-difference. In other words, the object is significant *for self-consciousness* in its *negativity*.

2] a] In the second instance, self-consciousness has *itself* for its object.

2] b] This second distinct object, namely, self-consciousness itself, is only possible through its *opposition* to the first object, namely, the object of self-certainty 1]a]

Thus, self-consciousness gains itself for its object only through its immediate object. In order to understand how this is the case, it is important to understand the *structure* of the doubled object of desire. While 1]a] maps onto 2]a], namely, the immediacy of the object corresponds to self-consciousness' certainty of itself, or its apprehension of itself as its object, this captures only one aspect of Desire, namely, the narcissist aspect of Desiring consciousness which seeks itself in its object. Thus, we are not yet in a position to understand the mechanism of narcissism itself. The logic of narcissism itself is revealed in the discovery that Desire is structured. Self-consciousness seeks its reflection in its object through the negation of the object (1]b]). But this negation cannot be immediate. This is so because self-consciousness only gains itself through its opposition to the first, immediate object. Thus, the operation of the negative, or of negation, is distinct from the object of sense-certainty. Negation is thus to be understood in terms of the structure of Desire such that the moment of the opposition is maintained. Understood along these structural lines, the play of negation and opposition form the determination of self-consciousness.

4 The account of civic life we are developing here through Hegel's historical account of ethical necessity diverges from a conceptualization of civic life that

is grounded in volunteerism. See Robert D. Putman, *Bowling Alone: The Collapse and Revival of American Community* (New York: Simon and Schuster, 2000).

5 Fred Dallmayr (1991) risks dismissing altogether the self-reflexive or critical self-knowledge of the state by virtue of its continual development through the civic institutions of citizenship. He is in particular skeptical of the role that Hegel assigns to the bureaucracy or the universal class in the investigation and generation of the social knowledge through which the state becomes objective to itself:

> . . . [H]egel's conception of the state cannot simply be attached to, or equated with, the modern state and especially the so-called "nation-state". Since his time, the flaws and "imperfections" of the modern-state—the "degeneracy (or putrefaction) of its flesh" (to use Marx's terms)—have become evident in manifold ways. Reduced to an instrument of bureaucratic controls or to a vehicle of chauvinist ambitions, the state has increasingly lost its Hegelian sense, instead approximating the external *Verstandesstaat* or models of collective immediacy (and unfreedom). *While implicit in the "march of God on earth" may be some kind of public Sittlichkeit, the latter no longer finds embodiment in statist structures.* In this situation, a plausible response may be to retain the impulse of Hegel's dialectic—-*without clinging to its institutional format* (Dallmayr, 1989: 340, my emphasis).

Sittlichkeit is better articulated, Dallmayr argues, in cross-cultural autonomous collectivities whose "open-ended and shifting alliances dedicated only to a generic and almost nonpurposive endeavor: the endeavor of healing the cleavages splitting society along racial, economic, and other lines (as well as the cleavage between society and nature)" (Dallmayr, 1989: 341). Our argument, however, is that the preservation of subjective difference, emphasized by Dallmayr, is only possible through the development of right or of subjectivity through the civic institutions of the state. Without such a structuration, as we shall see, we remain at the level of what Hegel refers to as "undifferentiated particularity," which, rather than preserve difference and the autonomy of subjective right, collapses under the weight of its own indifference, exacerbating racialized, classed, and gendered divisions within society. The institutional figuration of *Sittlichkeit*, then, is necessary for the preservation of difference.

6 We should recall here the dialectic we traced in Chapter 2 between *phronēsis* and emplotment or narrative. Where emplotment figures the attribution of an action to an agent, thereby placing emphasis on action over agent, *phronēsis* is a mode of practical deliberation or ethical evaluation that traverses the narrative configuration and thus constitutes the reflexivity of emplotment itself. This, we said, is a form of ethical evaluation wherein the reflexivity of narrative configuration with respect to its evaluations of the good life is drawn out. In this way, *phronēsis* is itself constitutive of narrative configuration. The dialectic between narrative and *phronēsis* constitutes the back-and-forth movement structured by the narrative configuration of practice, which allows for a continual evaluation between the whole and the part in life plans, in coordinated activity with others and finally on the institutional plane of civic narratives. This back-and-forth movement which Ricoeur likens to a hermeneutical approach to the reading of a text means that narrative is understood vis-à-vis the ethical aim in the teleological

tradition, namely, living the good life with and for others in just institutions. See note 11, Chapter 2.

[7] See Kenneth Kierans "The Concept of Ethical Life in Hegel's Philosophy of Right," *History of Political Thought* 13 (1992): 417–435.

[8] Ricoeur references Ewald's work in his examination of the relationship between responsibility and imputability in his essay entitled "The Concept of Responsbility," pp. 11–35 in *The Just*, trans. David Pellauer (Chicago: University of Chicago Press, 2000).

Chapter 6

[1] In *Time and Narrative* (1984), Ricoeur puts forth the idea that characters in a story are both identified and articulated by virtue of the mediation performed by the narrative structure; he refers to this as the "narrative configuration" of the character. Ricoeur develops his theory of narration through his analysis of fiction and tragedy whose essential task, he argues, is to imitate action, where the end towards which our life is oriented is itself understood in terms of action or activity (Ricoeur, 1992: 152). Just as identity or character in fiction is structured by the plot to such an extent that the character is itself understood as plot, so the individual in society is articulated by virtue of the (re)distributive principles and practices of that society. We can assert that there is no division between character and plot, on one hand, and individual and society on the other, precisely because of the essential mediation performed by narrative configuration. In other words, in order for this mediation to be possible, it must be understood in terms of a narrative structure. What Ricoeur is able to demonstrate is that the mediation performed by the narrative configuration is both structural and structuring (Ricoeur, 1984a: 44).

By broadening action into practice, Ricoeur seeks to reconcile the antinomy between freedom and necessity within the temporal realm by sublimating this necessity into the literary-cultural realm of responsibility. All of our beginnings and endings are culturally determined. But this necessity is of a different order than temporal necessity. That is, we only recognize ourselves, by virtue of our actions, practices and life plans, from within the broader cultural-political context in which our capacity to act, to live and to create with others, is defined and contextualized. Here, by submitting infinite freedom to a structuring narrative, the two moments of freedom and responsibility are brought together. It is the narrative that "grants" the character the "freedom" to begin an action precisely by structuring the beginning, middle, and end of the action. The freedom of the character is never absolute because the identity of the character, or, understood in Kantian terms, the responsibility of the character, only becomes intelligible if the freedom of the character is not absolute but structured or narrated. Recognition of self, or the identity of self, then, is only possible with reference to responsibility. But that this responsibility is not merely an individual(ized) responsibility is revealed by Ricoeur when he demonstrates that we are able to attribute an action to agent only by virtue of a narrative through which plot and character are articulated together. That is, there is a necessary connection between plot and character (Ricoeur, 1992: 146).

Borrowing from Aristotle's definition of "muthos" as it is developed in the *Poetics*, Ricoeur argues that narrative is structural insofar as it emphasizes concordance over discordance. By concordance we refer to the logical as opposed to the temporal ordering of events (Ricoeur, 1984a: 38). That is, muthos, or emplotment may be said to privilege concordance, or the ordering of events insofar as it is primarily concerned with the "wholeness" or the "completeness" of the story (Ricoeur, 1984a: 38). By emphasizing the whole, emplotment structures the story precisely by configuring or ordering the beginning, middle and end of a story. Thus, the structure or plot of the story cannot be understood apart from the practice or the activity of emplotment. Emplotment configures the discordances or the reversals in plot into a meaningful whole (Ricoeur, 1984a: 38–39).

2 See Chapter 5.

3 Nussbaum credits Sen's founding work on capability justice as grounding her own theory of capability justice, and the two thinkers are often paired together in references to capability justice. However, as we saw in Chapter 4, Nussbaum's conception of capability justice rests on a rejection of the distributive figuration of capability justice, and thus of the public figuration of capability justice. In contrast, Sen's theory of capability justice emphasizes the public-institutional figuration of citizens' capabilities for health and well-being.

4 In its discussion of the deleterious effects of the overly broad scope of Section 51(e), the majority notes that the punishment fails to take into consideration the social and political exclusion suffered by Aboriginal persons (*Sauvé*: §48). The over-breadth of the punishment would serve to exacerbate the over-incarceration of Aboriginal persons.

Bibliography

Adler, Nancy, Thomas Boyce, Margaret A. Chesney, Sheldon Cohen, Susan Folkman, Robert L. Khan, and Leonard S. Syme (1994) "Socioeconomic Status and Health: The Challenge of the Gradient." *American Pyschologist* 49: 15–24.

Arendt, Hannah (1998) *The Human Condition*. Chicago: University of Chicago Press.

Aristotle (1999) Trans. Terence Irwin *Nichomachean Ethics*, 2nd edn. Indianapolis: Hacket Publishing Company.

Aristotle (1999) Trans. Kenneth McLeish *Poetics*. New York: Theatre Communications Group.

Arneson, Richard (2003) "Perfectionism and Politics." *Ethics* 11: 37–63.

Avineri, Shlomo (1972) *Hegel's Theory of The Modern State*. London: Cambridge University Press.

Banting, Keith and Will Kymlicka (eds) (2006) *Multiculturalism and the Welfare State: Recognition and Redistribution in Contemporary Democracies*. Oxford: Oxford University Press.

Bentham, Jeremy (1962) *The Works of Jeremy Bentham*. New York: Russell & Russell.

Bommier, Antoine and Guy Stecklov (2002) "Defining Health Inequalities: Why Rawls Succeeds Where Social Welfare Theory Fails." *Journal of Health Economics* 21: 497–513.

Burns, Tony (1996) *Natural Law and Political Ideology in the Philosophy of Hegel*. Brookfield: Ashgate Publishing Company.

Butler, Judith (2005) *Giving an Account of Oneself*. New York: Fordham University Press.

Coburn, David (2000) "Income Inequality, Social Cohesion and the Health Status of Populations: The Role of Neoliberalism." *Social Science & Medicine* 51: 135–46.

— (2004) "Beyond the Income Inequality Hypothesis: Class, Neo-Liberalism, and Health Inequalities." *Social Science & Medicine* 58: 41–56.

Dallmayr, Fred (1991) "Rethinking the Hegelian State." In Drucilla Cornell, Michal Rosenfeld and David Carlson (eds), *Hegel and Legal Theory*. New York: Routledge.

Daniels, Norman (1981) "Health Care Needs and Distributive Justice." *Philosophy & Public Affairs* 10, 146–79.

Dauenhauer, Bernard (1998) *Paul Ricoeur: The Promise and Risk of Politics*. New York: Rowman & Littlefield Publishers.

Dupuy, Jean-Pierre (1988) "Les paradoxes de 'Théorie de la justice': Introduction à l'oeuvre de John Rawls." *Esprit* No. 134 (January).

Durkheim, Emile (1938) *Rules of Sociological Method*. New York: The Free Press.

Epsing-Anderson, Gösta (1990) *The Three Worlds of Welfare Capitalism*. Cambridge: Polity Press.

Ewald, François (1987) "Justice, Equality, Judgment: On 'Social Justice.'" In Gunther Teuber, ed. *Juridification of the Social Spheres*. New York: Walter de Gruyter.

Fiasse, Gaëlle (2006) *L'autre et l'amitié chez Aristote et Paul Ricoeur: analyses éthique et ontologiques*. Louvain: Louvain-la-Neuve Editions de l'Institut supérieur de philosophie.

Foster, Gary (2007) "Rawls and Ricoeur on Reconciling the Right and the Good: An Overlapping Consensus or an Ethical Aim?" *Philosophy Today*, 51, 159–76.

Foucault, Michel (1977) *Power/Knowledge: Selected Interviews and other Writings 1972–1977*. New York: Pantheon Books.

Fraser, Nancy (2002) "Recognition Without Ethics." In Scott Lash and Mike Featherstone (eds), *Recognition & Difference: Politics, Identity, Multiculture*. London: Sage Publications, pp. 21–42.

Fraser, Nancy and Axel Honneth (2003) *Redistribution or Recognition? A Political-Philosophical Exchange*. New York: Verso.

Hart, H. L. A. (1989) "Rawls on Liberty and Its Priority." In Norman Daniels (ed.), *Reading Rawls*. Stanford: Stanford University Press, pp. 230–52.

Hegel, G. W. F. (1967) Trans. T.M. Knox. *Philosophy of Right*. New York: Oxford University Press.

Hegel, G. W. F. (1977) Trans. A.V. Miller. *Phenomenology of Spirit*. Oxford: Oxford University Press.

Hobbes, Thomas (1946) *Leviathan or the Matter, Forme and Power of a Commonwealth Ecclesiasticall and Civil*. Oxford: Basil Blackwell.

Honneth, Axel (1995) Trans. Joel Anderson. *The Struggle for Recognition: The Moral Grammar of Social Conflicts*. Cambridge: The MIT Press.

—. 2002. "Recognition or Redistribution?: Changing Perspectives on the Moral Order of Society." In Scott Lash and Mike Featherstone (eds), *Recognition & Difference: Politics, Identity, Multiculture*. London: Sage, pp. 43–55.

—. 2010 *The Pathologies of Individual Freedom: Hegel's Social Theory*. Princeton: Princeton University Press.

Houlgate, Stephen (2001) "Hegel, Rawls, and the Rational State." In Robert R. Williams (ed.), *Beyond Liberalism and Communitarianism: Studies in Hegel's Philosophy of Right*. New York: State University of New York Press.

Ignatieff, Michael (1984) *The Needs of Strangers*. London: Hogarth Press.

Kant, Immanuel (1929) Trans. Norman Kemp Smith. *Critique of Pure Reason*. MacMillan & Co., Ltd.

— (1997) Trans. Mary Gregor. *Critique of Practical Reason*. Cambridge: Cambridge University Press.

Kearney, Richard (2005) *On Paul Ricoeur: The Owl of Minerva*. Aldershot: Ashgate Publishing.

Kierans, Kenneth (1992) "The Concept of Ethical Life in Hegel's Philosophy of Right." *History of Political Thought* 13(3): 417–35.

Kymlicka, Will (1988) "Rawls on Teleology and Deontology." *Philosophy and Public Affairs* 17: 173–90.

Lacey, Nicola (2007) "Criminal Justice and Democratic Systems: Inclusionary and Exclusionary Dynamics in the Institutional Structure of Late Modern Societies." *Harvard Center for European Studies Working Papers*, http://www.ces.fas.harvard.edu/publications/docs/pdfs/lacey.pdf

MacGregor, David (1996) *Hegel, Marx, and the English State.* Toronto: University of Toronto Press.

Machperson, C.B. (1964) *The Political Theory of Possessive Individualism.* New York: Oxford University Press.

MacIntyre, Alsadair (1981) *After Virtue: A Study in Moral Theory.* Notre Dame: University of Notre Dame Press.

Mann, Molly Harkirat (2009) "Ricouer's Principle of Civic Inclusion: An Aristotelian Interpretation of Rawls' Theory of Justice." *Philosophy Today* 53: 44–57.

— (2009) "The Course of Recognitive *Phronēsis*: Ricoeur's Response to the Moralization of Inequality." *Philosophy Today: Selected Studies in Phenomenology and Existential Philosophy* 53: 201–6.

— (forthcoming 2012) "Civic *Phronēsis*: Rawl's Anti-Sacrificial Ethics for Capability Justice." *Philosophy and Social Criticism* 38(6).

Marshall, T. H. and Tom Bottomore (1992) *Citizenship and Social Class.* Chicago: Pluto Press.

Navarro, Vincente (2002) "Health and Equity in the World in the Era of 'Globalization'." In Vicente Navarro (ed.), *The Political Economy of Social Inequalities: Consequences for Health and Quality of Life.* New York: Baywood Publishing Company, pp. 109–19.

Nelson, Eric (2008) "From Primary Goods to Capabilities: Distributive Justice and the Problem of Neutrality." *Political Theory* 36: 93–122.

Nozick, Robert (1974) *Anarchy, State, and Utopia.* New York: Basic Books.

Nussbaum, Martha (1992) "Human Functioning and Social Justice: In Defense of Aristotelian Essentialism." *Political Theory* 20: 202–46.

—. (2000) *Women and Human Development: The Capabilities Approach.* Cambridge, MA: Harvard University Press.

—. (2000) "Aristotle, Politics, and Human Capabilities: A Response to Antony, Arneson, Charlesworth, and Mulgan." *Ethics* 111: 102–40.

—. (2003) "Capabilities as Fundamental Entitlements: Sen and Social Justice." *Feminist Economics* 9: 33–59.

Nussbaum, Martha and Amartya Sen (eds) (1993) *The Quality of Life.* Oxford: Clarendon Press.

Olive, David (2008) "David Olive on the census: A country divided." *The Toronto Star,* May 2008.

O'Neill, John (2004) *His Majesty the Baby: Ego-Mimesis, Narcissism and the Politics of Love.* Paper presented at the International Social Theory Consortium, York University, Toronto, June 2004.

Pellauer, David (2002) "At the Limit of Practical Wisdom." In *Ricoeur as Another: The Ethics of Subjectivity.* Albany: SUNY Press, pp. 187–201.

Pierson, Paul (2003) "Big, Slow-Moving and . . . Invisible: Macrosocial Processes in the Study of Comparative Politics." In James Mahoney and Dietrich Reschemeyer (eds), *Comparative Historical Analysis in the Social Sciences*. Cambridge: Cambridge University Press, pp. 177–207.

Putnam, Robert D. (2000) *Bowling Alone: The Collapse and Revival of American Community*. New York: Simon and Schuster.

Raphael, Daiches D. (1950) "Justice and Liberty." *Proceedings of the Aristotelian Society, New Series* 51: 1967–196.

Rawls, John (1977) "The Basic Structure as Subject." *American Philosophical Quarterly* 14: 159–65.

— (1980) "Kantian Constructivism in Moral Theory." *Journal of Philosophy* 77: 515–72.

— (1985) "Justice as Fairness, Political Not Metaphysical." *Philosophy and Public Affairs* 14, 223–51.

— (1996) *Political Liberalism*. New York: Columbian University Press.

— (1999) *Collected Papers*, ed. Samuel Freeman. Cambridge: Harvard University Press.

— (2001) *Justice as Fairness: A Restatement*. Cambridge: Harvard University Press.

— (2003) *A Theory of Justice Revised Edition*. Cambridge: The Belknap Press of Harvard University Press.

Ricoeur, Paul (1978) "The Problem of the Foundation of Moral Philosophy." *Philosophy Today*, 22: 175–92.

— (1981) "The Model of the Text" in *Hermeneutics and the Human Sciences: Essays on Language, Action and Interpretation*, trans. John B. Thompson. Cambridge: Cambridge University Press.

— (1984) Trans. Kathleen McLaughlin and David Pellauer. *Time and Narrative: Volume 1*. Chicago, IL: University of Chicago Press.

— (1984) Trans. Kathleen McLaughlin and David Pellauer. *Time and Narrative*: Volume 3. Chicago, University of Chicago Press.

— (1987) "The Fragility of Political Language." *Philosophy Today* 31: 35–44.

— (1988) "Débat sur l'identité narrative." *Esprit*. No. 8 (August): 295–314.

— (1988) "Le Cercle de la demonstration". *Esprit*. No. 2 (February): 305–14.

— (1992) Trans. Kathleen Blamey. *Oneself as Another*. Chicago: The University of Chicago Press.

— (2000) Trans. David Pellauer. *The Just*. Chicago: The University of Chicago Press.

— (2005) Trans. David Pellauer. *The Course of Recognition*. Cambridge, MA: Harvard University Press.

— (2007) Trans. David Pellauer. *Reflections on the Just*. Chicago, IL: The University of Chicago Press.

Ross, Nancy A., Michael C. Wolfson, James R. Dunn, Jean-Marie Berthelot, George A. Kaplan, and John W. Lynch (2000) "Relation between Income Inequality and Mortality in Canada and the United States: Cross-Sectional Assessment using Census Data and Vital Statistics." *British Medical Journal* 320: 898–902.

Sandel, Michael (1982) *Liberalism and the Limits of Justice*. Cambridge: Cambridge University Press.

— (1984) "The Procedural Republic and Unencumbered Self." *Political Theory*. 12: 81–96.

Sauvé v. Canada (Chief Electoral Officer) [2002] 3 S.C.R. 519, 2002 SCC 68 (CanLII).

Sen, Amartya (1980) "Equality of What?" In Sterling M. McMurrin (ed.), *The Tanner Lectures on Human Values*, Volume 1. Salt Lake City: University of Utah Press, pp. 197–220.

Sen, Amartya (1985) *Commodities and Capabilities*. Oxford: Elsevier Science.

Siddiqi, Arjumand and Clyde Hertzman (2007) "Towards an Epidemiological Understanding of the Effects of Long-Term Institutional Changes on Population Health: A Case Study of Canada versus the USA." *Social Science & Medicine* 64: 589–603.

Sidgwick, Henry (1962) *The Methods of Ethics*. Chicago: Chicago University Press.

Smith, Steven B (1989) *Hegel's Critique of Liberalism: Rights in Context*. Chicago, IL: The University of Chicago Press.

Spiegelberg, Steven (1944) "A Defense of Human Equality." *The Philosophical Review* 53: 101–24.

Tawney, R. H. (1965) *Equality*. New York: Barnes & Noble.

Taylor, Charles (1994) "The Politics of Recognition." In *Multiculturalism*, ed. Amy Gutmann. Princeton: Princeton University Press.

Titmuss, Richard (1962) *Income Distribution and Social Change: A Study in Criticism*. London: George Allen & Unwi.

— (1981) *The Right to Welfare and Other Essays*. London: Heinemann Educational Books Ltd.

— (1997) *The Gift Relationship: From Human Blood to Social Policy*. New York: New York Press.

Wall, John (2005) *Moral Creativity: Paul Ricoeur and the Poetics of Possibility*. New York: Oxford University Press.

Walzer, Michael (1989) *Spheres of Justice: A Defense of Pluralism and Equality*. Oxford: Basil Blackwell.

Wilkenson, Richard and Michael Marmot (eds) (2003) *The Social Determinants of Health: The Solid Facts*. World Health Organization.

Wolff, Jonathon and Avner De-Shallit (2007) *Disadvantage*. Oxford: Oxford University Press.

Index

CPSIA information can be obtained at www.ICGtesting.com
Printed in the USA
LVOW080200211112

308275LV00005B/26/P

9 781441 198501